IN THE SHADOWS OF STATE AND CAPITAL

A book in the series

AMERICAN ENCOUNTERS/GLOBAL INTERACTIONS

A series edited by Gilbert M. Joseph

and Emily S. Rosenberg

IN THE SHADOWS OF

STATE AND CAPITAL

The United Fruit Company, Popular Struggle,

and Agrarian Restructuring in Ecuador,

1900–1995

STEVE STRIFFLER

Duke University Press

Durham & London

2002

Printed in the United States of America on acid-free paper ⊗
Typeset in Stone by Tseng Information Systems, Inc.
Library of Congress Cataloging-in-Publication Data appear
on the last printed page of this book. Portions of this book
originally appeared in a different form in "Wedded to Work:
Class Struggles and Gendered Identities in the Restructuring
of the Ecuadorian Banana Industry," *Identities* 6(1). Copyright
Overseas Publishers Association. Reprinted with permission
from Taylor & Francis Ltd.

AMERICAN ENCOUNTERS / GLOBAL INTERACTIONS

A series edited by Gilbert M. Joseph and Emily S. Rosenberg

This series aims to stimulate critical perspectives and fresh interpretive frameworks for scholarship on the history of the imposing global presence of the United States. Its primary concerns include the deployment and contestation of power, the construction and deconstruction of cultural and political borders, the fluid meanings of intercultural encounters, and the complex interplay between the global and the local. American Encounters seeks to strengthen dialogue and collaboration between historians of U.S. international relations and area studies specialists.

The series encourages scholarship based on multiarchival historical research. At the same time, it supports a recognition of the representational character of all stories about the past and promotes critical inquiry into issues of subjectivity and narrative. In the process, American Encounters strives to understand the context in which meanings related to nations, cultures, and political economy are continually produced, challenged, and reshaped.

CONTENTS

Acknowledgments

In producing this book, I contracted numerous personal and intellectual debts, a number of which are evident in the pages that follow. First, I would like to thank all of my Ecuadorian friends and colleagues who made the process of collecting documents, finding people, and learning about Ecuador both enjoyable and intellectually stimulating. Carlos Larrea not only shaped this project through his scholarship (as the bibliography attests), but suggested that United Fruit's Hacienda Tenguel might be an interesting place from which to understand twentieth-century Ecuador, the banana industry, and popular struggle. I agree, and am forever grateful. I am also in debt to him for having pointed me in the direction of two scholar-activists, Manuel Chiriboga and Padre Hernán Rodas. Manuel shared his time, knowledge, hospitality, and historical documents with uncommon generosity. Padre Hernán, as he is known to just about all of the protagonists in this book, not only opened his home and archive, but convinced a skeptical anthropologist that "the priest from the highlands" was and is as remarkable as everyone insists. To those who believe that one person cannot make a difference, I suggest spending a day with Padre Hernán.

I cannot possibly thank everyone in the region where I worked, but I would like to especially mention the Izquierdo-Chica family, the Zambrano family, Blanca, her mother, and the rest of the Arteaga family. Special thanks go to Humberto Eras and José Llivichusca for sharing so much of their time. I hope you enjoyed it as much as I did. I would also like to thank Joaquin Vásquez and his entire family, Sergio Armijos, the León brothers, Juan Ochoa, as well as the community of Shumiral. Finally, in Quito, I thank my Ecuadorian family, Blanca Tafur, Cynthia, Gaby, and (the late) abuelita. They did their best to keep me from working. For that, I am eternally grateful.

My deepest appreciation goes to (the late) William Roseberry. I am proud to say that for almost a decade he was my teacher, advisor, and mentor. He remains my intellectual guide. His warmth and understated humor made the process of graduate school, grant proposals, dissertation writing, and academia not only less difficult, but rewarding and enjoyable. His intellectual excitement, gentle critique, integrity, and careful research provided, and continue to provide, a model for meaningful scholarship. I hope that his understandings of (and commitments to) Latin America, Marxism, history, and anthropology are reflected in the following. If there is anything of value in these pages it is in large part because of Bill.

I would also like to thank three other mentors, Kate Crehan, Deborah Poole, and Gerald Sider, all of whom have continued to tolerate me long after I left graduate school. Kate provided insightful comments all along the way, and to a large extent introduced me to Marxist feminism. Debbie's knack for spotting intellectual sloppiness and her immense knowledge about Latin America have improved this project from its inception. Gerry's intellectual passion, as well as his unique ability to simultaneously confuse, frustrate, provoke, and stimulate, has been challenging me since I first took a class with him almost a decade ago. May it always be so.

Carlos de la Torre read the entire manuscript. His analysis and knowledge of Ecuadorian history and politics clarified my own thinking and prevented some serious mistakes. Catherine LeGrand read the manuscript several times, a task for which I can never adequately thank her. She has a unique ability to catch the tiniest of errors while simultaneously highlighting broader problems of argument and evidence. Although I was never able to adequately address all of her comments, the book has benefited immensely for having passed through her hands.

Many other friends and colleagues also suffered through drafts of these pages. Thanks to Avi Bornstein, Philippe Bourgois, Kristy Bright, Eliza Darling, Kirk Dombrowski, Lindsay Dubois, Oscar Espinosa, Liz Fitting, Gil Joseph, Robin Lebaron, Caitrin Lynch, Ricardo Macip, Lauren Martin, Carmen Martinez, Connie Miksits, Mark Moberg, David Nugent, Anthony Pereira, Aleeze Sattar, Joel Stillerman, John Uggen, and Lois Woestman for their encouragement and insightful comments. I would like to especially thank Kim Clark both for her intellectual insights and for "showing me the ropes" in Ecuador. Special thanks are also due to Lorraine Bayard-de-Volo, for many things, but most immediately for having invited me to present some of this work at a Latin American Studies colloquium at the University of Kansas. Thanks to all who participated. Charles Menzies, along with graduate students from the University of British Columbia, put together one of the most fruitful conferences I have ever been involved with. Thanks for letting me in on it.

Some of my debts are to institutions. The New School, for all of its financial problems, provided support during those moments when it was most difficult (and most crucial) to obtain funding. Generous grants from Fulbright and the Wenner-Gren Anthropological Foundation supported the bulk of my research in Ecuador. Special thanks to Helena of the Fulbright Commission in Ecuador for all of her help. I would have taken even longer to complete the original dissertation were it not for a write-up grant from the Harry Frank Guggenheim Foundation (Research for Understanding and Reducing Violence, Aggression, and Dominance). Similarly, I could never have turned the dissertation into a book were it not for a postdoctoral fellowship from the Program in Agrarian Studies at Yale University. My only complaint is that the position was not permanent. Jim Scott, Kay Mansfield, and Bob Harms, along with a number of other committed individuals, have made agrarian studies one of the truly special places in academia. I cannot thank you enough.

Some of the ideas and portions of the text appeared earlier in both *Identities* and *Plantation Society in the Americas*. The publishers kindly granted me permission to incorporate this material into the book. Thanks to Nina Glick Schiller, Louis Mazzari, as well as a number of anonymous reviewers for their insightful comments. Duke University Press has been great from the beginning. Miriam Angress answered all of my (at times silly) questions professionally, promptly, and with a sense of humor. Valerie Millholland was always encouraging. She is a wonderful editor, and has a sensibility that is particularly well suited for guiding and supporting first-time authors.

My greatest debt is to my parents, Chuck and Nancy, who kept me financially afloat, gave me a quiet place to write, and never asked when I was going to finish the damn thing. For their unconditional support, I save my deepest thanks and love.

Map 1   Ecuador

1 Capitalist Transformations

There is widespread agreement that something dramatic has been happening to the international economy over the past two decades: rapid and radical changes in production technology . . . , a major restructuring of world markets, and consequent large-scale changes in the policies of economic management at the international, national, and regional levels. At the same time there is a great deal of confusion about how to characterize these changes.
—Paul Hirst and Jonathan Zeitlin, 1991

Whatever the local peculiarities, contracting emerges with the full or partial decomposition of plantation-estate forms of production but often with the persistence, nevertheless, of the classical export commodities . . . now cultivated under contract by a variety local growers. Contracting . . . represents one fundamental way in which the twin processes of internationalization of agriculture and agro-industrialization are taking place on a global scale. The dispersion of contracting marks . . . a watershed in the transformation of rural life and agrarian systems in the Third World.—Michael Watts, 1994

I arrived in the small town of Tenguel for the first time in July 1994. Although it was several months past the rainy season, it was neither dry nor particularly cool and the intense sun was drying up the rain that had briefly covered the zone the previous night. In the southern coast of Ecuador, the heat, humidity, and rain are constants whose intensities vary within fairly predictable boundaries.[1] It is, as I would come to appreciate more fully in the coming months, this constant combination of intense sun and rain that make the area one of the most productive agricultural zones in South America. Yet, what seemed much more important at thc time—as I pedaled along on a borrowed bicycle—was the impact the sun and rain had on the town's dirt roads. The roads were a strange combination of dust and mud that choked conversations and made biking an especially tricky enterprise. To complicate things, large trucks packed with boxes of bananas sprayed an unpleasant mixture of mud, dust, and exhaust as they rambled through Tenguel on their way to oceangoing steamers owned by Dole and Chiquita.

Fortunately, Jacinto Lozano, a seventy-year-old man who had lived in the zone for most of his life, seemed to know just the path to take as he guided us along Tenguel's dirty streets. Obstacles aside, it felt good to be moving. Bicycling created an artificial breeze that provided temporary relief from the heat. Located on a flat, narrow, and extremely fertile coastal plain, Tenguel is about five kilometers from the Pacific Ocean and less than ten from the edge of the Andes. The wind from the ocean is, however, immediately suffocated by the sea of green trees that engulf the small town and much of Ecuador's southern coast. Despite their proximity, neither the ocean nor the mountains can be easily seen from Tenguel. Banana trees, with their huge green leaves and long stems, surround the town on all sides.

Although I had planned on visiting Tenguel during this first trip to the southern coast, it did not immediately strike me as the logical place from which to begin a social history of the region. I knew that the town had once been at the center of an immense banana *hacienda* owned by the United Fruit Company (since renamed Chiquita Brands).[2] But in a country where a relatively small number of foreign-owned plantations existed for only a short period of time, Tenguel did not seem particularly representative of anything but the inability of foreign banana companies to establish production sites beyond the boundaries of Central America. As it turns out, I never did become convinced that Tenguel, or the surrounding towns and hamlets that make up this study, are particularly representative of Ecuador's southern coast. In fact, throughout much of the following, I will insist they were not. However, as Jacinto Lozano convinced me that day, it is the specificity of Tenguel's past that makes it such an interesting place from which to begin a history of the region and rethink some of the concepts, categories, and dichotomies through which scholars have understood and talked about capitalism.

Only minutes before we had begun our tour of the town, Jacinto Lozano and a small group of men had been the victims of my well-rehearsed introduction. I was a historian interested in learning about the politics and economy of their part of the world. Because my frustratingly vague introduction almost always generated confusion and/or apathy, their collective excitement was encouraging. They quickly explained Tenguel's *historical* importance. During the "cacao epoch," as my new friends referred to the early decades of the century when Ecuador was the largest exporter of cacao in the world, the zone of Tenguel was the largest cacao plantation in the world before a disease destroyed both the hacienda's crop and the country's economy. Later, in the 1930s, the gringos came and transformed the entire zone, reconstructing the town of

Tenguel, building a number of smaller hamlets, bringing in modern machinery, developing a port, clearing cacao trees, and slowly planting the hacienda with bananas. It was during this period, as Ecuador was becoming the largest banana producer in the world, that Jacinto Lozano and the other men had come to Hacienda Tenguel. The wages, houses, and infrastructure offered by United Fruit had attracted migrants from both the coast and the southern highlands.

It was this discussion of the massive effort involved in developing a large agricultural enterprise in a relatively undeveloped frontier zone that led to the bicycle tour. Much of the infrastructure built by United Fruit in the 1940s and 1950s, from the system of railroads and network of roads to the homes and warehouses needed for housing, feeding, and otherwise maintaining thousands of workers, was still standing in one form or another. It did not take long to realize that Tenguel was unlike any other town I had seen in Latin America. To begin, there is no *parque central*. The town center, if one could call it that, is a full-size soccer field that is lined on each side by a series of neatly spaced wooden buildings. All are of equal size and once housed three families. Some families have since constructed cement foundations, but many of the houses are still made of the same wood that United Fruit imported some fifty years earlier. The houses, in fact all of the buildings, have survived the rain and humidity remarkably well. Additions, deteriorations, and renovations notwithstanding, the town's layout still reflects the company's obsession with order and hierarchy. The roads are neatly laid out and lined with dozens of nearly identical houses. Differences are quickly explained. The smaller, almost slave-like quarters, were for single men. The larger homes were for field bosses. Across the river one finds what used to be the administrative compound, the mansions, headquarters, and facilities used by the foreign administrators (now home to a military encampment and some of the zone's largest capitalists).

Both the tour and the history lesson piqued my interest. Although Tenguel's history differs significantly from much of the southern coast, it is nonetheless an excellent place from which to view the principal changes that have transformed Ecuadorian society during the twentieth century. The zone has played a central role in two of the country's three export booms, cacao and banana (the third being oil), and has been a center of popular political activity for most of the century. In fact, it was at Tenguel where the large-scale production and export of bananas first began in Ecuador.

Nevertheless, I still had questions about Tenguel's more recent past. Was Tenguel nothing more than a historical anomaly, an interesting but ultimately failed attempt on the part of a multinational to establish a banana enclave? Ecuador did become the largest producer of bananas in the world, but (unlike in Central America) the overwhelming majority of fruit has come from domestic producers rather than multinational enclaves. By 1965, foreign-owned plantations ceased to exist and direct production was left in the hands of Ecuadorians (Larrea 1987). My concerns led to a rather obvious question that has guided this research project to the present day. As I posed it on that July day: What happened to United Fruit?

Judging by the pained expressions on my friends' faces, the question was neither comfortable nor particularly easy to answer. It generated two basic responses. The first came in a hushed, almost apologetic, tone. The workers, I was informed, invaded the hacienda in 1962 and pushed United Fruit out of the zone. The Ecuadorian state subsequently intervened, took over the hacienda, and delivered a large portion of the property to the workers through the country's first agrarian reform project. Not only did banana production effectively begin at Tenguel, but so too did agrarian reform and a regional peasant movement for the land that would exist in varying degrees of intensity until the late 1970s. The second, almost contradictory response, was suggested by Jacinto Lozano himself: "United Fruit never left." To be sure, the company was forced out of the zone and the workers received a large section of the fertile coastal plain. Yet the workers-turned-peasants were not given the resources necessary to work their newly acquired holdings and subsequently lost their land to an emerging class of landlords. Despite their long struggle against a major multinational, the military, local capitalists, and the state's agrarian reform apparatus, they currently possess little land. Most of their sons now work on banana plantations in conditions far worse than they themselves had experienced during the time of the company. Worse yet, many of the large plantations that now control the zone—on land once owned by United Fruit and later by the workers—have contracts with multinationals such as Chiquita Brands (United Fruit), Dole (Standard Fruit), Del Monte, and Bonita Banana (Noboa). In this sense, Jacinto Lozano was right. United Fruit never left, even if both its name and its control over land, labor, and production have changed dramatically.

In a simple sense, this book tells the story of how Jacinto Lozano got from there to here. How did one system of producing and marketing bananas (large foreign-owned enclaves) give way to another (contract farming), and in what ways were the political struggles and daily practices of people like Jacinto Lozano central to this transformation? As we will see, this process of agricultural restructuring was extremely uneven, transforming a variety of interconnected spaces over nearly an entire century. It involved considerable conflict between and among factions of capital, the state, and popular groups, as well as nearly two decades of agrarian reform, a regional peasant movement, and the uneven emergence of both a semi-proletarianized class of cacao producers and a much smaller group of plantation owners and shrimp growers. The process of capitalist transformation examined below has been *political* at its core.

The point of the following is not simply to understand how peasants and workers such as Jacinto Lozano have experienced a series of political-economic processes, but to demonstrate that their political struggles lie at the core of the production process and its transformation. At the heart of both enclave production and contract farming—their emergence, maintenance, and transformation—has been the continuous formation of, and struggle between, a number of quite differentiated actors, including capital, the state, peasants, workers, lawyers, communists, and others. Marxists have been arguing that class struggle is at the core of the production process and capitalist transformation for quite some time. What the following does—through the historical and ethnographic analysis of a particular area—is place politically engaged human actors at the center of this assertion by examining a particular process of agrarian restructuring that unfolded during the course of the twentieth century.

"NEW TIMES"

There has recently emerged in scholarship, political discourse, journalism, and popular imagination a general consensus that the contemporary period represents a "radical break" from earlier historical moments (Smith 1991). Above all, this break (generally understood as beginning at some point in the early 1970s) has been characterized by increased fragmentation and movement on a global scale, whether seen as a cultural rupture from modernism to postmodernism, a political shift from class-based movements to identity politics, or an economic transformation from Fordism to something called post-Fordism. There is little agreement over the nature, extent, and meaning of these changes, let alone the terms with which to classify them, but there is nonetheless a broadly held belief that there is something decidedly "new" about the period in which we live.

It is not surprising, given agrarian studies' traditional concern with capitalist transformation, that the radical break metaphor quickly entered into debates on agricultural restructuring. In fact, when Jacinto

Lozano remarked that "United Fruit had not left" but had merely changed the way in which it controlled the zone's land, labor, and markets, he was implicitly referring to a global transformation that has recently caught the attention of a growing number of scholars (Carney and Watts 1990; Clapp 1988; Little and Watts 1994; Korovkin 1992; Grossman 1998; Collins 1993; Watts 1994). The growing importance of contract farming is, according to Little and Watts, "a crucial means by which agriculture is being industrialized and restructured" in the late twentieth century (1994: 6). Similarly, as Lawrence Grossman notes, contract farming is "one of the most significant and powerful means by which peasants have been integrated into national and international commodity markets and agro-industrial complexes" during the post–World War II period (1998: 1). The "world of plantations," in which a large and often foreign capital engaged in the direct production of classical export commodities such as sugar, cotton, and bananas, has been "crumbling and reconfiguring itself in important and novel ways" (Watts 1994: 24). In "the same way that industrial enterprises, driven by competition and global market volatility, disperse risks and costs by subcontracting," multinationals involved in agribusiness have avoided the risks of direct production by contracting with domestic planters (Goodman and Watts 1994: 34). We have, it seems, a "new times" for agriculture (ibid.).

At this point, the purpose is not to enter into any specific debates regarding the "newness" of the contemporary period, the particular locations where such changes are most conspicuous, or even the significance of certain phenomena whose existence I am most concerned with here (i.e. contract farming, alternative forms of peasant organization, etc.). Instead, I would simply like to make a number of broader arguments about how capitalism, and particularly its latest manifestations, should (and should not) be studied. To begin, it must be noted that despite the wealth of terminology, including a wide array of terms for characterizing both "the past" (Fordism, monopoly capitalism, etc.) and "the present" (post-Fordism, flexible accumulation, etc.), few studies have traced capitalism's most recent transformation in any detail. This is not to suggest that a range of "new" phenomena, from social movements, sweatshops, and the decline of labor unions to the dismantling of particular industries and the reconfiguring of urban space have not caught the ethnographic eye of anthropologists and others. However, although much of this literature, and particularly that on contract farming, has pointed to a number of interesting problems and questions, and forced researchers to situate local forms of agriculture, industry, identity, and culture within broader political economies, surprisingly few studies have combined historical, comparative, *and* ethnographic analysis.

In the case of contracting, macro-historical discussions tend to locate its emergence in broader, largely economic, changes. Contract farming, or the transformation of agriculture more generally, seems to emanate from the logic of capitalist expansion in which class conflict plays little role. All the important struggles and actions take place within or between major corporations and a handful of national governments (Glover and Kusterer 1990; Kim and Curry 1993; Bonanno 1994; McMichael 1991, 1994). Moreover, as a number of scholars have noted, this literature has tended to draw uncritically from debates on *industrial* restructuring, often imposing a Fordist/post-Fordist dichotomy onto agriculture (Goodman and Watts 1994; Grossman 1998). In such a scenario, "Fordist" agriculture is represented by large agro-industrial plantations which, at some point in the 1970s, are replaced by a "post-Fordist" and more flexible system of production based on contract farming. As Goodman and Watts (1994) and Grossman (1998) point out, this Fordist/post-Fordist periodization breaks down when applied to agriculture. Simply put, most of what has been taken as evidence for the emergence of post-Fordism — in particular, contract farming — was already present in the (so-called) Fordist period. However, in all the commotion over labels (i.e. is it or is it not Fordist/post-Fordist?), the basic question of how and through what processes certain changes have occurred becomes lost. If the Fordist/post-Fordist periodization is too simplistic, and debates on industrial restructuring do not explain recent changes in the organization of agriculture, how should such changes be understood?

Unfortunately, ethnographic studies have been of little help in addressing this question. Most have focused on the impact that contracting has had on local groups, whether it be in terms of the household (Carney 1988; Collins 1993), income differentiation (Korovkin 1992), or control over the production process (Clapp 1988; Grossman 1998). These ethnographies do help us understand how a particular group, generally peasants, have *responded to* contracting, either by undermining the terms of the contract or subverting the method of production (Jackson and Cheater 1994; Grossman 1998). The historical emergence of contract farming, however, is either used as a contextual point of departure, taken for granted, or explained by "changes in the world economy." There is an admirable attempt to reinsert agency, but it is a form of agency in which subordinate groups simply respond to broader structural forces. In the end, we learn little about the role that popular struggle plays in processes of global capitalist transformation, and even less about how such changes shape the range of identities and struggles that are open to, cut off from, and manipulated by various groups.[3]

Although scholars, and particularly anthropologists and historians, have become increasingly adept at situating the "local" in relation to the "global," we have been less successful in showing how the local has shaped the global. How do people's actions propel *global* transformations? Although this conceptual void can be traced back to an earlier (1960s/70s) literature on the world-system and dependency, it has become particularly conspicuous in a contemporary period where global capitalism is seen as an unstoppable force. In such a scenario, the global becomes structure and the local agency. One of the central goals of this project is to place politics at the heart of "economic" processes and seemingly abstract categories such as capital, the state, and class struggle. More simply, I show how the local struggles of Ecuadorian peasants and plantation workers, in combination with similar struggles in other banana-producing regions, decisively shaped broader processes of production, marketing, and accumulation within the global banana industry. Shifts within this global industry were not simply the product of an all-powerful transnational capital or the changing needs of the "world-system." Rather, such changes, and the choices and constraints faced by multinational corporations, were conditioned by local struggles over land and labor in places like Tenguel. By placing these struggles at the heart of global transformations, we are not only left with a more meaningful understanding of agency—one in which people are central to broader processes of transformation—but are forced to reveal the political and social content of capitalism (something that is all too often seen only in its economic manifestations; see Wood 1995).

This is not to suggest that multinational corporations have not imposed contracting on an industry-wide level. They have. This is precisely why the banana industry is such an interesting case. Despite the fact that a handful of corporations have maintained a stranglehold over the production and marketing of bananas, the global restructuring of the industry—indeed, the decision by multinationals to pull out of direct production—was ultimately rooted in class conflict. The "world of plantations," its uneven formation, reproduction, and transformation, was constituted through the (often local) struggle between differentiated factions of capital, the state, and popular groups (among others). The sad irony is that peasant-workers' success in undermining one system of production (i.e. the foreign-owned plantation) helped generate a subsequent system (i.e. contract farming) that has undermined their own capacity to effectively organize (at least in the short run).

All of this is not to suggest that nothing is "new" about capitalism in the late twentieth century. To the contrary, one of the reasons why the southern coast of Ecuador is an interesting place from which to examine "late capitalism" is because so many of the changes that have caught the imagination of scholars, journalists, politicians, and others can be seen there in such sharp relief. The region's dominant industry *has* been restructured along the lines predicted by economists and geographers. The large foreign-owned plantations are gone and contract farming has become the dominant method of producing bananas. Similarly, the state's presence in the zone *has* gone through a series of transformations that can be seen throughout much of rural Latin America. A period of intense state investment, most frequently under the guise of agrarian reform or "development," has been followed by a neoliberal period characterized by the withdrawal of state resources and an almost religious turn to the market. And finally, the peasant movements that shook the region in the 1960s and 1970s *have* disappeared, giving way to distinct forms of popular political organization (what some have called "new peasant movements").

The question is not whether these changes in forms of production, state intervention, and popular organizing have happened, but how we characterize and understand them—whether we see them as an automatic response to the changing needs of the "world-system," as an inevitable outcome of "globalization," or as part of a conflict-laden process in which local struggles play a central role in determining the constitution of global outcomes, actors, and histories (to the point where the dichotomy between local/global or above/below becomes increasingly blurred). To understand these transformations requires not only a historical perspective—one that reveals and explains the changes within the continuities—but an ethnographic one that, by placing political struggles at the center of abstract categories and "economic" processes, allows us to see how capitalisms have emerged, been maintained, and transformed (Roseberry 1995). Once actual participants are placed at the center of structured processes it becomes difficult to talk of capital, the state, and the peasantry in abstract terms (or oppose structure to agency). Capital is no longer seen as an omnipotent and nameless force, but comes in a variety of differentiated forms, from United Fruit officials and local capitalists to technical experts and small-time con men. The state is not a faceless structure, but a series of fragmented relationships comprised of heads of ministries, local police forces, labor inspectors, and agrarian reform officials. The peasantry, in turn, is not a like-minded rural mass, but a squatter trying to persuade local officials, a worker hoping to start an organization, and a woman confronting hacienda police. Similarly, the conflicts, struggles, and alliances between *and* among these differentiated groups become much more complicated than formulaic understandings of dependency, the world-system, or (more recently) global-ization suggest (where an infinitely mobile and unchecked transnational capital dominates an increasingly irrelevant state as it exploits an unorga-nized and defenseless working class). The challenge, then, is to under-stand *and* explain the historical specificity of a capitalism in which poli-tics and culture are viewed not as secondary phenomena that operate on a separate level from "the economy," but where human agency is seen as a central component of structured processes that evolve unevenly over time and space. To recognize the social and political content of capi-talism is, as Ellen Meiksins Wood suggests, "to illuminate the terrain of struggle" through which history is made and capitalism transformed (Wood 1995: 25).

THE SETTING

Located on the Pacific coast of South America between Colombia and Peru, Ecuador is divided into three geographic regions: the Oriente or Amazon, the sierra or highlands, and the coastal lowlands. The Oriente occupies about half of the national territory and is a combination of subtropical and tropical Amazonian rainforest that is home to less than 10 percent of the country's twelve million people. The sierra, which sepa-rates the Amazon from the coastal plain, covers about one-quarter of the national territory and is comprised of two parallel mountain chains that run north to south and are separated by an elevated plateau. The historic center of Ecuador's population, the sierra is now home to slightly less than half of the nation's population, of which about one-fifth live in Quito, the nation's capital and second largest city.[4]

Home to almost half of Ecuador's twelve million people, the Ecuador-ian coast—beginning with the humid subtropical zone at the Colombian border, continuing south through the exceptionally productive basin of the Guayas River, and terminating in almost desert-like conditions at the Peruvian frontier—is one of the most fertile agricultural plains in the Americas. Although the production of bananas, shrimp, cattle, rice, and cacao are the most important economic activities, there are few crops that cannot be produced in the coastal region. Small producers, many of whom migrated from dry, rocky zones in the highlands, have a saying that aptly describes much of the coastal plain: "The only thing that does not grow is that which you do not plant."

This is particularly true of the southern coast between Guayaquil and the Peruvian border. Despite the southern zone's relatively small size, it is arguably the most important region in the country. In the north (part of the southern coast), the zone is dominated by Guayaquil, the country's largest city, most important port, and financial-industrial center. At the southern end is the Peruvian border and Machala, the second most important port, a major regional center, and the "banana capital of the world." Around and between these two city-ports lies one of the most productive agricultural zones in the world. Ecuador is the world's largest producer of bananas, one of the largest shrimp exporters, and a major cacao producer. The majority of *each* of these products—the country's most important exports excluding oil—are produced in the southern coast.

The southern coast is shaped like an hourglass. There are two wider sections dominated by Guayaquil in the north and Machala in the south. The northernmost section, moving south from Guayaquil, is warm and relatively dry all year round. Some cacao, a sprinkling of banana, and a little rice can be found, but the area is dominated by large cattle ranches. At the southern end, as one enters the province of El Oro, approaching the regional center of Machala and then finally arriving at the Peruvian border, the Andes slowly move away from the ocean and the coastal plain opens up. Cattle ranches disappear and every hectare of land appears to be covered by banana trees until the fertile zone turns into desert near the Peruvian border (see Map 2).

Linking the northern and southern agricultural areas that surround Guayaquil and Machala is a long, narrow strip that stretches well over 100 kilometers in length but rarely extends more than 15 kilometers in width. Traversed by a series of rivers that cut east to west across the zone, the middle section of the southern coast, or what I shall call Tenguel-Balao, is home to a range of agricultural activities. Small cacao producers occupy considerable quantities of marginal land along the Andean foothills to the east.[5] They are bordered by cattle ranches which eventually give way to banana plantations as one moves further west. Continuing in this direction across the main highway that runs north to south from Guayaquil to Machala, banana plantations dominate the zone before shrimp farms and the Pacific Ocean swallow the landscape. Thus, from the shrimp pools on the Pacific Ocean to the cacao farms in the Andean foothills, virtually the entire middle section of the southern coast is utilized in some way.

This book is not a social history of the entire southern coast. It does not include Guayaquil, Machala, or the agricultural zones immediately surrounding these important cities. Instead, I focus on the cities, towns, hamlets, and haciendas that make up the zone between Naranjal and El Guabo, the thin narrow strip that connects the country's most important

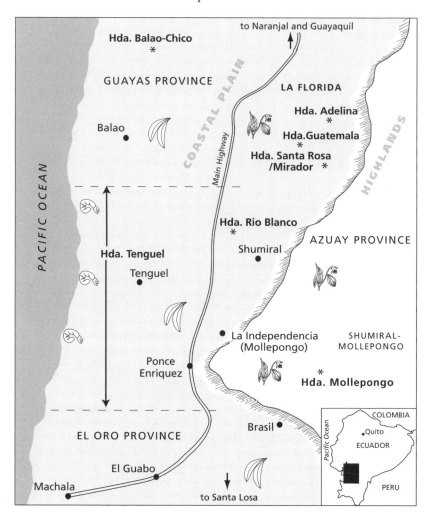

Map 2   The region that I call Tenguel-Balao. It is not drawn exactly to scale but does show the relative position of towns, haciendas, and other markers. The map covers an area that is roughly 100 kilometers in length and 25 kilometers in width.

ports. I have concentrated on the zone of Tenguel-Balao, and particular communities and haciendas within it, not because they are particularly representative, but rather because they played central and early roles in the development of both the region and peasant-worker movements.

Since the turn of the century, the zone of Tenguel-Balao has been at the center of the southern coast's principal transformations, including the cacao boom (1880–1922), the development of the Ecuadorian banana industry (1930s–present), and the region-wide construction of shrimp pools (1970s–present). During the first two decades of the century, as Ecuador became the principal producer of cacao in the world, much of the zone was planted with cacao trees, including Hacienda Tenguel.[6] After the cacao boom collapsed, the United Fruit Company purchased the 100,000-hectare hacienda and introduced the large-scale production of bananas both to the region and Ecuador as a whole. By the early 1950s, as Ecuador was rapidly becoming the largest producer and exporter of bananas in the world, over 80,000 banana stems were leaving Tenguel's port every week.

Not surprisingly, Tenguel was not the only hacienda in the zone that participated in the two booms. A number of large cacao haciendas flourished and then collapsed in the first decades of this century. United Fruit subsequently brought many of these properties under its control and into banana production through a system of contracts (well before contracting would come to dominate the industry in the 1970s). However, one of these holdings, Hacienda Balao Chico, remained outside the company's control and was transformed into an immense banana plantation by a Chilean multinational, Compañia Frutera Sudamericana (Larrea 1987c: 51).

The entrance of these exceptionally large and foreign-owned agricultural enterprises led to the recruitment and reproduction of not only labor forces but also peasant-worker communities and organizations, the formation of which have followed a geographic division that structures this book. On the one hand, peasants, whether as squatters on the fringes of foreign-owned enclaves in the 1940s or as smallholders producing cacao in the 1970s, have occupied marginal lands along the Andean foothills. They have also formed some of the most militant organizations and communities in the southern coast. On the other hand, workers have been concentrated near banana plantations in the fertile coastal plain just to the west. The social division between these two groups is not rigid. Peasants often work on banana plantations and workers frequently own small plots. Nor, as we will see, have their attempts to organize been entirely disconnected. Nevertheless, there has been a politics of space. Geography has profoundly shaped the type of political and economic opportunities that have been open to, created by, and closed off from peasants and workers in different times and places.

Two of the country's strongest agricultural labor unions emerged in Tenguel and Balao Chico in the 1950s, towns located in the heart of the coast's most fertile sections at United Fruit's Hacienda Tenguel and the Compañía Frutera's Hacienda Balao Chico. Moreover, at the same time as the two multinationals were struggling with organized groups of plantation *workers* at the core of their respective properties, they became involved in land conflicts with independent *peasants* located on the margins (see Map 2). About five kilometers to the southeast of Tenguel lies the small hamlet of La Independencia, founded during the 1940s and 1950s when neighboring peasants confronted United Fruit, formed one of the earliest peasant organizations in the region (the Mollepongo Commune), and won marginal sections of the hacienda at the foot of the Andes (chapter four). Inspired by their neighbors in La Independencia, ex-workers of Hacienda Tenguel would go through a similar process of struggle and community formation in the late 1950s (chapter five). The result of this struggle, the small community of Shumiral, lies just northeast of La Independencia, or about ten kilometers northeast of the town of Tenguel. Here again, the struggle involved the formation of a peasant organization (the Colonia Agrícola Shumiral), the creation of a community through land invasion, and the dismantling of a foreign enclave (United Fruit lost 2500 hectares). These early peasant land invasions also provided the foundation on which subsequent popular struggles for the land would emerge in the late 1960s. Not only did the peasants inspire plantation workers to invade the core of Hacienda Tenguel in 1962, but they themselves reemerged as political actors after three years of military dictatorship (1963–1966), challenging the region's elite by forming organizations, invading lands, and establishing new communities during the late 1960s and 1970s (chapter seven). One of these conflicts forced Hacienda Balao Chico to cede almost 4000 hectares of marginal land to peasant invaders and led to the formation of Luz y Guia, a community and organization located about ten kilometers north of Shumiral (chapter eight).

In each of these locales the peasantry's movement for land and community would have its own logic and timing. The strategies employed and the violence used depended on the peasants and landlords involved, as well as the alliances they formed with local military forces, state agencies, and other outside groups. Yet, when these local organizations and communities briefly came together in the mid-1970s, they formed a regional movement that would play a key role in determining how and by whom the zone's marginal lands would be utilized. Plantation workers, on the other hand, have seen their labor unions thoroughly dismantled since the 1960s as contract farming and associated forms of state regulation have taken hold of the more fertile sections of the coastal plain.

Indeed, as integral a role as popular struggle has played in the disintegration of foreign-owned plantations, peasants and workers were not able to dictate the subsequent terms through which land would be distributed and agricultural products cultivated and sold. Just as the dismantling of enclaves took place through an unequal struggle between differentiated factions of capital, the state, and peasant-workers, so too did the uneven emergence of a system of capital accumulation based on contract farming. Both peasants and workers were, more often than not, simply outmatched.

The large foreign-owned plantations have long since been dismantled, but agricultural labor unions and peasant movements for the land have also disappeared. Today, the zone of Tenguel-Balao is dominated by large producers of bananas who possess *relatively* secure contracts with multinational exporters. Existing alongside these large agro-industrial enterprises are both plantation workers and a semi-proletarianized class of small cacao producers who occupy the Andean foothills. The political-economic process through which this constantly changing human geography has unevenly emerged is the subject of this study.

ORGANIZATION AND SOURCES

The first half of the book examines the emergence and eventual decline of a system of capital accumulation characterized by large banana enclaves directly owned and operated by multinationals such as United Fruit. Using correspondence between United Fruit's representatives and the American Consulate's office in Ecuador, chapter two begins by outlining some of the international and national factors that first drew United Fruit to the southern coast of Ecuador in the 1930s. Although this correspondence provides a somewhat biased look at a multinational's attempt to secure the broader conditions necessary for a capitalist enterprise, it forces us to reconsider what we mean by the "penetration" of "foreign capital" into a Third World nation-state. Chapter three—based on over 100 interviews with former workers, administrators, and labor organizers—continues the discussion of United Fruit's uneven entrance into Ecuador from the local perspective of Hacienda Tenguel. By importing significant quantities of materials and people into a largely undeveloped zone, United Fruit's entrance involved the creation of popular organizations, systems of labor control, and forms of state intervention. Chapter four explores the first of a series of popular attacks—orchestrated by neighboring peasants located in the marginal area of Mollepongo—that eventually made it impossible for United Fruit to continue its operations at Tenguel. Although complemented by interviews with the peasants themselves, this chapter is based largely on correspondence between two employees of United Fruit, the company lawyer and the general manager of Ecuadorian operations. These letters provide a unique, "insider's" view into the relationships between a major multinational, the Ecuadorian state, and a small group of persistent peasants. Chapter five explores the second successful attack on the territorial integrity of Hacienda Tenguel. In the late 1950s, recently laid-off workers invaded marginal sections of the hacienda in the zone known as Shumiral. This invasion not only made it impossible for United Fruit to expand the geographic scope of its operations, but provided the workers at the core of the property with an inspirational example. Chapter six then returns to the heart of the enclave and examines the 1962 workers' invasion of the entire property. Using workers' own narratives to interrogate newspaper accounts of the invasion, this chapter concludes the first half of the book. The invasion of Hacienda Tenguel brought an end to enclave-style production in Tenguel and ushered in agrarian reform at both local and national levels. With United Fruit forced from the zone, a wide range of groups intensified the struggle over how and by whom the coastal plain would be distributed and utilized.

The second half of the book, chapters seven through ten, explores the protracted emergence of a "new" system of capital accumulation that has been defined first and foremost by contract farming. Chapter seven examines the agrarian reform project at the core of Hacienda Tenguel, a process that saw the ex-workers first acquire and then lose a large portion of the property to domestic capitalists. Once again, oral accounts from the ex-workers and their families are used to interrogate agrarian reform reports and court documents. Chapters eight and nine return to the more marginal zones near Mollepongo and Shumiral where independent groups of peasants first confronted United Fruit in the 1940s and 1950s. It was in these zones—at the same time as Tengueleños were enmeshed in the country's first agrarian reform project—that groups of peasants began to (re)organize in the late 1960s, pressure the state for a more meaningful reform, and invade marginal haciendas located at the edge of the Andes. These chapters, based both on oral accounts and a "popular" archive,[7] examine the slow emergence, regional expansion, and eventual decline of a peasant movement during the 1960s and 1970s. Finally, chapter ten examines the present system of contract farming, particularly its implications for popular struggle and organizing.

A CONCLUDING NOTE

Throughout this history I try to demonstrate how the political struggles of peasants and workers have been central to broader processes of transformation. Part of the story necessarily involves moments of "victory" when peasant-workers came together and defeated a large company, scared off a local landlord, or sent the police running. Indeed, the temptation to end the historical narrative with the takeover of Hacienda Tenguel, or the subsequent emergence of a region-wide peasant movement, was seductive. Upbeat histories in which the downtrodden are victorious —if only for a day—are pleasant to both read and write. However, peasants and workers, both in the southern coast of Ecuador and elsewhere, do not shape history only during those dramatic (and sometimes revolutionary) moments when their actions demand the attention of elites. Nor is their political and economic influence limited to what have been called "everyday forms of resistance," those thousands of individual, anonymous, and unorganized acts of subordination that silently transform the socioeconomic landscape (Scott 1985). We must, in short, begin to understand how the *failed* (yet conscious and organized) struggles of subordinate groups shape historical processes. Histories of partial and sometimes total defeat must be traced alongside and within what are almost always *partial* victories.

It was clear from my first day in Tenguel that Jacinto Lozano and the others who contributed to this story would not allow me to end a history of the southern coast with the invasion of Hacienda Tenguel or the successful struggle for agrarian reform. Most people eagerly recounted the histories of their political activities and organizations, but few were nostalgic about past struggles and almost no one overstated the implications of their successes. The pained expressions on their faces—generated by a simple question regarding the departure of United Fruit—suggested that although they had successfully invaded Hacienda Tenguel in 1962, they had yet to acquire the autonomy and dignity that had motivated them in the first place. New forms of domination, exploitation, and dependence were formed almost as rapidly as old ones were broken. They knew then, and certainly understand now, that—as peasants and workers—victory and success would often be short-lived and almost always incomplete.

Yet they tried. Peasant-workers formed organizations, petitioned the state, denounced their oppressors, and invaded the properties of large multinationals and local capitalists alike. Most often, their attempts to organize were carried out with considerable reluctance, were often crushed, rarely lasted more than a short period, and never fulfilled all of their authors' aspirations. Regardless of their relative success and almost inevitable failure, the political activities and organizations of peasant-workers mattered, both individually and collectively. They formed through struggles that not only shaped state power and transformed processes of capital accumulation in the southern coast, but that provide the basis on which subsequent popular organizations will emerge and continue to struggle for a more equitable existence.

Decades before United Fruit introduced the large-scale production of bananas to Ecuador's southern coast, the region—and Hacienda Tenguel
in particular—played a central role in the first of the country's agricultural booms: cacao. Although cacao is indigenous to the Americas and
was traded throughout the precolonial and colonial periods, it was not
until the latter half of the nineteenth century that a significant luxury
market for chocolate developed in the United States and Europe. Consequently, production expanded rapidly. The major sites of cultivation
gradually drifted south in reaction to plant diseases and soil depletion,
with semi-organized production beginning in Mexico and then peak-
ing first in Venezuela during the mid to late 1800s, in Ecuador at the
turn of the century, and in Brazil by the first decade of the 1900s. After
1910, the dominant production site moved across the Atlantic to the
Gold Coast of Africa (Wickizer 1951: 12). Between 1900 and World War I,
world cacao exports more than doubled, and by 1931 they had surpassed
500,000 tons (Wickizer 1951: 263). Unfortunately, by the time chocolate
had been transformed from a luxury item at the beginning of the century
to a major industry after the first World War, Ecuadorian production had
been devastated by diseases and the rapid rise of competitors in Brazil
and Africa.

Although the country could not take advantage of the growing demand for chocolate after World War I, the Ecuadorian cacao boom, last-
ing roughly from 1880 to 1920, nonetheless had a dramatic impact on the
political economy of both the coastal region and the country as a whole.
By 1904, or less than two decades after Ecuadorians began to seriously
cultivate cacao, the country itself was the largest producer in the world
and cacao represented between 60 and 70 percent of Ecuador's total exports. Because production remained largely in the hands of domestic producers, cacao shaped the entire political-economic landscape, speeding
up the country's integration into the world economy, financing state expansion, and altering power relations on national, regional, and local
levels.[1]

The most conspicuous consequence of Ecuador's rapid entrance into the world of export agriculture was the emergence of a new economic and political elite. From 1895 and Eloy Alfaro's "Liberal Revolution" until the end of the cacao boom in the early 1920s, the national government was a relatively coherent instrument of class rule under the control of a landowning export elite based in the coast. Coastal landowners, a handful of whom owned most of the cacao-producing land, dominated the Liberal party, the government, major banks, and significant sectors of the Ecuadorian economy during the first decades of the century (Crawford de Roberts 1980; Cueva 1982).

The rapid expansion of cacao production after 1880 served to solidify and even exacerbate existing inequalities in rural areas of the coast. Cultivation expanded rapidly as established families extended the boundaries of their already immense properties at the expense of both state lands and peasant holdings. Although contemporary Ecuadorian cacao production has, since the 1970s, been largely in the hands of peasants (i.e. small producers), it was cultivated on immense plantations during the boom years at the turn of the century. Haciendas were owned and managed by a small group of Ecuador's wealthiest families, even if—as in the case of Hacienda Tenguel—they often contracted with peasants to clear, plant, and then care for trees during the initial stages of cultivation.

Although the expansion of cacao production integrated Ecuador into the world economy, expanded the state's resources, and shifted the center of power from the highlands to the coast, it is important to keep the first of Ecuador's export booms in perspective. Cacao production remained concentrated along major rivers, in large part because the development of roads, the rapid growth of regional population centers, and the massive migration from the highlands to the coast would not occur until the banana boom and the 1950s. The expansion of cacao at the turn of the century did open new areas of the coast to agricultural development, particularly in the Guayas River basin and along the southern coast (i.e. areas where transportation could be handled by boat). But it was bananas, not cacao, that would ultimately bring "development" to much of the coastal region. The Guayaquil-Machala highway, the main artery linking Tenguel and the southern coast to the rest of the country, was little more than a dirt path until the late 1950s when much of the coastal jungle was replaced by banana plantations.

More importantly, by 1915 it was clear that the Ecuadorian cacao boom would not last forever. Although Ecuador had its largest harvest ever during the first year of World War I, a number of problems were becoming apparent. Cacao trees in West Africa and Brazil had matured, making

Table 1   Cacao Production on Haciendas in Tenguel-Balao

		NUMBER OF QUINTALES		
Haciendas	Trees	1918	1921	1925
Tenguel	3,000,000	22,984	30,626	883
San Rafael	300,000	3,781	4,067	3
Mercedes	800,000	6,711	11,078	81
Balzillar	850,000	5,915	8,702	348
Adelina/Mirador	300,000		1,500	

Source: Crawford de Roberts 1980: 201, 203

Ecuador an increasingly minor producer. Moreover, World War I had devastated the world trade in cacao. Supply began to outpace demand and surpluses rapidly built up around production sites. To complicate matters, an agricultural disease—the "Witch's Broom"—was devastating Ecuadorian trees by the early 1920s. Some areas such as Tenguel-Balao were completely destroyed, and few zones were left unaffected (Crawford de Roberts 1980: 199–205; see Tables 1 and 2).

The impact of the cacao crisis was felt differently by the various groups involved in the crop's production and marketing. Workers were laid off en masse. In Tenguel-Balao, labor forces were cut between 50 and 90 percent and some people recall large groups of fired workers wandering the zone in search of food, jobs, and land. As a group, however, workers survived the crisis better than elites. After a difficult period of transition, workers simply (re)expanded their subsistence holdings to make up for the loss of wages.

The collapse of cacao devastated the bourgeoisie's economic and political power. Coastal elites quickly lost control of the national government and in 1925 a group of low-ranking military officers instituted what is known as the Julian Revolution. The "Revolution" ushered in a period of instability characterized by two important features. First, the central government would never again be so clearly controlled by a single faction of the dominant classes. For over two decades, from the end of liberal rule in 1925 until the beginning of the banana boom in 1948, no single group (from either the sierra or the coast) could maintain control over a central government that changed hands over twenty times. Crisis and instability became institutionalized. Second, the Julian experiment represented the beginning of a political period in which popular classes had to be taken into account by those who ruled. The cacao boom had generated enough wealth and expanded the government sufficiently to create a growing middle class of professionals, bureaucrats,

Table 2   Number of Workers on Haciendas in Tenguel-Balao

Hacienda	1922	1925
Tenguel	540	238
San Rafael	75	24
Mercedes	134	81
Libertad	280	19

Source: Crawford de Roberts 1980: 201, 203

and intellectuals. A small proletariat also emerged around public services, small industry, and Guayaquil's port (Cueva 1982).[2] By challenging the landed elite's monopoly over political power, these groups transformed and complicated the political terrain in which United Fruit found itself in the 1930s and 1940s.

THE COLLAPSE OF A CACAO HACIENDA: TENGUEL, 1900–1934

It was just prior to and during the cacao boom that Tenguel was transformed into Ecuador's largest and most developed hacienda. Owned by one of the country's elite families (Caamaño), and located to the south of Guayaquil, Hacienda Tenguel was already the country's largest producer of cacao when its owner went in search of foreign capital in the first part of the twentieth century.[3] In 1910, Hacienda Tenguel became *Caamaño Tenguel Estate Limited,* a British-based and -backed corporation. Within a short time after its British incorporation and the infusion of foreign capital, Tenguel expanded to three million cacao trees. In addition to vast groves of cacao, the hacienda was exceptionally well maintained and boasted an expansive infrastructure. There were over three hundred workers' houses spread out over seven or eight population centers. Foreign experts were brought in and the system of production and management was modernized during the 1910s (Crawford de Roberts 1980; Chiriboga 1980; author interviews).

Despite working from a relatively high level of investment, the system of *sembradores* that was used throughout much of coastal Ecuador was also adopted in Tenguel. In general, the *sembrador* (subcontractor) would clear, plant, and then care for cacao trees while planting food crops on the same or nearby lands. Upon termination of the contract (generally four to six years), the sembrador would turn over the planted area to the landowner who would pay a cash sum for each tree. The landowner would then work the plantation with hacienda peons who were paid in a combination of cash, access to land, and other benefits. This system not only allowed landowners to plant their land with relatively little capital, but shifted all of the production risks to the sembrador; if the trees died or were of poor quality, the sembrador could lose all or part of his investment (Crawford de Roberts 1980; author interviews). In Tenguel, a sembrador could often stay in the same general area for up to twenty years, working a subsistence plot while clearing and planting different zones with cacao. With an impressive infrastructure, housing, and considerable land, Hacienda Tenguel was able to attract sembradores and workers during the first quarter of the century. By the early 1920s, the zone was home to migrants from all over Ecuador and the hacienda was employing over five hundred wage laborers (Crawford de Roberts 1980: 203).

Even at its peak (1912–1922), however, Caamaño Tenguel Estate Limited was not devoted exclusively to cacao. In addition to some three million cacao trees, former workers recall the production of nearly everything, from sugar and cattle to basic food crops such as yucca and plantains, as well as a wide range of fruits. The hacienda's isolation from both Guayaquil and highland population centers, as well as the underdevelopment of local markets, made it economically impossible to have a completely proletarianized workforce. Cacao was shipped to Guayaquil, and some basic goods were brought in by boat. In general, however, workers sustained themselves through a variety of activities ranging from wage labor and the production of food crops to hunting, fishing, and small-scale marketing.

Despite *relatively* high levels of wage labor and capital investment, forms of labor control and social relations remained decidedly "archaic" and Tengueleños refer to this period as "the time of slavery." Arrests and jailings, as well as forms of punishment and torture, were both frequent and arbitrary. The hacienda's relative isolation and the absence of state authorities contributed to the random (though purposeful) nature of hacienda violence. The system of production also shaped plantation management and forms of labor control. Maintaining a relatively secure hold on small but fertile subsistence plots, the peasants' need for wage-labor did not match the hacienda's demand for wage-laborers. Because the hacienda's ability to control production and appropriation was limited by the "autonomy" that peasants derived from their subsistence plots, the owners and administrators found it necessary to use non-economic forms of coercion to insure a docile and available workforce. As one ex-worker recalls:

> The administrator controlled everything. If you did not want to work they would beat you or put you in jail. The women had to work also, cooking meals and washing clothes in the main house. It was their

> obligation. We had to bow when he came around on his horse. The
> people really had no respect for themselves. If you wanted to punish
> your woman you had to ask the administrator. We were like slaves.
>
> Yes, there were some good things too. They gave land to work and
> meals when we worked for wages. The patron would also help with
> a loan or when someone was sick. But it was a tough period. We had
> few options and could not leave. (L.V. 8/95)[4]

In order to secure control over appropriation, the hacienda thus extended its system of domination beyond the work process itself and into
social relations at the community and family level. As the preceding
quote suggests, punishment was often administered in order to force
"peons" to carry out tasks they had no economic incentive to complete.
At the same time, random and arbitrary forms of violence were equally
common and conveyed a broader message: despite a certain autonomy
derived from subsistence plots, the very existence of community and
family were largely under the control of the patron. Forms of benevolence, equally arbitrary, conveyed a similar message: the peasant's world
was dependent on the patron's kind heart (Sider 1986: 55). As we will
see, although Hacienda Tenguel's next owner, the United Fruit Company, would implement a much more "rational" system of production
and domination, it also had a profoundly cultural component.

In terms of trees, volume of production, number of workers, and production techniques, Hacienda Tenguel was an immense and exceptionally modern hacienda at the time of cacao's collapse. In 1920, Hacienda
Tenguel produced some 30,000 quintales of cacao, making it the largest
single producer in the country. Less than five years later, in 1925, the
hacienda had been effectively destroyed by agricultural disease and produced only 883 quintales (Crawford de Roberts 1980: 199–205). As a significant producer of cacao, Tenguel, and in fact the whole southern coast,
was finished until the postwar period when peasants would reintroduce
the crop to marginal lands that were unsuitable for banana production.

Between 1922 and 1925, Tenguel's workforce was cut in half, with other
major plantations in the zone such as Mercedes, Libertad, Adelina, and
Mirador being similarly affected. Many of the fired workers were forced
to leave the zone. Some left for Guayaquil where conditions were often
worse, while others found arrangements on nearby haciendas or on sugar
plantations that emerged in the Guayas basin during this period (ibid.;
author interviews). A large portion had few options and were forced to
stay. Aside from Guayaquil, which remained more than a day's journey, there were no cities of any importance in the region. Machala,
which would emerge as a major regional center during the banana boom,

was little more than a tiny port and offered workers few opportunities. Consequently, many stayed in Tenguel, occupying and cultivating marginal areas of the hacienda that remained outside of the administration's reach.

Hacienda Tenguel went into default and the Banco Territorial took it over in 1926 (Crawford de Roberts 1980: 233). At the time of its takeover, the hacienda had an immense infrastructure that reflected a large capital investment. According to the Remate de Hacienda Tenguel (conducted during the early 1930s),[5] the hacienda was home to hundreds of horses and nearly 1000 head of cattle. There was the main house, the administrative building, several houses for field bosses, a church, a bakery, as well as hundreds of workers' homes. Storage facilities and other buildings related to cacao production and cattle raising were also spread throughout the hacienda. Moreover, despite the devastation of the disease, there were still over two million cacao trees covering the property.

The Banco Territorial was not in a position to manage a hacienda of this size and continued to rent out sections to sembradores. Other sections were simply left abandoned and taken over by peasant families. Few Tengueleños recall the change in ownership, from a British-backed corporation to an Ecuadorian bank, and almost no one remembers it as anything significant. Opportunities for wage labor were less frequent, though still available, and access to land became less difficult. As one of Tenguel's longtime inhabitants recalls:

> I remember when the bank took over. But really little changed. The more important change was the [earlier] destruction [of the cacao trees]. When the bank took over few of the ex-administrators departed. Even Don Stagg remained and managed the area around Tenguel. The employers were just as bad but we worked less [for wages] and had more time on our plots. Things really did not change until the Colombian came and the United Fruit Company took over in 1933 or 1934. (J.C., 7/95)

When United Fruit arrived in the 1930s, it confronted a complicated political terrain—characterized by general economic crisis, a politically bankrupt elite, the growing political activity of popular classes, and the fracturing of an already fragmented state—in which Ecuador's ultimate populist, José María Velasco Ibarra, received 80 percent of the vote and was swept into the presidency for the first of five times in September 1934 (Cueva 1982; de la Torre 1993). In Tenguel, United Fruit found a zone with few inhabitants and almost no roads or other substantial infrastructure. By the time the company arrived, the hacienda had existed in a state of semi-abandonment for over a decade, but nonetheless possessed thousands of hectares of naturally irrigated and exceptionally fertile coastal plain. Although the full-scale development of the zone and Ecuador's emergence as a major producer of bananas would have to wait until the end of World War II, United Fruit's purchase of the property in 1934 signaled the beginning of a new era both for the southern coast and the country as a whole. It is to this period that we now turn.

2   The Banana Boys Come to Ecuador

From 1900 until the 1960s, the global banana industry emerged and became quickly defined by the control and direct involvement of multinational corporations in every phase of banana production, transportation, and distribution. The production of bananas revolved around extremely large foreign-owned plantations or enclaves. Multinationals such as the United Fruit Company and the Standard Fruit Company bought immense quantities of land, made extremely large investments in machinery and other resources, and began the agro-industrial production of bananas. Almost from the beginning, however, this enclave form of production was threatened by a number of factors. Due to agricultural diseases, labor problems, and hard-to-manage governments, multinationals slowly abandoned their own plantations throughout much of Latin America. By the 1960s, the leading corporations were withdrawing from direct production and implementing a system of contract farming that has since restructured the geopolitical landscapes of banana producing regions (Larrea 1992; Bourgois 1989; FLACSO 1987; Botero and Sierra 1981; Bucheli 1997; Lopez 1986; Slutsky and Alonso 1980; Moberg 1997; Grossman 1998; Soluri 1998; Striffler 1998, 1999).[1] How do we understand this global restructuring of the banana industry, or the spread of contract farming more generally in the latter half of the twentieth century?

The present chapter examines this process from its earliest moments when United Fruit and other foreign capitalists were attempting to establish the necessary conditions for the direct production and export of bananas in Ecuador. Although the company's problems would multiply once it arrived in Tenguel and began to manage the hacienda (chapters 3–5), United Fruit had to first secure a number of guarantees from the Ecuadorian state before purchasing land or planting banana trees. The company had the resources to enter and leave as many as a dozen Latin American countries, but when it was *there*—whether *there* was Guatemala, Costa Rica, Colombia, or Ecuador—it had to deal with the peculiarities of particular states and political landscapes. The "penetration" of foreign capital was never as smooth and one-sided as the metaphor often seems to imply.

Scholars interested in the relationships between Third World states and foreign capital have tended to fall into one of two camps. On the one hand, there are those who argue that Third World states are "weak," lacking the power to shape the nature, timing, and impact of foreign capital (Murray 1971; Cox 1981). Although this argument has become particularly pervasive in the contemporary period (a moment defined in large part by the mobility/flexibility of capital), it has also been applied to earlier historical periods in which foreign companies operated with relative freedom in many parts of the Third World (Ohmae 1990; Horsman and Marshall 1994; see McMichael and Myhre [1991] and Weiss [1994] for interesting discussions). In fact, United Fruit and "the banana republic" are often taken as the quintessential examples of this phenomenon in Latin America. On the other hand, there are those who insist that Third World states can and do achieve a certain degree of independence from foreign capital, influencing the nature and impact of capital's entrance into national political economies (Gordon 1988; Evans 1985; Picciotto 1991; Pooley 1991; Weiss 1997).

In this chapter, as well as in subsequent chapters, I attack the problem from a slightly different angle, suggesting that both approaches make incorrect assumptions about the state. States *do* matter, but not simply because they are (or are not) strong, independent, or nationalist, understandings that misleadingly view "the State" as an autonomous and discrete policy-making actor that stands apart from "society" or "economy" (Mitchell 1991). United Fruit's difficulties in securing favorable tax concessions or acquiring help from the local police did not so much stem from the independent, anti-imperialist, or "strong" nature of the Ecuadorian state. In fact, due to the collapse of cacao, the Ecuadorian state was in constant financial crisis during this period and elites were desperately searching for an alternative export. If there was ever a time and place when United Fruit could have dictated the terms of its presence, it was in Ecuador during the 1930s and 1940s.[2]

The state played decisive roles in United Fruit's ability to purchase land, export fruit, and control peasant workers, but the roles it played were ambiguous, contradictory, and divided because the state itself was so fragmented. "It" rarely shaped legislation and conflicts in coherent, single-minded, or planned ways. This lack of cohesion, which had a decisive impact on United Fruit's operations, was due not so much to the weakness of the Ecuadorian state during this period, but to the extent and manner in which it was permeated by a wide array of competing interests. Put another way, the state did not frustrate United Fruit's operations because it was strong (with the power to facilitate, inhibit, or shape the "penetration" of foreign capital), but because its organizational terrain was characterized by contradictions that were intimately linked to broader conflicts and interests that even a company with the resources of United Fruit could not predict, let alone control.

A FRUIT GOES GLOBAL: BANANAS BEFORE ECUADOR, 1900–1934

The political activities of workers and peasants, along with agricultural diseases and Latin American governments, have decisively shaped the movement of capital in the global banana industry. In the first decades of the industry, from about 1900 to 1930, there were a number of factors inherent in the production and marketing of bananas that contributed to the emergence of large multinationals. The opening up of new lands, the development of extensive canals, the scientific research demanded by tropical agriculture, the construction of railroads, the purchasing of machinery, and the global transportation and distribution of a perishable commodity all required an investment well beyond the range of most capitalists (Kepner 1936: 40–41). Writing in 1936, Kepner and Soothill characterized United Fruit's rise in the following terms: "this powerful company has throttled competitors, dominated governments, manacled railroads, ruined planters, choked cooperatives, domineered over workers, fought organized labor, and exploited consumers" (Kepner and Soothill 1935: 336). By 1930, United Fruit had total assets of close to $250 million and was the "unquestioned lord of the banana industry" (ibid.: 341).[3]

Due to their susceptibility to disease and the rapidity with which they depleted soils, bananas were cultivated in an almost semi-migratory fashion prior to the introduction of disease resistant varieties in the 1960s (Bourgois 1989: 6). As a former United Fruit engineer noted:

> The Panama Disease used to kill everything. The only solution was to get a hold of new lands. It was not possible to maintain bananas once the disease struck. So when one farm died off another was planted, one would die another was planted. . . . That's how we ended up in Ecuador. (ibid.: 7)

Because bananas (before the 1960s) could not be cultivated on the same land for more than about ten years, the industry was ideally suited for large companies that had the resources to spread production throughout a number of countries. United Fruit was continually moving from one production site to the next. During the first decade of its existence (1900–1910), the company's most extensive banana cultivations were in

Costa Rica and Panama. The Panama Disease then devastated production in both countries, leading the multinational to search out disease-free production sites in Guatemala, Honduras, Colombia, Mexico, and eventually Ecuador (Bourgois 1989: 7–8; Kepner 1936: 44–50; LaBarge 1959: 20–40).[4]

In addition to spreading its cultivations over multiple sites, United Fruit dispersed the risks involved in agricultural production by contracting with local producers. Although the push toward contracting would be greatly intensified in the mid-1970s (in a quite different form), the practice has been an integral part of the banana industry from its inception. In general, United Fruit would develop its own plantations while establishing relationships with local planters (i.e., extending credit, expertise, etc.). Then, as diseases inevitably reduced productivity on United Fruit's own lands, "independent" planters would make up the difference, supplying a larger and larger portion of the company's exports from any given site.[5]

Once United Fruit or Standard Fruit installed the basic infrastructure, including ports, railroads, and processing centers, banana production required relatively little capital during the first half of the century. As a result, the majority of contracted planters were peasants who owned little or no land. Quite often, the producer leased the land from the company, borrowed money from the company, traveled on the company's railroads, depended on the company store for food, and was beholden to local officials who received their salaries from the company (Kepner 1936: 55). United Fruit could do almost anything to the contractee's land, but was under no obligation to buy the fruit. Such planters were, of course, devastated when the company inevitably moved to another zone (ibid.: 90–105).

The ability to move from site to site has also helped United Fruit control labor. With production sites spread throughout Latin America, United Fruit had considerable flexibility when dealing with labor problems on any particular plantation. Confident that banana exports would continue to flow from a variety of sources, United Fruit could afford to wait out the isolated strike, repress workers, or simply abandon production in particular locales. This strategy became increasingly important as labor strikes became more common during and after the Great Depression. Although the first major strike of the period occurred in Colombia in 1928 (Kepner 1936; Herrera Soto and Romero Castaneda 1979), smaller-scale actions, many of which were linked to broader revolutionary movements, were carried out during the same period on company plantations in Panama, Costa Rica, and Honduras. For example, in Honduras, strikes occurred continuously after 1930 and were often associated with broader political movements. Similarly, the 1934 strike at Limón, in Costa Rica, not only included over 10,000 workers but involved the Communist Party (LaBarge 1959: 36–37). These strikes drew their strength both from labor's broader growth during this period and the increasingly independent nature of Central American governments. United Fruit could no longer assume that generous land concessions and tax policies would be extended without a fight, and labor laws were strengthened in virtually all of the banana-producing countries during the 1930s.[6]

Thus, by the 1940s, and certainly by the 1950s, all the traditional problems faced by United Fruit had not only worsened, thereby cutting into profits and scaring shareholders (Bucheli 1998), but could be found in virtually every country and region where the company was involved in the production of bananas. To be sure, United Fruit's ability to move from site to site served to spread risk and maintain a sufficient level of profits; but the fact remained that labor problems, agricultural diseases, and Latin American governments were making it increasingly difficult to reproduce a system of production based on the corporate-owned and -operated plantation.

It was out of this continual search for disease-free lands and a cheap, docile labor force that United Fruit entered Ecuador and began exploring production sites in the late 1920s. At least initially, Ecuador seemed ideal. Not only were labor organizations relatively underdeveloped compared to those in Colombia and Central America, but cacao production had collapsed, leaving large quantities of land and labor available in the coastal region (Chiriboga 1980; Crawford de Roberts 1980; Guerrero 1980). Since Ecuador had never produced bananas on a large scale, the Panama Disease was largely absent and workers had no experience in dealing with foreign banana companies. Moreover, the collapse of cacao, the country's primary export during the first decades of the century, meant that both elites and the state were looking for an export alternative. The problem, however, was that between the late 1920s, when United Fruit first began to explore production sites in the coastal region, and 1934, when the multinational purchased Hacienda Tenguel and a number of other properties, Ecuador's political climate changed dramatically, making life complicated for multinational corporations engaged in direct production. Before turning to these broader changes, and their local manifestations in Tenguel, the next section explores United Fruit's entrance into Ecuador on the national level during the late 1920s and early 1930s.

THE FIRST BITE

In November 1922, just as the full effects of the cacao crisis were beginning to be felt, the American consul general at Guayaquil reported that a new law had been passed by the Ecuadorian Congress in order to encourage the production and export of fruit. Although the first known presence of United Fruit representatives in Ecuador was still two years away, the law was clearly directed at, if not generated by, multinationals. It granted "special facilities" to steamers appropriate for the ocean transport of fruit, gave potential planters access to virtually unlimited quantities of land, and allowed producers to construct railroads and other infrastructural works necessary for the production and transport of fruit. The law also contained a clause specifically directed at bananas. They would be exempt from all export duties for the first two years of production and subject to very low taxes thereafter.

It took about two years, but the build-it-and-they-will-come strategy of the Ecuadorian government produced results by the end of 1924. In early December, rumors began to circulate that United Fruit experts were in the northern province of Esmeraldas, the U.S.-based South Pacific Banana Corporation was thought to be exploring possibilities around Guayaquil, and two Chilean companies had even begun small-scale exports (NA RG59, 822.6156/1, 12/5/24).[7] Rumors surrounding United Fruit became stronger, leading the American consul to report:

> Mr. Sinners spent several weeks in Guayaquil and his presence became a matter of interest in business circles because of the secrecy with which surrounded his movements. I now have reason to believe that Mr. Sinners represents the United Fruit Company and that he was negotiating for the purchase of the plantation "Tenguel". . . . I believe he will stop in Esmeraldas . . . to investigate the property owned by the Ecuador Land Company [British]. If the United Fruit Company should purchase lands and establish banana plantations in Ecuador, it would mean much to the country. (NA RG59, 822.6156, 12/26/24)

Sinners's loyalties aside, United Fruit exported no bananas and did not purchase Tenguel or any other property during this initial intervention. In fact, it would be another four years before the consulate reported additional activity on the part of U.S. banana companies:

> Arrival in Ecuador of Clarence L. Chester reported to be a representative of the American fruit syndicate. . . . Mr. Chester is alleged to be interested in entering into contracts with Ecuadorian fruit growers

with a view to exporting such products to the United States. According to unconfirmed reports, [Mr. Chester] is representing the United Fruit Company. (NA RG59, 822.6156/3, 12/4/29)

The presence of Chester, who had worked for President Leguía of Peru in the mid-1920s and had twenty years of experience in Latin America, caused "considerable interest . . . in local business and financial circles." He was reportedly trying to make an agreement with domestic fruit growers "for the exportation of bananas to the United States on the boats of the Grace Line." He had promised to finance domestic planters and offered higher prices than the Chilean exporters. Like Sinners, however, Chester refused to reveal whom he represented, insisting that he had no reason to fear the United Fruit Company (NA RG59, 822.6156/4, 3/1/30).

With the support of Ecuadorian Senator Manuel Navarro, Chester had met several times with top government officials, including the Minister of Finance and President Isidro Ayora Cueva himself. In fact, by October 1930, a law was pending before the Ecuadorian Congress that would give Chester the exclusive right to export bananas. Outraged, national newspapers noted that Congress should at least take bids from other foreign capitalists before it sold off the country. Why should this one man be given the exclusive right to export bananas?

In response, Chester assured Senator Navarro and President Ayora that he and his associates did not want to acquire land, control railways, or, "like the United Fruit Company," establish a monopoly. He agreed that the presence of United Fruit would ruin domestic planters and insisted that his group wanted to help *Ecuadorians* grow a high-quality fruit. His company would not produce bananas, but would facilitate Ecuadorians in the development of a truly national industry. In fact, he could not reveal the names of his investors because they were strong competitors of United Fruit, and thus allies of Ecuador (NA RG59, 822.6156/8, 6/12/31).

The attention served to reveal some of the mystery surrounding Chester. He was the vice president of the Pacific Fruit Company based in New York. The company's president was former U.S. Ambassador Poindexter and one of its directors was none other than Ecuadorian Senator Manuel Navarro. Senator Navarro had been acting as Chester's "disinterested" ally in negotiations with both President Ayora and the Ecuadorian Congress. Charles Weinberger, who had worked for United Fruit for over thirty years, was also on the company's board.

Due to opposition from the press and sectors within Congress, Chester could not get the exclusive right to export bananas. Nevertheless, by February 1933, Senator Navarro had managed to push through a series of laws that allowed Congress to sign eight-year contracts with fruit exporters (NA RG59 822.6156/7, 11/18/30). The laws, which promoted the development of ports and gave large land concessions and tax exemptions to foreign companies, generated cries of "Yankee imperialism" and "dollar conquest" from sectors within the press and government. Such opposition was fueled by the fact that at the same time as Senator Navarro was pushing the laws through (his) Congress, he was also negotiating a contract for (his) Pacific Fruit. According to the proposed contract, the Pacific Fruit Company, run by Chester, Navarro, and Weinberger, was to deal directly with domestic planters who could finance themselves. Entrepreneurs looking to begin production could get loans through the State Mortgage Bank which would be partially funded by Pacific Fruit (ibid.).

One of the nation's major newspapers, *El Telégrafo,* immediately suggested that Chester's project was monopolistic, that a number of politicians had serious conflicts of interest, and that government negotiations should be made public. According to the newspaper, the government contract was so ridiculously generous that it would violate the constitution and sovereignty of the country. Most important, Ecuadorian planters would be given little capital to begin farms that would be left wholly unprotected (NA RG59 822.6156/10–13, 2/33). Indeed, the most consistently expressed fear among opponents of foreign banana companies was that Ecuador would become another Central America—that exporters would produce and export their *own* bananas, do nothing to promote domestic planters, and then eventually leave altogether.

Interestingly, it seems as though United Fruit was actually fueling these fears. According to the consulate, "opposition [in the Cabinet] and hostility in the press" were due to "efforts being made by the United Fruit Company to block [Chester's] project" (NA RG59 822.6156/11, 2/13/33). Frank Coleman, the recently appointed representative of United Fruit in Guayaquil, had been spreading information in the United States to discredit the Ecuadorian government, Ecuadorian bananas, and Chester's entire venture.

By March 1933, Chester's project was doomed by opposition from a variety of sources and he returned to New York to meet with the board of directors of the Pacific Fruit Company. The entire project was abandoned. Chester resigned as vice president and was eventually arrested in New York for misusing company funds (NA RG59, 822.6156/13, 4/12/33; 6156/14, 4/28/33). The Pacific Fruit Company closed its New York office and, somewhat suspiciously, moved to Boston, home of United Fruit's corporate headquarters.

United Fruit's campaign against Chester was just one of a number of indications that the company was expanding its operations. It was widely believed, and subsequently confirmed, that company representatives Frank Coleman and Arcesio Echeverri had purchased a number of properties in the southern coast (ibid.). In addition, United Fruit's *SS San Mateo* arrived in Guayaquil in January 1934 and company officials announced that three of their steamers would be definitively assigned to the Guayaquil-Panama-Mobile (Alabama) run. Finally, the clearest signal that United Fruit was committed to Ecuador was the arrival of Richard Goodell. Goodell, who had run company operations in Mexico, was the first real "banana man" sent to Ecuador (NA RG59, 822.6156/21, 8/10/34; 6156/24, 11/24/34). With land, steamers, and personnel in place, United Fruit had officially arrived and Ecuador instantly became a *potentially* important producer and exporter of bananas.

As this brief story about the initial entrances and retreats of foreign banana companies into Ecuador suggests, the process was much more complicated than the metaphor of penetration implies because what constituted both "capital" and "the state," as well as the relationships between them, was exceptionally complex.[8] Although United Fruit was feared, seduced, and attacked by a wide range of groups, including the American consulate's office, foreign and domestic capitalists, sectors within the Ecuadorian state, the national press, as well as peasants and workers, it was only the most important actor among what we commonly refer to as "capital"—a differentiated bunch that in this case included major multinationals, domestic capitalists, and small-time con men (and con men working for multinationals). Moreover, despite the fact that Ecuador's economy was extremely vulnerable during the 1930s, capitalists confronted a variety of national level obstacles *before* they could engage in production. Even multinationals such as United Fruit—which possessed immense resources, could manipulate governments, and had the luxury of operating within as many as a dozen different countries— had to function within quite complicated political arenas.

One of the key factors shaping the Ecuadorian political landscape and the arrival of foreign banana companies was the state. Although the Ecuadorian state of the 1930s was "weak," both because it lacked resources and was constantly changing hands, such a characterization does not help us fully understand the rather complicated story outlined above. As the incestuous relationships between foreign capitalists and members of the Ecuadorian state suggest, the idea that a "weak/strong" state stood apart from and (neutrally) regulated the participation of foreign companies in the Ecuadorian "economy" is largely a fiction. It was not simply the case that the state was weak or divided, that there were internal conflicts within "the state" over the formation and implementation of policies designed to regulate an important sector of "the economy." The image of an internally differentiated state that debates, regulates, and favors certain business interests over others is certainly preferable to one that assumes a unified state that unambiguously facilitates the penetration of (an equally unified) foreign capital.

However, this minor set of disputes, involving a major multinational, a pseudo-capitalist, an Ecuadorian senator, members of Congress, the Cabinet, the president, a former U.S. ambassador, and various state institutions/agencies not only suggests that the Ecuadorian state was highly divided, extremely biased, and easily influenced by a range of interested actors. It indicates that the state can in no way be seen as a discrete policy-making actor that stands above or apart from entities called "society" and "economy." It is worth remembering that Senator Navarro was negotiating a contract between (his) Congress and (his) Pacific Fruit Company in which the latter would purchase bananas from entrepreneurs/congressmen who could obtain financing through the *State* Mortgage Bank, which was partially funded by the Pacific Fruit Company. This complex collusion between members of the Ecuadorian government and the emerging banana industry contradicts the notion of a sharp distinction between state and society/economy.

In addition, the metaphor of a weak/strong state does not help us explain United Fruit's success at outmaneuvering Chester and company, or the subsequent difficulties the company would face at national, regional, and local levels. Regardless of the relative weakness of the state, even one of the largest and most experienced multinationals operating in the region could not simply impose the legal apparatus on which the Ecuadorian banana industry would evolve. Competition and contradictions between and among domestic and foreign capitalists were felt within the terrain of the state and served to complicate the political arena. Legal problems came in a variety of forms and once "resolved" by a particular state agency were almost always subject to review by subsequent governments or different ministries within the same government (who were connected to different factions of the dominant classes).[9]

In short, the success or failure of "foreign capital" in "penetrating" Ecuador, or in this case the ability of a single multinational to set up the conditions necessary for its operations, may have less to do with the relative strength of a particular state than with its internal contradictions—the manner in which its organizational terrain is permeated by wider interests (and how foreign capitalists are able to negotiate those interests). The fragmentary nature of the state, and the key role that those fragmentations played in shaping production systems, property patterns, and forms of conflict, will become even more apparent as we turn to the local level and United Fruit's attempt to plant bananas, control labor, and evict squatters. Despite, or perhaps because of, its internal contradictions and divisions, the state was a key relation of production that contributed to the eventual dismantling of foreign-owned enclaves and the emergence of contract farming.

3   The Birth of an Enclave: Labor Control and Worker Resistance

Disputes over export policies, the legality of land purchases, and a whole range of other problems would continue to preoccupy United Fruit representatives during the 1940s, 1950s, and 1960s. Nevertheless, by the 1930s the company was sufficiently confident in the Ecuadorian political landscape to purchase several large haciendas, secure the rights to a number of others, and begin to establish the *local* conditions necessary for the production, processing, and export of bananas.

United Fruit began production in Tenguel, or what would become the centerpiece of the company's Ecuadorian operations from 1934 until the workers' invasion in 1962. The company's tenure in Tenguel corresponded to, and in many ways helped propel, the Ecuadorian banana boom. When United Fruit first purchased the immense property in 1934, Ecuador was exporting virtually no bananas. Although the presence of United Fruit's steamers in Guayaquil helped stimulate banana production in the 1930s and early 1940s, it was not until after World War II and the expansion of world demand that Ecuador would begin producing and exporting bananas in large quantities. A minor player prior to 1948, Ecuador was producing more bananas than any other country in the world by the mid-1950s. Banana production spread through the Ecuadorian coast, with important production sites in the northern province of Esmeraldas (near the Colombian border), the Guayas River basin, and the zone south of Guayaquil. In contrast to Central America, where production was concentrated on foreign-owned enclaves, the majority of Ecuadorian bananas were produced on medium sized holdings (generally less than 200 hectares) owned by domestic producers (Larrea 1987). To be sure, multinational corporations played a decisive role during the Ecuadorian banana boom from the late 1940s to the mid-1960s. Not only did they control shipping, but a handful of extremely large foreign-owned enclaves dotted the coast from the Colombian border to the southern zone of Tenguel-Balao. Although production from these enclaves never represented the majority of Ecuador's exports, they were important sites around which Ecuadorian capitalists developed their own plantations.

Foreign-owned enclaves were the places where Ecuadorian producers, including large capitalists and poor peasants, sold their bananas, received advice, obtained credit, and secured the necessary inputs to start and maintain banana farms of varying sizes.

Nevertheless, when United Fruit first began in Tenguel in the late 1930s, it was confronted with a semi-abandoned zone covered with neglected cacao trees and dense jungle. The banana boom was still more than a decade away and the state had done little to connect the southern coast to the rest of the country. Guayaquil, which by the 1930s was a bustling port city of well over 100,000 people with a rich history of political unrest, was still more than a day's journey from Tenguel (it is currently less than a two-hour drive; Pineo 1996). Towns that would become important regional centers during the banana boom—including Naranjal, El Guabo, and Santa Rosa—were not yet on the map (see Map 1). Even Machala, the country's second major port and the future banana capital of the world, would not reach a population of 30,000 until as late as 1960 and was only accessible by boat during the 1930s (it is currently about a one-hour drive; Martz 1972: 9). As a result, United Fruit was forced to bring in virtually everything by plane or boat. In addition to the necessary facilities for banana production, including a system of railroads that covered cultivated portions of the hacienda, the company reconstructed the entire town of Tenguel and built a number of smaller hamlets from scratch. Wood and other materials for the workers' homes, the Catholic church, the hospital, the port, and the company store were all imported from the United States. Movie theaters, one for the workers and one for the employees, as well as clubhouses and an employees' pool, were built with imported materials and company-paid labor. Administrators, mechanics, agronomists, and other experts were also brought in from United Fruit's Central American plantations.

Even agricultural laborers had to be brought in from outside the immediate zone during the first years of the hacienda's operation. Although company representatives made occasional forays into the Guayas basin in order to recruit workers, most of the earliest migrants to Tenguel were found in Guayaquil. Many had migrated to the city from rural areas of the coast after the collapse of cacao in the 1920s. Most were poor, had considerable experience in agriculture, and welcomed the opportunity for steady work. The earliest migrants tended to be single men, or at least traveled to the zone without their families. During the 1930s and early 1940s, the zone was thought to be unsuitable for women and children. Later, as Hacienda Tenguel developed and got a reputation for being a fairly attractive place to live and work, workers increasingly came from the southern highlands and arrived with their families. As one former worker and early arrival to the hacienda remembers:

> I came to Tenguel around 1940. My family had moved to Guayaquil in the 1930s because there was no work in [rural areas of] the coast. A friend told me there was this American company that was hiring workers. I got a job and the company took me and some others to Tenguel by boat. There wasn't much here when I arrived, and many people left right after they got here. We had to build everything. But later things improved and I brought my wife and we made a family here. After the second World War, things really picked up and men would arrive with their families from Loja and Cuenca [in the south-central highlands]. (A.F. 8/2/95)

Despite obstacles, much of the infrastructure was in place when world demand for bananas expanded after World War II. Beginning in the mid-1940s, thousands of hectares of bananas were planted and Hacienda Tenguel quickly became the largest producer in the country. By the mid-1950s, at a time when Ecuador was exporting more bananas than any other country in the world, Tenguel was producing over 5 percent of the country's total exports (Sylva 1987: 116). Thousands of workers were hired to not only maintain and expand the hacienda's infrastructure but to produce, clean, harvest, and transport as many as 80,000 stems of bananas every week.[1] Employing nearly 2000 workers by the late 1940s, the hacienda grew to a permanent workforce of close to 2500. In particularly intense periods of expansion, the number of employees could often reach well over 3500. Of the 2500 permanent workers, about 1500 had families living in Tenguel as well as the surrounding hamlets of San Rafael, La Esperanza, Pagua, Chimborazo, and Cotopaxi (IERAC 1964).

There was a relatively high degree of worker specialization and the hacienda's geographic organization reflected the fairly rigid hierarchy found on all United Fruit plantations. Life and work revolved around the town of Tenguel. The company constructed a number of smaller hamlets, but most workers lived in Tenguel itself and those who did not came there almost every day for work assignments, food, medical attention, news, social events, entertainment, and just about everything else. Access to certain areas, services, and houses depended on one's location within the occupational hierarchy. Administrators, engineers, artisans, dock workers, railway operators, and field workers all experienced quite different living conditions and privileges. At the same time, over 70 percent of the permanent workers were classified as "agricultural laborers" (IERAC 1964). Despite a relatively high degree of job specialization, occupational-based divisions among this mass of field workers were relatively minor. Most former laborers remember moving from one specialized task to the next and from one work gang to another. Tasks were specialized, but workers were not.

Before turning to the internal workings of the company's enterprise, it is important to stress that although Hacienda Tenguel shared many of the attributes normally associated with enclaves, including relative isolation, a massive capital investment, and a sizable workforce, such a characterization can be misleading if it hides the hacienda's impact on the regional economy. The emergence of Haciendas Tenguel and Balao Chico, two immense foreign-owned enclaves, stimulated the development of the southern coast in much the same way that the broader growth of the banana industry propelled the development of Ecuador's entire coast during the 1950s and 1960s. Hacienda Tenguel's presence generated, in fact required, *regional* markets and transportation networks that were oriented around the hacienda's quite substantial consumer population. This broader regional development occurred slowly and unevenly, and was partially halted by World War II, but local merchants, peasants, as well as relatively large landowners all took advantage of the opportunities opened up by the hacienda.[2] The political implications of the company's *regional* presence will be explored in subsequent chapters. First, however, we must turn to heart of the hacienda and the forms of labor control and resistance that defined United Fruit's productive operations during the 1940s and 1950s.

LABOR CONTROL AT THE CORE OF AN ENCLAVE

The labor practices employed by United Fruit in order to maintain an available and relatively docile workforce during the 1940s and 1950s are central to any understanding of the workers' invasion and the end of enclave production in the 1960s. The workers and their families would rework the forms of discipline and benevolence utilized by the company, transforming them into an oppositional culture that would eventually force United Fruit from the country and contribute to the withdrawal of multinational corporations from direct production on a global level.

Although a number of the company's labor practices were relatively elaborate, even underhanded, one of the principal factors working on the side of United Fruit was the size and isolation of the hacienda. United Fruit owned everything within the zone, from the machinery and infrastructure to the workers' houses, water, and electricity. Control over points of entry into the core of the hacienda was facilitated by the fact that the company owned the means of transportation for traveling to, from, and within the hacienda. Those workers who were not recruited from outside the zone were screened by company security when they appeared at the hacienda's gates. All workers were interviewed and placed on a period of probation. If they did not conform or were seen as a potential political problem, they were sent back to Guayaquil or Machala.

In addition, because there was a sufficient pool of new workers by 1950, overseers had little need to utilize repressive measures. "Troublemakers" were simply fired. The self-contained nature of the hacienda served to keep workers in line. Loss of a relatively well-paying job was compounded by the fact that being fired meant having to leave the zone. Even if they could have stayed on the hacienda after being let go, workers had no subsistence plots or other sources of employment, nor did they own the houses they lived in, the streets they walked on, or the water they drank. As one former worker recalls:

> It is hard to imagine what the zone was like in the time of the company. Most of the area was still jungle. There were hundreds of hectares of bananas, but this was all surrounded by jungle with wild animals. There were no roads or other towns like today. The only way to move around or leave the hacienda was by rail or boat. It would have taken days to walk off the property. When a worker was fired, or wanted to leave, he was taken by the company's boat to Machala or Guayaquil. New workers were brought in the same way. Everything was controlled by the company. (A.S. 5/95)

United Fruit's control over a large and relatively isolated zone also made it difficult for regional labor organizations. As one former labor leader from Guayaquil pointed out: "Sure, we had continual contact with some of the workers' leaders but only when they came to Guayaquil. We were aware of what was going on in Tenguel because of the presence of a foreign company and the large number of workers. But it was impossible to promote our organization or our ideas amongst the mass of workers because we were prohibited from entering. The whole area was private property of the company" (J.V. 1/4/96). Members of political organizations were prohibited from entering and workers with suspected ties to labor were quickly dismissed and removed from the zone.

Such control was enhanced by the fact that United Fruit had its own police force in Tenguel. Local police forces located in Balao, a small town just north of Tenguel, remained relatively independent of United Fruit and exercised considerable authority at the margins of the property where the boundaries between land owned by United Fruit, the state, and third parties were far from clear. At the core of the hacienda, however, United Fruit and its police force were given the complete freedom to arrest, discipline, and control Tengueleños—all of whom were completely dependent on the company for their survival. The police in Tenguel took their orders directly from the superintendent and kept a tight control on all forms of behavior. Drinking was strictly controlled as was gambling and other suspect activities. As one ex-worker noted, "Here in Tenguel the houses were company houses; the police were company police; the *teniente politico* was of the company; even the priest was a company priest" (V.M. 8/25/95).

The Stable Family as a Relation of Production
From the very beginning, United Fruit equated a stable and disciplined labor force with a married one. The nuclear family, as sustained and supported by the company, was a form of labor control that was integral both to the hacienda's profitability during the 1940s and 1950s *and* the workers' invasion in 1962. The company not only wanted to attract men, but men who would bring their families and reside in the zone permanently. Although it was difficult to seduce families during the initial years of the hacienda's development, once the infrastructure was installed the zone became relatively attractive. High wages, cheap food, good schools, and well-maintained houses served to attract close to 2000 married workers by the early 1950s. One former administrator explained the company's policy as follows:

> Married men were always preferred. Some men would come by themselves and be put in single quarters. But this was with the idea that their family would quickly follow and they would move into houses for families. [After the hacienda was established] the only single men we hired were sons of workers. It was felt that the community would be easier to manage if there were families instead of single men. (M.G. 1/3/96)[3]

The plantation labor force was exclusively male. Even company stores and food halls were run by male workers. Petty commerce was strictly controlled by the company and the right to market products within the zone was given to former male workers. Women, however, did not seem to mind the lack of employment opportunities. As one explains:

> There were no jobs for women. But we had plenty of money and a good home. There was no need for women to work. My husband was making more money than ever and the work was consistent. And we

had children. I had to go to the company store and keep the house clean. And we [women] were involved with the schools, churches, and community. (T.R. 6/96)

For most, the middle-class ideal of a family model based on a male breadwinner and female housewife was unattainable prior to arriving in Tenguel. Regardless of their origin, migrant families were poor and women were accustomed to working outside the home. Once in Tenguel, however, women no longer "needed" to work (in fact, could not work) and their economic dependence on men grew.

At the same time, women clearly benefited from the higher wages and benefits received by their male relatives. They ate better, lived in well-maintained houses, had electricity, and paid less for basic goods. In addition, because the company saw the nuclear family as a key to its productive enterprise—as a way to secure *and* reproduce a permanent labor force—women's claims on their husband's wages, homes, and benefits were strengthened.[4] The relatively high salaries obtained by male plantation workers were predicated on women's exclusion from the labor market and the assumption that men would maintain their families. It was a family wage in every sense of the term. Men could not obtain a house without a wife and family. Due to prevailing understandings of "women's work" and masculinity/femininity, men "needed" a wife to acquire food from the company store, care for children, and wash laundry. They also "needed" women to maintain the home at a level of cleanliness required by the company's rigid standards.[5] Because women, as housewives and providers, were essential to the jobs, high wages, and benefits received by their husbands, and because the company actively supported the nuclear family, women could make quite serious demands on their partner's wages and benefits. If a male worker did not maintain his family, he faced the possibility of losing his job or home; if he abused his wife or children, he was visited by the company police, company priest, or administration.[6]

The Father Figure
United Fruit did not simply want a stable labor force, but one that was disciplined, reasonably content, and organized in a particular way. Domestic arrangements based on male workers, a family wage, and the exclusion of women from the labor market were part of this equation. Other practices, such as a company police force, limitations placed on the movement of single women, and the regulation of fiestas, were clearly repressive. Nevertheless, the development, maintenance, and reproduction of the entire enterprise depended quite heavily on forms of benevo-

lence and paternalism. Some version of the following was echoed by virtually all of the former workers and their wives:

> Tenguel was a paradise during the time of United Fruit. There was plenty of work and we didn't lack anything. The food was extremely cheap and of good quality. The company sold us meat and rice at cost. We had pasteurized milk and one of the best hospitals in the country. Rich people would come here for operations. The company maintained everything in good conditions. The houses were painted frequently, the streets were cleaned regularly, and we had light, good water, and entertainment. Tenguel was a paradise. (R.B. 7/1/95)

This remarkably positive evaluation of the "time of the company" must be read in relation to Tengueleños' experiences and understandings of both the past and the present. Few Tengueleños remember the pre–United Fruit era with any fondness. Commonly referred to as the "time of slavery," this earlier (cacao) period is most frequently characterized by extreme paternalism and daily indignities. According to one elderly woman, "it was only with the arrival of [United Fruit] that we could begin to breathe" (A.I. 7/9/95). United Fruit's tenure is also remembered against a more recent period in which basic necessities and services such as light, water, and shelter have deteriorated in quality and regularity almost as rapidly as they have increased in cost. To a certain extent, then, the fact that Tengueleños' memories of United Fruit are so positive serves as a commentary on the conditions in which they currently live as wage-laborers, peasant producers, and owners of small businesses.

Nonetheless, although Tengueleños glowing perception of the "time of the company" may seem to contradict much of what we know about working and living conditions on other United Fruit plantations,[7] it would be wrong to dismiss such accounts as nostalgic memories that illuminate nothing more than current insecurities and vulnerabilities. Mixed among the generalizations—such as Tenguel is a paradise—are a wealth of quite concrete memories, memories that speak to a historically specific, if relatively isolated, moment in the (enclave) production of Third World export crops. Workers on United Fruit's Hacienda Tenguel were the recipients of benefits unheard of in rural Ecuador during the 1950s (or 1990s). Rice, milk, and meat were provided "at cost" by the company.[8] Few ex-workers forget that cattle were slaughtered and fresh meat delivered on Tuesdays and Fridays. Tenguel had the best hospital in the country, cheap medicine, as well as company-sponsored sports teams and social clubs. United Fruit even offered a version of paid vacation and sick leave. Most importantly, peasants and workers from provinces throughout the country migrated to Tenguel because the company offered wages up to four times higher than those received by agricultural laborers in other parts of Ecuador. In addition to providing such tangible benefits, United Fruit also offered predictability and security. As one former worker recalls: "One had to work hard and long as before, but that was all that was expected. Show up on time and do the job right or you were out. On the third warning you were flown out of the zone. For some this was hard. But most recognized the benefits and conformed" (M.A. 8/13/95).

In many respects, this Fordist system of management and discipline— including high wages, exceptional benefits, and considerable paternalism—was a direct product of three factors: (1) the Ecuadorian economy, where lower costs allowed the company to extend a range of benefits to its labor force; (2) the Ecuadorian political landscape, where populist-nationalist forces kept the company's more egregious excesses in check; and (3) the history of Central American banana production, where increasing problems with workers led the company to adopt a more conciliatory approach in Ecuador.[9] In this sense, United Fruit's attempt to sustain family and community in Tenguel differed significantly from company practices in Central America prior to the 1940s—practices that not only supported a social system characterized by single male workers, drunkenness, fights, and prostitution, but that provided a recipe for political disaster. In short, United Fruit paid its workers in Tenguel relatively well in order to secure a politically docile labor force and maintain good relationships with the Ecuadorian state. High wages, well-maintained services, and a considerable range of benefits removed the need for more repressive forms of labor control.

The majority of workers at Tenguel were poor migrants in search of steady employment. As one former worker remembers: "We heard about Hacienda Tenguel and decided to leave. What little land we had [in the sierra] was dry and rocky and would not support five brothers. We arrived with nothing. I did not even have shoes or a machete when I arrived in [the company port]" (J.M. 1/16/96). Given these conditions, workers were content with such luxuries as regular wages, a house, and cheap food. Similarly, most found their new employers to be a somewhat milder and more predictable version of past bosses. As long as the hacienda retained its profitability, the company seemed to have preferred the carrot to the stick. One former worker noted: "Yes, there were some cases of employees hitting workers. This was not unheard of. But there was really no need for violence. People worked hard because they wanted to stay. The company just fired people they didn't want" (L.V. 8/13/95).

United Fruit's benevolence extended far beyond areas that would normally be considered within the realm of worker-company relations. As part of a broader effort to create an enduring community, United Fruit supported a wide range of services and benefits, including not only schools and theaters but clubs and sports teams. As one ex-worker remembers:

> The company sponsored all the soccer teams. They provided us with uniforms, balls, and the necessary equipment. They maintained the field. They would give the best players better food and make sure they were given easier jobs. They would also train them. They did this with boxers as well. We had a national champ in boxing here from Tenguel. Some of the gringos would train and fight him. Not all gringos played with us. Some kept their distance. But others played. There was one guy, a Bill, a big man with huge shoulders. No one could box him. And he was a great soccer player. A real man. (J.C. 10/7/95)

Similarly, another recalls:

> Yes, the company financed the social clubs. There were social clubs for all the different groups. The field bosses had their buildings and furnishings. Some were given better things than others. But different groups of workers had social clubs as well. The railworkers and carpenters, as well as different groups of laborers. The clubs would have meetings and sponsor different things. Perhaps to help with the community or the school. And of course they had parties. Part of the money the company gave to the social clubs went to dances and the election of queens. Most fiestas went through the clubs. (F.A. 10/6/95)

One of the most interesting aspects surrounding the sponsorship of sports teams and social clubs is that of all the company's acts of benevolence, none are remembered with more fondness. From the company's perspective, it was money well spent. With practices such as sports teams and social clubs, the company moved well beyond work and subsistence-related areas and into the more culturally delineated (and community-forming) occasions during which workers, and to a lessor extent their families, exercised, drank, and socialized. Ironically, these were the occasions and events which the company often disapproved of and only ambiguously participated in.[10] The company was afraid of large groups of drunken workers and almost never directly sponsored fiestas. Isolated drunks, in fact, were put in jail. Nonetheless, the company was aware that such events would occur. Introduced in the early 1950s, the social clubs were an attempt to control the timing, scale, and nature of fiestas and other social occasions during a time when the community and the hacienda were rapidly expanding.

Quite clearly, such acts of benevolence, although culturally shaped, were not culturally prescribed (Sider 1986). Company-sponsored sporting events and social clubs were embraced quite seriously by the workers but were not traditions with century-long histories.[11] Nevertheless, sports and social events were and are customary, significant, and semi-ritualized occasions during which peasant-workers come together. By providing the very basis through which these customary occasions took place (the uniforms, equipment, athletic training, special diet, fields, social meeting places, music, and beer), the company was sending a subtle, but nonetheless clear, message: We not only control your source of labor, your basic subsistence, but directly provide you with the means through which you are able to interact during special events such as fiestas and sporting events. We are the source of everything (Sider 1986).

In what appears to have been a rather blatant attempt to keep its labor force politically divided, United Fruit created separate clubs for railworkers, administrators, field bosses, and different groups of field workers.[12] Members of particular clubs not only worked, partied, and exercised together, but established long-lasting familial ties. In this sense, although the divisions inherent in the social clubs did not emanate from intercultural differences, *the clubs themselves created and came to depend on different sets of cultural practices.* Few workers failed to note the importance of the social clubs in everyday life. As one recalls:

> Everything was done through the clubs. Parties, elections of queens, events to help the community, even classes, were all done through the clubs. The clubs got money from the company. And people from the clubs generally played on the same soccer team. This is because we worked in the same jobs. Carpenters had their own clubs. Administrators . . . It was like a small community. People from the same club married each other. (J.T. 3/96)

Such practices, sponsored as they were by United Fruit, seemed to have served two rather contradictory purposes. On the one hand, they allowed United Fruit to create and maintain a hierarchy. Even as they improved the workers' lives, the social clubs and other services sustained divisions, undermined more political forms of organization, stabilized the workforce, and enabled the company to extend its sphere of control into the daily life of the workers. They were creative forms of labor control in a situation where—in the absence of a sustained state presence—the company had to induce (not coerce) workers into remaining on the hacienda.

On the other hand, the social clubs also provided the setting through which recently arrived migrants were able to meet and develop bonds of friendship and dependence. As sociocultural creations, the clubs, like the nuclear family, were *simultaneously* a source of company control and worker autonomy. The clubs, regardless of their form—as company creations, workers' organizations, or, later, state cooperatives—were simultaneously a source of worker resistance and the framework through which workers were incorporated and controlled by state and capital. That the organizations endured and proved effective both as sources of resistance and oppression is due in no small part to the fact that the social clubs were the sites where workers forged cultural, political, and economic ties in the realm of daily life (Sider 1986).

THE WORKERS TALK BACK

In the late 1940s, or about a decade after the company first entered Tenguel, United Fruit created a pro-management workers' union. This rather insidious form of labor control, common to many of United Fruit's plantations in Central America, was a preemptive effort on the part of the company to weaken attempts by workers or outside groups to form independent, anti-management labor unions (Bourgois 1989; Moberg 1997). With a workforce of over 2000 men and a changing political climate, paternalism was no longer sufficient and outright repression was simply impossible. As company documents demonstrate, United Fruit administrators were concerned with a number of real and imagined factors, including the spread of communism, popular organizations, and the unpredictability of Ecuadorian governments, that had transformed the political landscape in the ten years since the company had first purchased Hacienda Tenguel.

Most significantly, the political excitement and agitation surrounding Velasco's first election in 1934 served to stimulate a dramatic growth in peasant organizations and labor unions during the latter half of the 1930s. Before 1929 there were four labor unions in all of Ecuador; in 1939 there were almost seventy (de la Torre 1993: chap. 2). Urban-based worker strikes became an institutionalized feature of Ecuadorian life, centering on the expansion of the national labor code and the improvement of working conditions.[13] This process only intensified in the 1940s—especially after the May Revolution of 1944 and Velasco's return to power —as the workers' movement strengthened and radicalized. The major national unions, including CEDOC (Confederación Ecuatoriana de Organizaciones Cristianas, 1938) and the Communist Party's trade union the CTE (Confederación de Trabajadores del Ecuador, 1944), along with the Socialist Party (1926), women's and students' organizations, and early peasant organizations (FEI, Federación Ecuatoriana de Indias), all formed during this period (de la Torre, 1993).[14] Street demonstrations, increasingly violent, occurred with growing frequency near United Fruit's main offices in Guayaquil, which by now had close to a quarter of a million people and was the country's main center of popular political activity and unrest (Pineo 1996).

From the company's perspective, the fact that *rural* popular organizations had also begun to form during this period was even more troublesome. In 1929, there were thirty-four legally formed popular organizations. Despite a decade of repression, nearly 800 popular organizations formed in the 1930s, most of which were constituted in rural zones by peasants and agricultural workers (ibid.). Peasant organizations, most of which were designed to confront the region's landowning elite and acquire property, began to form at the same time as labor unions emerged on the region's larger haciendas. In the coast, most of these local organizations, such as the Mollepongo Commune (chapter four) and the Colonia Agrícola Shumiral (chapter five), were linked to the national CTE through the regional FPTG (Federación Provincial de Trabajadores del Guayas). Based in Guayaquil, the FPTG was the most important and radical labor union operating in Ecuador at the time.[15] It was communist, intensely nationalist, and trying to infiltrate Tenguel by the time the banana boom began in the late 1940s.

It is important to note, however, that although labor unions, left-wing political parties, and peasant organizations were all emerging during this period, they never coalesced—either in the 1940s/50s or the 1960s/70s—into anything resembling a social movement that had the power, numbers, or organization to take over the Ecuadorian government or carry out a "communist revolution." (Velasco's populism was the most powerful "popular" political force, but it was ultimately conservative in orientation and never posed a serious threat to the social order.) Ecuador was not, nor did it ever pose the threat of becoming, another Cuba (or even a Peru or Colombia). This is not to suggest that the CTE, on the national level, or the FPTG, in the coast, did not make significant interventions. As we will see, although the CTE/FTPG was unable to provide on-the-ground support, it was absolutely crucial to peasant-worker struggles—as a source of legal aid, information, and moral support—from the 1940s through the 1970s. But such support came at a heavy price. The limited, but vocal, presence of communists within Ecuador, as well as the more genuine spread of communism in other parts of Latin America, fueled elite paranoia and legitimized their rhetoric about the spread of communism within particular governments and locales. Anti-communism proved to be an effective justification for squashing land invasions and overthrowing governments (1963).

Nevertheless, given the growing (though still quite limited) strength of labor unions in Ecuador during the 1940s, United Fruit officials had reason to believe that a labor union would be formed at Tenguel. The only real questions were who would organize it and how would it be run. For most of the hacienda's workers, unions were still quite foreign and the company's sponsorship went unquestioned. It controlled everything else. Furthermore, United Fruit created two factions of workers whose yearly battles for control gave the union a certain legitimacy and obscured the fact that neither group seriously challenged the company. As one ex-worker put it:

> In the beginning there were two groups battling for control of the union. The group of Paulino Sánchez and the group of Elso Ascencio. One year Sánchez and his group would have control and the next year Ascencio and his group. Sánchez was an agricultural laborer and Ascencio was in construction. The two groups were antagonistic, but they were both pro-company. The company supported both groups through their control of Macini. It was really Macini who was in control of the union. He led both factions. With him there was no discussion. If it was Sánchez, Macini was the leader. If it was Ascencio, Macini was the leader. (A.N. 3/96)

Whether or not Juan Macini, the union leader, was in the company's pocket from the beginning, or was only later seduced, is somewhat immaterial. Macini himself, and the aura of confrontation he created, gave the union its credibility, making it impossible to create a more authentic workers' organization. According to one former worker,

> Macini would come out in the plaza and start ranting and raving against the company. This and that he complained about. Others would get up and join him, really agitating the workers. They would denounce abuses or make demands on the company to do this or that. Then a day or so later he would announce that the company had agreed to our demands. The company never agreed to all of them, but the majority. This made it seem more genuine. It was only later when other people came into the zone that we began to realize that Macini was a traitor. We began to wonder why he would

always eat with the administrators. When we found out that he was accepting money from the company we demanded to have our own leaders. Imagine, he was working for the company. (V.M. 8/95)

The workers' collective questioning of Macini, who had come from the highlands and was relatively well educated, would take years and had less to do with his relation to the company than his relation to the workers. Under Macini's control, the union was limited to agricultural laborers. Mechanics, railworkers, carpenters, and administrators were considered part of the company and hence not allowed to unionize. They were instead organized into the social clubs described above. More importantly, under Macini's reign, the majority of agricultural laborers were not unionized. It was this fact more than any other that led a number of workers, including Arturo Mejilla and Adolfo Nieto, his uncle Ernesto, his brother Gustavo, as well as others such as Segundo Lima (his brothers), José Cobos, and Jacinto Lozano, to begin organizing an opposition movement, the Frente de Unidad Sindical Independiente (hereafter Frente).

Under the guidance of Arturo Mejilla, the Frente developed a plan to separate Macini and United Fruit from the labor union. The union elections always had two opposing slates of five candidates each. The 1958 election included a Macini-controlled slate that ran in opposition to the slate sponsored by the Frente. The election, then, was the first real one in the sense that one of the slates was not under Macini's direct control. More importantly, two of the individuals on Macini's slate, Mejilla and Jacinto Lozano, actually belonged to the Frente. They had infiltrated Macini's group. In effect, then, the Frente was running seven candidates: five on its own slate along with the two who had infiltrated Macini's group. As a result, the Frente won a majority on the union's ruling body and Macini's hold was definitively broken. Worker outrage to this electoral sleight of hand was quickly quieted when Macini's all-too-close connections with United Fruit were confirmed and exposed. The union was subsequently audited, revealing further improprieties committed by Macini and his inner circle.

The significance of Macini's unmasking went beyond the personalistic squabbles of union leaders. The labor union, which had essentially been a company-sponsored tool for over a decade, was transformed into an increasingly militant organization as the Panama Disease spread and the company was forced to lay off more and more workers. Ironically, the rapidity of this transformation is in part explained by Macini's own role in organizing the workers. He helped provide the next set of leaders with an organization and the skills to run it. It was largely a matter of shifting the union's political direction.

From Clubs to Union

As important a role as the new leaders played in transforming the union into an authentic workers' organization, the dramatic radicalization of the workforce in the late 1950s was tied to two factors: the spread of the Panama Disease and the resulting deterioration of working conditions on the hacienda, and an increasingly unstable political climate characterized by calls for agrarian reform, the growing strength of popular organizations, and Velasco's return to power.

United Fruit's decision to purchase Hacienda Tenguel in 1934 was at least partially connected to the fact that the Panama Disease had not yet arrived in Ecuador's southern coast (Larrea 1987). Its arrival, however, was inevitable, and its southern movement along Ecuador's coast during the 1950s devastated an industry that was characterized by medium-sized producers who lacked the resources to either combat the disease or shift production to alternate sites. Although the disease was present in small quantities on Hacienda Tenguel by the end of World War II, it was not until the end of the 1950s that it began to seriously damage the hacienda's banana groves, thereby threatening the entire enterprise. Once it began to cut into the company's profits, United Fruit turned increasingly to the "stick." Services were cut back and less friendly methods of labor control intensified. New hirings stopped and layoffs began. Some recall up to 150 workers being fired in a week. Rules that had never been enforced were suddenly cause for dismissal and workers who were seen as political problems were the first to go.

At the same time as the workers were being laid off in Tenguel, the country was in the midst of an intense discussion regarding agrarian reform. Such debates have a long history in both Latin America and Ecuador, but it was with the Cuban Revolution (1959), the subsequent response by the United States (Alliance for Progress), and the 1960 Ecuadorian presidential election that the "agrarian problem" entered into public discourse and became the country's most urgent question. Between 1959 and 1961, at the exact moment when Hacienda Tenguel began to fall apart, peasants, students, intellectuals, labor leaders, left-wing parties, and even sectors of the dominant classes increased the pressure on landlords and the state for serious land reform.[16]

That the call for agrarian reform was adopted and intensified by Velasco Ibarra should be of no surprise. As Ecuador's most infamous populist, Velasco was the first presidential candidate to take the campaign to rural areas of the country. Agrarian reform was a central component of the 1960 presidential election—a campaign in which, according to Peter Pyne, "the words 'revolution' and 'reform' were the leitmotifs" (Pyne 1975: 112). All of the candidates made extravagant claims and promises.

The sparring between Velasco and his chief rival, Galo Plaza Lasso, was particularly intense. Plaza, who had been president from 1948 to 1952, had not only been the first president to complete a full term since 1924, but had been one of United Fruit's staunchest supporters during the early years of the Ecuadorian banana boom. In fact, Plaza had coauthored *The United Fruit Company in Latin America* (1959), an extremely sympathetic work on the multinational. Not surprisingly, Plaza's pro-American stance attracted the political-nationalist ire of Velasco and drew unwanted attention to United Fruit. More important, Velasco won the June 1960 election by the largest plurality in the country's history.

Once Velasco assumed office, however, the political situation deteriorated quickly and he would remain in office for only about a year. He immediately dismissed forty-eight high-ranking military officers, fired thousands of state employees, and installed his own supporters throughout the government. Those that he did not fire, he quickly alienated through misguided foreign and economic policies. His neutral stance toward Cuba angered the Right, the military, and the U.S. government which held up much-needed loans. Moreover, once Velasco succumbed to U.S. pressure and changed the policy, he immediately alienated the CTE, the major labor organization in the country, which then began to organize a national strike. On the economic front, Velasco's fourth administration was the victim of an economic downturn that, by 1960, had made the relative prosperity of the previous decade seem like a distant memory (Pyne 1975). Regardless, his ineffective, and at times nonexistent, economic polices solidified widespread opposition to the regime.[17]

An important source of this opposition came from Congress. Velasco's reform program posed a direct threat to elite interests and his Agrarian Reform bill was seen by some members of Congress as evidence that "communists" had infiltrated the government. Congressional opposition to Velasco coalesced around Velasco's own vice president, Carlos Julio Arosemena Monroy, who actively positioned himself as the only sane alternative. The conflict between the president and the vice president became public when Arosemena refused to cancel a trip to the USSR at the exact moment when U.S. officials were in Ecuador convincing Velasco to sell out Cuba (Pyne 1975).

Thus, by the middle of 1961, or what corresponded in Tenguel to the height of the layoffs, the country was in political chaos and it was clear that Velasco would not complete his term. The only question was how, when, and under what circumstances he would leave office. After a period of confusion in which three men simultaneously claimed the presidency, Vice President Arosemena, with the support of Congress and the Air Force, assumed office in November 1961. Velasco, in turn, fled to Mexico and would not return to the presidential palace for almost a decade (Pyne 1975). With Arosemena in office, the discourse of agrarian reform rose to a new level. The necessity of reform was now well established and, with the exception of certain landowning sectors, almost universally accepted.

The problem, however, was that there was no consensus as to when, how, and where land reform should be carried out. These questions would be partially addressed in Tenguel during the first half of the 1960s as the Panama Disease worsened, the company slowly withdrew from the zone, and the workers invaded the hacienda. In the meantime, however, virtually everyone, from demagogic presidential candidates and national congressmen to labor organizations, landowners, and newspaper reporters, had an opinion about agrarian reform. Certain sectors of the military and dominant classes favored a limited reform either as a political solution to the "spread of communism" or as a way to stimulate large-scale commercial agriculture (at the expense of inefficient haciendas). Others felt that a more equal distribution of land would promote peasant agriculture and improve living conditions in rural areas. Not surprisingly, the voices of peasants and agriculture workers were rarely heard in the five years leading up to the passage of Ecuador's first serious piece of agrarian reform legislation in 1964. Nevertheless, the debate over agrarian reform provided a crucial space in which—under the right circumstances—peasants and agricultural workers could initiate and justify a greater range of political actions.

In this sense, although the decline of Hacienda Tenguel served to politicize the workforce, it was through the language of agrarian reform that the workers would express themselves. In appropriating the discourse of agrarian reform—as they did with the formation of a cooperative and would continue to do during the next two decades—the workers were drawing on a political language that emanated from far beyond the boundaries of the hacienda. Not only was the discourse surrounding agrarian reform increasingly loud in the late 1950s, but it came from a variety of sources and was filled with numerous contradictions. It was a resource that peasant-workers drew on, but it could—as we will see in sharp relief in chapter six—also be used by elites to repress popular political activity and root out "communism."

As the Panama Disease worsened and discussions of agrarian reform circulated within Tenguel, fired workers began spending less time in the social clubs, participating more and more in the revitalized union. By 1960, close to 80 percent of Tenguel's agricultural laborers belonged to a labor union that confronted the company at every corner and had ambiguous links with regional labor organizations. Ironically, the strength of the labor union did little to save the workers' jobs, instead providing the company with increased incentive to pull out. By 1961, most of the agricultural laborers had been let go, leaving the company with a workforce of less than 400. Over 2000 workers had been fired, more than half of which remained in their company-owned housing (IERAC 1964). Because United Fruit maintained virtually everything, from housing and education to health and basic services, the situation became increasingly intense as the withdrawal of the company led to the inevitable reduction in services.

The loss of jobs, reduction in wages, cuts in electricity, and disappearance of the company store were threats to a way of life that sustained work, family, and community, and in which both men and women had much at stake. As interviews with former workers make clear, masculinity was based on men's perceptions of themselves as family providers engaged in a quintessentially masculine occupation. They were not simply involved in agriculture, but a form of industrial agriculture that explicitly excluded women. As one man explained,

> Only men worked for the company. The work was too hard for women. Yes, you are correct, women work on banana plantations today. But it was different back then. A whole different process. The banana was different, much larger. It was shipped by stem [as opposed to box] and was much heavier. We had to carry stems much further than they do today. Also, the company had big machines. A woman could not operate one of those. (C.E. 5/96)

Although it is true that the contemporary production process is much different from earlier forms, the work itself was more highly valued and masculinized during the time of the company not simply because it was a male domain, but because it was directly associated with a tangible set of benefits. As the hacienda collapsed and men lost the benefits and status associated with plantation labor, their sense of themselves *as men* was threatened. One former worker explained:

> The work during the time of the company was very hard. It was not for everyone. Only strong men. But it was worth it. We were paid well. The company gave us cheap food, free houses. We could take care of our families. It was a good life. When the hacienda began to decline many could not believe it. We thought the company would never leave. It was not just our jobs that were gone. We were going to lose everything, our houses, access to food. . . . I could not take care

of my family. And there was no other work. My wife did not work and we had little children. If I could not care for them what would happen? (J.F. 2/96)

This sense of loss quickly turned political. The set of shared experiences that surrounded plantation life had forged a certain solidarity among the workers. However, once the economic benefits and privileges that sustained not only those experiences but the particularities of men's domination over women and notions of masculinity, were withdrawn, forms of solidarity, community, and even family took on a much more politicized form. One worker conveys this politicizing sense of loss and his own movement from the social clubs to the workers' union in the following terms:

> I did not know what to do when I was fired. How was I going to feed my family? They closed the store, then the hospital, then the building where our club met. They said we had to leave our [company-owned] houses. Where would we go?
>
> This is when I left the social club and began participating in the union. I had never been political. I didn't even know what communism or Cuba was! But when the company tried to force us from our homes! They were attacking my family. They would not let us use the land. How could we survive? This is when I left the club and joined the union. (A.C. 3/96)

The cutback in services produced a similar, though somewhat different, reaction among women. Women's roles in organizing fiestas, supporting schools, and managing their families' consumption took on a more political form as the economic basis of those activities was undermined. Or, rather, those activities themselves became key points of contention between the community and the multinational. As supplies disappeared from the company store and the men were laid off, women organized communal kitchens, took over the running of schools, and led the effort to produce subsistence crops. Thus, although men and women continued to participate in the same gendered activities and roles that they had in the past, those activities themselves took on politicized meanings.

The withdrawal of services undermined the nuclear family supported by United Fruit, including both the male provider and female housewife. Consequently, women joined the men in strikes and talked at rallies. As conditions worsened, women organized a support committee that eventually evolved into one of the first women's political organizations in the coast. As one woman explains:

> When the company started to leave we were lost. We had no food
> and my husband just sat around the house. It was like someone died
> after he got fired.
>
> Some women began organizing committees, getting the people
> together. Our main concern was food. But we kept the streets clean
> and took over the school too. The company had done all of this
> before. We also went to the administrators to make demands. We
> worked with the union but the men didn't want women. We kept
> organizing on our own, sometimes with the men, other times with-
> out. (J.A. 2/96)

The basis for women's increased political activity and presence in the
public sphere was rooted in, and legitimized by, their role as housewives
—a social form whose particularities had been shaped by United Fruit
and the hacienda's production regime. The type of family and community that had been supported by the company created a unity of interests among men and women that was based on a broadly similar sense
of emotional and material loss and entitlement. As Hacienda Tenguel declined, the struggle for wages, food, health services, schools, and other
benefits became, more than ever, a (gendered) class struggle rooted in
the family and plantation community. Once their stability was undermined, both the household and the social clubs, forms of social organization directly supported by the company itself, became critical sources of
labor militancy and union solidarity. Integral forms of labor control became crucial sources of resistance and the company's paternalistic utopia
collapsed.

4   On the Margins of an Enclave: The Formation of State, Capital, and Community

> The court said that the [disputed] land belonged to [the United Fruit Company]. At this point the company thought it had won—that the conflict was over. It was just the beginning. We [the peasants] were not leaving vacant land that we had cleared and cultivated through our own efforts. We did not know what to do so we waited, made contacts with [labor organizers]. Then we formed the Mollepongo Commune and renewed our claim with [another branch of government]. When this failed we tried [another branch] (laughter). All along we controlled the land and kept on good terms with the local police. Only force could remove us from the land.
> —José Llivichusca, founding member of the Mollepongo Commune

The workers did not carry out the first invasion of Hacienda Tenguel. Independent groups of peasants in Mollepongo, Shumiral, and Brasil, uncultivated areas along the foothills of the Andes on the eastern fringes of the hacienda, beat them to it. The peasant invasions in these areas were the first serious threats to United Fruit's agricultural enterprise and the system of capital accumulation based on enclave-style production. Once agricultural diseases inevitably destroyed banana groves at the core, United Fruit had to expand into previously uncultivated areas of the hacienda (thus turning the margins into the core). In the case of Tenguel, the company's ability to expand banana production was surprisingly limited given the initial size of the hacienda. Although the original property was close to 100,000 hectares, United Fruit donated around 80,000 hectares of mountain to the Ecuadorian government only two years after purchasing the property (UFC 7/23/47). The 1936 donation was both a public relations ploy and a failed attempt to establish more definitive boundaries over the remaining 22,000 hectares. Further expansion was then complicated by geography and property patterns. There was the Pacific Ocean to the west and relatively fixed boundaries to the north and south. It was only in the east, where the coastal plain quickly turned into mountainous terrain unsuitable for banana production, that additional land existed. Characterized by dense forest and no infrastructure, the soil in the eastern section of the hacienda was of poorer quality, and irrigation was made difficult by a number of factors. In fact, before the Panama Disease began to affect the core of the hacienda in the late 1950s, the company made no effort to cultivate or even control most of the eastern third of the hacienda. To the contrary, United Fruit tolerated peasant squatters in these areas because they supplied the hacienda with much of its food. However, when the multinational was finally forced to extend production in this direction due to the Panama Disease, the peasants in Mollepongo, Shumiral, and Brasil not only made expansion impossible, thereby threatening the very core of United Fruit's operations, but laid the groundwork for the emergence of a region-wide peasant movement that would cover much of the zone during the late 1960s and 1970s.

Almost immediately after purchasing Hacienda Tenguel in 1934, the company became embroiled in a struggle with a small group of peasants living in an area known as Mollepongo. The conflict, which lasted some twenty years, led to the formation of one of the first peasant organizations in Ecuador's southern coast—the Mollepongo Commune—and contributed to demise of United Fruit's operations in Ecuador. How did this happen? How was the Mollepongo Commune, a peasant organization comprised of less than a dozen families, able to successfully "invade" over 3000 hectares of land owned by an extremely large and experienced multinational? The answer, as this chapter suggests, lies in the state and the relationships that both United Fruit and the Mollepongo Commune were (and were not) able to form with various actors and agencies within its organizational terrain. As José Llivichusca's statement suggests, the Ecuadorian state was at the center of this territorial dispute from the initial court case in the late 1930s until the commune's final victory in the mid-1950s. The state made legal rulings, passed legislation, determined property boundaries, sent commissions, and ordered police actions, all of which had a direct impact on the commune's formation and successful invasion of marginal sections of Hacienda Tenguel. Based on interviews with peasants (conducted in the 1990s) and correspondence between United Fruit officials (written in the 1940s and 1950s),[1] this chapter examines the state's role in the conflict from the perspective of both United Fruit and the Mollepongo Commune.

In so doing, we will once again question the image of a "weak/strong" state that simply inhibits or facilitates the "penetration" of foreign capital. As we will see, United Fruit's inability to illicit state support in evicting a small group of squatters did not so much emanate from the strength, independence, or anti-imperialist nature of the Ecuadorian state during this period. In fact, United Fruit officials *were* able to influence all of the agencies, commissions, and institutions involved in this relatively minor conflict. The company's difficulties—in obtaining favorable export policies at the national level or evicting a group of peasants on the local level—were rooted in the fragmented nature of the state. In short, the Ecuadorian state could not "facilitate the penetration of foreign capital" both because it was politically divided (i.e. its organizational terrain was fraught with turmoil and confusion during a period when populism was on the rise and the central government was constantly changing hands) and because it was geographically thin: there was no "State" in the sense of a unified actor that could make and implement a coherent set of policies with respect to foreign involvement in the southern coast.

At the same time, it is important to stress that many of United Fruit's difficulties with the Ecuadorian state were exacerbated by the peasants. The Mollepongo Commune proved particularly adept at maneuvering through, even manipulating, forms of state power in ways that continually frustrated the company's efforts. United Fruit was unable to "win" this particular conflict because it was defeated by peasants who were, or rather became, experts at navigating internal divisions within the Ecuadorian state. At times, what appeared to company officials as bureaucratic delays were really conflicts between different branches of government— conflicts and divisions that had been cultivated by the peasants.

And, yet, the peasants' victory—and education—came at a price. The creation of a commune brought the Mollepongo peasants into increasing contact with the routines, rituals, institutions, and offices of state power. An important part of this story involves the effectiveness with which the peasants negotiated these modes of rule; but so too is the uneven way in which domination was secured. Following Philip Corrigan and Derek Sayer (Corrigan and Sayer 1985; Sayer 1994), this chapter suggests that the Ecuadorian state's attempt to establish a common discursive framework was most effective when it was enacted *through practices*, and not words or other more transparent schemes to manipulate beliefs and achieve ideological consent. As William Roseberry notes,

> The power of the state [for Corrigan and Sayer] rests not so much on the consent of its subjects but with the state's regulative and coercive forms and agencies, which define and create certain kinds of subjects and identities while denying, ruling out, other kinds. . . . Moreover, the state accomplishes this not simply through its police and armies but through its offices and routines, its taxing, licensing, and registering procedures and papers. (Roseberry 1994: 355)

In fact, it may be the case that rule is most effectively accomplished when state forms and agencies are experienced not as coercive but enabling (Sayer 1994). The primary form of state regulation examined here was a seemingly innocuous law regulating the formation of communes. Although this law can be seen as part of a larger, albeit ill-defined and incoherent, state project to incorporate rural areas into the nation-state, it was not particularly repressive in intent or implementation. The 1937 Law of Commune Organization (Ley de Organizaciones de Comunas) invited rural population centers of more than fifty people to petition the state to become communes, a legally recognized form of organization (much like a town or city) that formalized the relationship between rural peoples and the Ecuadorian state. The law, then, had to be embraced and enacted by groups of peasants in order to be effective. In could not be implemented or imposed by the state. More important, the law *allowed* peasants, both in Mollepongo and throughout Ecuador, to confront and defeat landlords. Instead of restraining popular action, this state form empowered and enabled the Mollepongo peasants to obtain significant quantities of land from the most powerful landowner in Latin America.

Nevertheless, by embracing the law and forming a commune, the peasants placed themselves in a formal and subordinate relationship to the state. As we will see, the creation of the commune brought the Mollepongo peasants into increasing contact with the routines, rituals, institutions, and offices of state power. What made this form of rule so effective was the inconspicuous way in which it was accomplished. It was adopted, even manipulated, by the peasants, and enabled them to achieve certain goals. The commune, and the interclass conflicts that led subordinate groups to adopt this state form, served to organize, even create, organizations and communities of peasants. But it was a peasantry that was organized by and into the state; peasants became increasingly dependent subjects (*comuneros*) inhabiting a particular geopolitical space (the commune) that could be managed, granted rights, denied resources, disciplined, or simply ignored. It was through such laws, and the series of contacts, conflicts, and processes that they entailed and initiated, that rule was enacted and the state itself was physically constructed (in the creation of agencies, ministries, and commissions) and imagined (as an arbiter that stood apart from the interclass conflicts taking place within "the economy"). Although the long-term consequences of the peasants' uneven incorporation into the nation-state would not become clear until the expansion of state power and the implementation of agrarian reform in the 1960s and 1970s (part two), the Mollepongo affair, and other land conflicts occurring throughout Ecuador during the 1930s, 1940s, and

1950s, set the unstable framework on which clientalistic relationships between the state and peasant-workers would develop in the postwar period.

FIRST CONTACT, FIRST CONTRACT

After purchasing Hacienda Tenguel in 1934, United Fruit began to build the necessary infrastructure for the production, processing, and distribution of bananas at the core of the hacienda while securing territorial control over the margins of the property. Much of the hacienda's land was, however, being rented to peasants such as Jacinto Llivichusca. As his son José explains: "When the company came it bought out all of the tenants, including my father. There was no choice, you had to sell to the company. But it was fine. The company gave us a good price which allowed my father to buy part of Hacienda Mollepongo" (J.L. 12/10/95).

Along with Manuel Illescas, Llivichusca took the money he received from United Fruit and purchased some rights and shares in what was commonly known as Mollepongo, the immense hacienda on Tenguel's southern border. Through purchasing shares, Illescas and Llivichusca acquired a *right to possess* (and through possession own) a certain amount of land within the immense boundaries of Hacienda Mollepongo. As the peasants admit, and United Fruit's documents confirm,[2] they not only began to plant the flatter portions near Hacienda Tenguel, but sold smaller sections to friends and family who promised to cultivate and populate the zone.

It was their growing numbers that motivated Hacienda Tenguel's new owner to take action. In 1938 United Fruit initiated and won a court case against Victor Velez, a fellow shareholder and friend of Illescas. The court's ruling forced Velez to legally recognize the company's dominion over the disputed property located on the frontiers of Tenguel-Mollepongo. Velez, as well as the other Mollepongo shareholders (Illescas, Llivichusca, Barros, etc.), were forced to sign rental agreements for the area they had under cultivation when the company arrived. These lands, according to the court, were located within the boundaries of Tenguel and not Mollepongo. As the contracts noted, the peasants were owners of shares in Mollepongo and had mistakenly occupied and cultivated part of Tenguel (J.L. 4/22/1996; UFC 9/5/45, 4/40).

The cultivations of the "mistaken" peasants were quite substantial. Between Torres, Barros, and Eras, they had close to 7000 cacao trees, 4000 plantain trees, and significant quantities of cultivated pasture. This was at the time the contracts were signed. Bermeo and Vergara's cultivations were at least as extensive and included coffee and a variety of fruits. By signing the contracts, the peasants explicitly recognized that (1) the lands in question belonged to the company and that they had no rights or claims to the area, and (2) that the lands of Mollepongo and Tenguel had never overlapped. The shareholders of Mollepongo thus became tenants of Tenguel and, in so doing, affirmed United Fruit's legal ownership. Although the company was not looking to rent out sections of the hacienda, the ruling, by turning squatters into tenants, had satisfied its primary goal—undisputed legal control over its recently acquired property (UFC 4/40). Or so it seemed.

Although the peasants signed the contracts, they believed that the disputed lands belonged to Hacienda Mollepongo. As shareholders of Mollepongo, they felt they were within their legal rights to cultivate the land. More importantly, despite signing the contracts, they believed the lands were theirs by virtue of the fact that they had cleared and cultivated vacant forest. As José Llivichusca remembers, "We did not recognize the contracts even though we signed them. We needed time and wanted the company to leave us alone" (J.L. 1996). The contracts, then, were signed in 1940 by a small and unorganized group of peasants who sought to avoid a conflict with a large company. Regardless of their legal status (shareholder, tenant, squatter), each held onto the idea that had brought them to the zone in the first place—owning their own piece of land. By 1945, this idea, combined with a strategic alliance with political activists from Guayaquil, would generate one of the first peasant organizations in the zone: the Mollepongo Commune.

CONFRONTATION AND ORGANIZATION: THE COMMUNE'S FIRST ATTEMPT

The peasants' subsequent decision to form a commune—as opposed to some other form of organization—did not occur by accident. Of the nearly 800 popular organizations that formed during the 1930s, close to 600 were communes (de la Torre 1993: chap. 2). This wave of organizing was propelled by the Law of Commune Organization in 1937. The expressed goal and motivation behind the law was to extend the state's control beyond the parish head and into smaller population centers. The myriad rural hamlets and communities that existed throughout Ecuador were instructed to appeal to the state and become communes—a geopolitical form of organization that would formally establish the existence of rural populations and legalize their relationship to the state. Each commune would be run by a council of five town elders and placed under the jurisdiction of the Ministry of Social Welfare. The only restriction was that at least fifty people had to be permanently inhabiting a single population center (Barsky 1984: 31–33).

Communes were clearly an attempt on the part of the state to extend its administrative and legal reach into those rural areas that up until the 1930s had remained outside its control. Such legalistic measures reflected two important facts. First, many rural areas were only loosely incorporated into the nation-state in the late 1930s.[3] Second, because the state lacked the practical resources to move further into rural areas (build roads, open government offices, etc.), it was forced to pass laws whose effectiveness depended on the active participation of rural groups in their own integration. As we will see, the multiplicity of state ministries, agencies, commissions, and boards that were based in either Quito or Guayaquil were quite often working through the same local official. The local Teniente Político, as well as the provincial Intendente, could and did receive orders from a variety of government branches, including the president himself. In this sense, both the Teniente and the Intendente were much more than the simple extension of police power. These local state figures wore many hats and had considerable control in deciding which Quito-based ministry, agency, or actor would get to speak and act in rural areas (and when, how, and to what extent). In the zone of Tenguel-Balao, such power also made these local state agents key factors in determining how bananas would be produced, labor organized, and conflicts resolved. Although United Fruit utilized its own police force to deal with plantation workers at the core of the property, the company was forced to rely on local state authorities from the small town of Balao in order to handle problems on the margins of Hacienda Tenguel.

In the case of communes, there were a number of reasons why peasant groups actively embraced the state's initiative. First, it fell under the jurisdiction of the relatively supportive Ministry of Social Welfare. Labor activists, as well peasants in the region, insist that this particular ministry was peopled by socialists prior to the military dictatorship of 1963 and thus more sympathetic to their cause than other branches of government. Second, and more importantly, because they provided a collective, organized, and legal form of representation before the state, communes were quickly adopted by peasants involved in land conflicts. As a weapon against landlords, hundreds of communes were formed despite the fact that the initiative was only given serious state support for a short period of time (de la Torre 1993). The commune, then, was simultaneously a legal form used by the state in order to geographically organize and politically incorporate the rural population *and* a popular form of organization adopted by peasants in their struggles with landlords.

The peasants' attempt to form the Mollepongo Commune was clearly part of this wave of commune formation and popular organizing. The legal confrontation with United Fruit had two immediate effects on the peasants of Mollepongo. First, they formed a community in order to confront future aggressions as a collective. The peasants moved off of their individual plots of land and into La Independencia, a community created on the exact site of the boundary dispute. It is worth noting that the Mollepongo peasants did not view this move as a "land invasion," a term whose use did not become politically acceptable or available until the agrarian reform period. Rather, they explained their decision to form a community first through legal argument (i.e. we own this land) and then in moral terms (i.e. the land is uncultivated). Once developed, this moral argument would be the rationale that more progressive sectors within Ecuadorian society would use to justify both a national agrarian reform and the peasantry's invasion of underutilized lands during the 1960s and 1970s. At the time of the Mollepongo conflict, however, an "invasion" was neither politically possible nor part of the peasantry's language. Second, the court case forced the peasants to make contacts with labor activists from the CTE/FPTG. These contacts were primarily in the form of advice and legal aid; national labor organizations did not have the resources to develop a sustained presence in rural zones during this period. Even by the 1970s, when the southern coast was more fully integrated into the nation-state and national peasant-labor organizations were expanding, local peasant-worker groups were largely on their own when it came to on-the-ground conflicts. Nevertheless, the information and legal resources provided by national popular organizations often proved decisive. In the case of the Mollepongo conflict, the FPTG quickly informed the peasants that informal organization was not sufficient. A commune, which by definition assumed the existence of a population center (whose members owned the site on which the commune was located), would give the peasants a legal presence before the state.[4]

Unfortunately, the legalization of the commune was anything but routine. Knowing that their request would go through the Teniente Político's office in the nearby town of Balao, the peasants sent a petition to the subsecretary of the Ministry of Social Welfare in Quito. The petition requested that someone from the ministry be sent to Mollepongo in order to verify the presence of at least fifty inhabitants living and working in the zone. The Ministry of Social Welfare, as expected, sent a communication to the Teniente, ordering him to carry out the investigation. Victor Velez, the commune's secretary (and the same man who had lost the court case in 1938), arrived at the Teniente's office at just about the same time as the telegram and generously offered to conduct the study himself. As a longtime friend of the Teniente, he was duly deputized, carried out the "impartial" study, and subsequently informed the Teniente that there were, in fact, fifty-one inhabitants living and working in the zone—or, coincidentally, just one more than required by law. The Teniente, in turn, sent the report to the ministry in Quito (UFC 9/45). Had the company not been tipped off by someone in the ministry, the commune would probably have been legalized. The question of ownership—were the lands of Tenguel or Mollepongo?—still would have remained unresolved, but the legalization of the commune would have put the peasants on a near legal par with the company.

The peasants' attempt to form a commune within the boundaries of Hacienda Tenguel in 1945 did not worry United Fruit officials. It represented the extension and escalation of an affair that had been festering for some time, but which the company believed had been legally settled in 1938. That the court case did not resolve the problem is best explained by a combination of circumstances, including the peasants' legal-moral belief that they owned the land; their continued possession of the disputed property and remarkable ability to manipulate local representatives of state power; and the company's misplaced confidence that the issue would be rationally resolved through a judicious reading of the legal facts by state authorities in Quito. In short, the peasants' occupation of the land, their ability to access information, and their deep understanding of local and national power made it difficult for the company to resolve the issue.

Nevertheless, United Fruit had a number of reasons to be quite confident. First, its ownership of the land, established by land titles and strengthened by the 1936 donation, seemed indisputable. Second, the leaders of the commune had signed contracts recognizing the company's ownership over the disputed property. As *comuneros,* they were trying to appropriate the very same lands they were renting as *tenants.* These contracts, especially when removed from the context within which they were signed, were powerful pieces of evidence. From the company's (legal) perspective, the commune's formation and movement onto hacienda lands was no different than the case they had won against Victor Velez eight years earlier. Legally, it mattered little that Velez was an individual and the commune an organization.

On a legal level, then, company officials were not worried. But they were confused. The formation of a commune and its attempt to acquire lands was not unusual. The question nevertheless remained: Why were the company's own tenants trying to form a commune on lands which they had legally recognized as belonging to the company? What were they possibly thinking? A complete answer to this question would have many dimensions, including the peasants' need for productive lands with access to markets; the comuneros' desire to remain in the zone; and a local knowledge that said the lands in question were of Mollepongo and not Tenguel. In retrospect, however, it seems clear that the most important factor was the quite different understandings the two combatants had regarding the land. For the company, the problem was simple precisely because it was legal. The peasants had begun work on private property. They were squatters who, if necessary, should be removed by force. For the peasants, the problem was also about legal rights, but rights that were grounded in possession. As José Llivichusca explains: "My father always told us that if he were taken to jail we should remain on the land. If we left the land, he said, we would lose our right of possession" (J.L. 1996). Part of their argument, then, was that the disputed territory was part of Mollepongo and thus belonged to its shareholders. For the peasants, however, the most important fact was that they had cleared and worked a sector that had been vacant prior to their arrival. Land, first and foremost, was something to be used. These conflicting and largely irresolvable understandings defined the parameters of the conflict for the next fifteen years. However, even a partial understanding of why the peasants attempted to form the commune in 1945 does little to help us understand why and how they were successful in 1955. For this, we must turn more closely to local, regional, and national politics.

THE COMMUNE'S SECOND ATTEMPT

During the next decade, even as they became experts in manipulating networks of power in Quito and Guayaquil, the peasants never forgot that local control could often be decisive in a zone where national authorities exercised a partial and uneven authority. In contrast, the company's inability to resolve the matter, and the frustration that resulted, betrayed a confusion regarding the nature of local politics, the Ecuadorian state, and the changing relationship between the two. Legal rights and influential contacts in Quito could be made meaningless by a stubborn Teniente Político or Intendente on the local-regional level. In theory, a call from the company to the responsible ministry in Quito would result in a telegram ordering the Teniente or Intendente to carry out a particular action (i.e. eviction of squatters). As we will see, this chain of command almost never worked, or at least not in the way the company envisioned.

In this sense, the "impartial" investigation conducted by Victor Velez was, in retrospect, a microcosm of the problems that United Fruit would continue to face with both peasants and the state. In 1938, the Teniente, on orders from the court, removed Victor Velez from company land. In 1945, a group of peasants, now organized, almost succeeded in taking a large step toward the acquisition of these very same lands—an act that was done through the same Teniente's office by the same man who had been evicted. Indeed, as the company would finally come to learn, the Mollepongo matter would not be judicially resolved by delivering the right map or legal document to the correct person in Quito.

To a large extent, local officials such as the Teniente had to be controlled locally. At the core of the hacienda, in Tenguel itself, this posed little problem. United Fruit had its own police force and was left alone when dealing with workers. However, on the fringes of the property, where banana groves faded into uncultivated jungle, the situation was much different. The economic viability of banana cultivation was still being established during this period; local landowners—most of whom made *claims* to poorly demarcated and uncultivated land—were leery of a new neighbor that possessed immense resources, was expanding production, and actively sought to define property boundaries. The area's largest landowners had retreated to Guayaquil after the collapse of the cacao boom and would not be lured back into the zone until the profitability of banana production had been established. As a result, not only did state officials—who were based in the local government seat of Balao—operate outside the consistent and immediate control of any single sector within the national government (or political party); they were also not under the thumb of local landowners. That is, they were not directly and unequivocally controlled by United Fruit's traditional allies. The Tenientes during this period were, according to José Ilivichusca, "normal people."

> Tenientes here were different from those in the highlands. In the highlands they were *caciques* who helped the *hacendados*. Here they were more independent because most of the large landowners were absent. One Teniente here [in Balao] was a small farmer (*pequeño agricultor*) like my father. A peasant. Another owned a small store. They were never the poorest; most had some land. Sometimes they even had trouble finding people to take the job. There wasn't much money to be made during this period [in being a Teniente]. They were always from Balao and usually helped us against the company. (J.L. 7/5/96)

Encouraged by the company and incensed by Victor Velez's dubious report "verifying" the presence of fifty-one inhabitants, the Ministry of Social Welfare decided to carry out a study to resolve the problem once and for all (UFC 9/7/45). On September 13, 1945, only a month after the attempted formation of the commune, Dr. Adriano Cobo, lawyer for United Fruit in Quito, confidently wrote General Manager Estrada that the labor inspector was being sent by the ministry in order to settle the Mollepongo matter. According to Dr. Cobo, "with his report and our [petition] requesting refusal to their claim, the Ministry will deny their petition" (UFC 9/13/45). How could it be otherwise? The tables were now turned and, unlike the first report, the second "impartial" study would not be conducted by the peasants, but by United Fruit and its allies within the Ministry of Social Welfare. The report, in short, would justify a decision that was already made.[5]

Interestingly, signs of trouble emerged immediately after Labor Inspector Morán conducted his investigation. Morán had been trying to contact Dr. Cobo, a fact that worried United Fruit's General Manager Carlos Estrada: "I have no idea why Morán wants to contact you. . . . If he hits you up for more expense money, you may let him have up to 100 more. We paid him 400 here [in Guayaquil/Tenguel]." As it turned out, the glitch was not about money. United Fruit had simply bought the wrong official. The governor of Guayas did not like the report (or Morán himself) and forced the inspector to resign, thereby jeopardizing the entire investigation (UFC 10/2/45). United Fruit nevertheless continued to push the tainted report through the ministry. Writing in frustration in mid-October, United Fruit's lawyer, Dr. Cobo, noted the "report has been there for awhile sitting around—once the legal dept gets the report a decision will be made in favor of UFC. This Ministry is a tough babe, I mean they don't know how to decide on anything and matters just lay there for months and months without any decision" (UFC 10/18/45). Continuing in the same tone several days later, Cobo wrote from Quito that the report "from the legal dept of [Social Welfare] is ready. This report goes to the Minister where undoubtedly it will remain on his desk for only God knows how long. It is almost impossible to get the Minister to act on anything" (UFC 10/23/45).

From the peasants' perspective, such delays were critical in that they allowed them to strengthen their hold on the land, acquire additional allies, and pressure the state from a variety of angles. On the day before the report passed through the ministry's legal department, Hacienda Tenguel's superintendent reported that two of the peasants, Illescas and Barros, were in Guayaquil trying to get the land considered as part of Mollepongo. He also noted that they had been in the area with communists from Guayaquil (the FPTG) who had publicly declared that they would return to divide the disputed lands among the peasantry. The commune had also acquired a lawyer who, having connections within the government, requested that the matter be (re)investigated due to the biased nature of the labor inspector's report (UFC 10/25/45). At the same time as they were involved in a range of legal maneuvers, the peasants had expanded their cultivations and some of their animals had destroyed the company's banana groves. With each delay, solutions involving the forced removal of the squatters became increasingly unrealistic.

The conflict festered with little legal change well into the new year and by March 1947 the company's situation seemed weaker. President Velasco had himself received a telegram from Illescas and Llivichusca complaining that United Fruit's thugs had attacked them (UFC 3/17/47). Llivichusca, accompanied by Marco Oramas, lawyer and secretary general of the FPTG, had taken his complaint directly to the new governor of Guayas who then forwarded it to the president. The company, of course, viewed the attacks quite differently. According to General Manager Estrada, a company engineer had been threatened with violence and prevented from working in the zone near the commune. As a result, the engineer was sent again, this time with an armed contingent. Barros and Llivichusca subsequently threatened both the engineer and his guards, noting that they had thirty armed men ready to protect their lands. Estrada immediately appealed to the governor for police protection, complaining that the company could no longer complete works on its own lands (UFC 3/47). The appeal was in vain (UFC 3/18/47).

It was during this period between late 1946 and early 1947 that the company's optimism began to wane, especially in Guayaquil and Tenguel. United Fruit officials felt their case had been proven, but that the state was nonetheless unwilling to enforce their property rights. Estrada, clearly frustrated with his own lawyer, told Dr. Cobo that one more "study" was not the solution to a problem which "the Ministry has studied . . . from all sides many times. Barros and his accomplices have demonstrated themselves to be unscrupulous people that only want to bother us, and it appears as though each time there is a change in the Ministry they are going to renew their unfounded claims" (UFC 9/12/46). That was the point. The peasants had no desire to resolve the issue through a company-backed study of boundary titles and, as long as they physically occupied the lands and pushed the right state buttons, they were able to discourage the government from enacting legal resolutions. As Estrada's frustrated statement highlights, the peasants had become experts at negotiating state power at both local and national levels, continually pressing their claims at a variety of points along the fragmented lines of state power. As Llivichusca explains:

> We would not take no for an answer. If the Ministry of Social Welfare
> rejected our claim, we went to the Ministry of Government. If they
> would not listen to us, we went to some other bureaucracy or got law-
> yers from the FPTG to push our procedures through [the state]. We
> even went to the Ministry of Defense! The FPTG always knew where
> [in the state] to go. They had friends throughout the government. All
> along we were cultivating crops, harassing company employees, and
> maintaining good relations with the Teniente. We would not leave
> the land regardless of what someone said in Quito. (J.L. 5/18/96)

It was through these ongoing peasant-state contacts, and the conflicts
out of which they emerged, that the state was not only formed (i.e.
agencies were created and transformed, commissions were sent, studies
were conducted, etc.) but also imagined. It should be clear that peasants
such as Llivichusca never imagined the state a *neutral* arbiter. A single
trip to a particular state branch almost never resolved a conflict. Multiple trips to a range of different and quite biased state sites were absolutely essential for successful encounters with the state. Nevertheless, the
clarity with which the peasants understood state power betrays the extent to which they were being exposed to its routines and procedures.
The peasants' success at cultivating the state simultaneously served to
further their own interests while increasing their dependence on state resources and intensifying their dialogue with state practices, agencies, and
routines. This dialogue, although relatively innocuous (and even benefi-
cial) during these early stages, would become increasingly intense and, as
I will argue in the second half of the book, ultimately disempowering for
peasant-workers as the banana boom (and then oil boom) developed, the
state expanded into rural areas during the 1960s and 1970s, and popular
organizations struggling for the land were transformed into clients of the
Ecuadorian state.

United Fruit, whose representatives seemed to have personal or familial relationships with almost every ministry or subsecretary involved
in the dispute, was also pressuring the state from many angles, but
remained overly focused on national-level authorities who not only
changed office on an almost yearly basis during the 1930s and 1940s but
seemed unwilling or unable to exercise authority in local zones such as
Tenguel. Frustrated with the ministry and worried about the peasants' recent contact with Velasco, the company became increasingly determined
to take its case to the president or any other channel *outside* the Ministry
of Social Welfare (whose offices were, according to peasants, labor organizers, and company officials, staffed by socialists during this period).
Most frequent among their new contacts were close advisors to the presi-

dent and sympathetic officials within the Ministry of Government. Like the Ministry of Social Welfare, each set of authorities expressed open support and sympathy for the company. In one attempt to reach President Velasco, the company wrote that "with every change in authority, assembly, Minister, Governor, etc. this group of persons returns to press their false claims. Perhaps it is time to resolve this problem once and for all because later on if leftish authorities come to power the affair will become more difficult" (UFC 3/18/47). By March 1947, the company had learned several lessons about the Ecuadorian state and the persistence of the peasants that led them to conclude that no resolution without the involvement of the president would be successful in definitively resolving the problem.

But the shift in strategy involved a whole new series of bureaucracies and delays. Through developing connections with Dr. Carrion, advisor to the president, the company had direct access to Velasco. This pressure, in turn, forced the Ministry of Social Welfare to propose (yet again) the creation of a commission that would go to Tenguel and resolve the problem. But another month passed and in May the reports of peasant activity continued. Company workers had been threatened with violence and prevented from working (UFC 5/5/47). The company could no longer gain access to over 10,000 banana trees and the peasants had defiantly declared that they had the formal support of local police forces. Such acts reinforced Estrada's belief that the ministers of Social Welfare and Government had to be contacted directly and in conjunction with the president in order "to defend the rights of the company" (UFC 5/47). He also noted that the conflict could no longer be resolved by sending "a dozen or so civil guards" because the peasants were sufficiently organized and armed to resist such a contingent. A more "energetic form" of protection was necessary to insure the company's rights. But this was exactly what the populist government was not prepared to do (UFC 5/5/47).

The peasants now had a well-established community, the very name of which—La Independencia—suggested their willingness to insert themselves into nationalist-populist discourses. La Independencia, including houses and something of a town center, was located at the heart of the disputed property. The peasants had extensive cultivations, and even claimed (and prevented company employees from working) a portion of land that United Fruit had planted with bananas. The peasants were, as Llivichusca makes clear, entrenched: "We had our families, with homes and other buildings. We were clearing land and cultivating crops. And we were on constant alert. If one of us saw someone from outside the community, he quickly alerted everyone else and we grabbed our shotguns and machetes and came to see who it was. The company could not just walk in here" (J.L. 8/11/96).

By May 1947, inaction on the part of local police forces had become a chronic problem for the company and one that seemed to be worsening as the peasants' hold on the land grew more secure. When serious action was ordered it was never completed. On May 7th, for example, the Ministry of Social Welfare telegraphed the Intendente from the province of Guayas, instructing him to send sufficient troops to control the intruders and take them to jail. But just when the ministry seemed determined to resolve the problem in favor of the company, it received additional reports about the peasants' increased activities. After years of handling the problem, the Ministry of Social Welfare suddenly declared that the issue was now under the jurisdiction of the Ministry of Government. It was no longer a social problem, but a legal one that should be handled by the police. The Ministry of Government immediately telegraphed the Intendente, instructing him to send troops in order to rectify the problem. Claiming that he had not received either telegraph (from either ministry), the Intendente insisted that he talked personally with President Velasco who ordered him not to comply with the orders (UFC 5/47). United Fruit officials, in turn, were simply confused. Which, if any, part of the state was responsible for handling this relatively minor conflict?

The governmental delays and confusions continued, company employees were prevented from working, and the peasants became increasingly confident. In early May, two company employees submitted the following report:

> When we arrived to the first section of bananas, Illescas left saying that we were not going to use a machete in his lands, because he doesn't believe the Company. . . . Just then Llivichusca, Illescas and Ruben and Tobias Guerrero arrived (one with a shotgun). Llivichusca threatened us and said we would not touch the land because it would be disgraceful; Illescas said the Intendente promised that the hacienda wouldn't bother them any more and that he would not send the civil guard. And Llivichusca said when they took him to jail he talked personally with Estrada who said the company wouldn't bother them any more.
>
> They also said that these men are going to reclaim some 200,000 cacao trees that they have in San Fran[cisco], on lands of theirs, that the company is taking out to plant banana. (UFC 5/6/47)

Attempts by United Fruit's lawyer, Dr. Cobo, to talk directly with the president only served to buy the peasants more time. Cobo had the feeling that President Velasco was avoiding him, but nonetheless felt that a "showdown" with respect to the conflict would occur soon (UFC 5/17/47). The company's new strategy—to tap as many government channels as possible—served to confuse things as new proposals were thrown on top of old ones. The Intendente from the province of Guayas suggested to the president that a military engineer be sent to resolve the problem; President Velasco continued to support an additional commission and hoped to avoid a conflict; the various ministries, in turn, continued to put forth a variety of postures and poses. The situation became so ridiculous that General Manager Estrada became seriously concerned about a potential conflict, not between the company and the peasants, but "between the Intendente, the Minister of [Government] and the President, if the Intendente continues to disobey the minister's order" by hiding behind his personal relationship with President Velasco (UFC 5/15/47).

On May 21, after numerous postponements, Dr. Cobo finally got his meeting with President Velasco who said he would immediately order the Intendente to evict the intruders and organize a commission to go to Tenguel and resolve the issue. However, somewhere between the company's meeting with the president and the president's own communications with the various ministries, things became confused. On May 21, Cobo had been told personally by the president that the commission would be run through the Ministry of Social Welfare. A day later, on May 22, he was informed that the matter had been referred by the president himself to the Ministry of Government. The minister of Government was out of town, but the order to evict the intruders had been sent to the Intendente (yet again). The Intendente, it seems, was "sick" and could not carry out the order.

In June 1947, things went from bad to worse for United Fruit. Reports from the hacienda indicate that the peasants were escalating their efforts.

> When we arrived we found [peasants] Llivichusca, Illescas, Eloy Barros, José Sinche, Tobias Guerrero, Filiberto Guerrero, Ruben Guerrero, and Mesias Guerrero. They surrounded us. Barros and Sinche were armed with 2 barreled shotguns and the rest had machetes.
> Llivichusca asked us what we were going to do. We said to clean the bananas of the hacienda; he said the company had no bananas, nor land in this sector and we would not touch it with a single machete; these lands were theirs; they said they had orders to capture anyone sent by the hacienda and send them to Santa Isabel, Pucara—which they would do to us if we returned.
> Illescas then said: "He said he would not take us to jail because

we were just poor folk and that we were making a living and were sent by the company, but he warned us that this was the last time, because if we came back again he would capture us and send us to Pucara. He also said that the Intendente of Guayas said he would not send the Civil Guard because this was not Guayas but Azuay. And that he had been to the Ministries of Government and Defense and that everyone knows these lands belong to them. (UFC 6/5/47)

As the above highlights, the peasants had sought and obtained support from provincial authorities in Azuay, thus exploiting the fragmented nature of the state in yet another way. The peasants argued that the company, located in the province of Guayas, was invading not only their land but the province of Azuay. The Intendente in Guayas, at least for the moment, was accepting this interpretation and suggested the zone was not in his jurisdiction. Whether or not authorities from Azuay had instructed the peasants to arrest company employees is not clear, but they were nonetheless supporting the peasants' claims (inasmuch as they coincided with the province's own interests). Based on legal support garnered by sympathetic lawyers, the peasants were now arguing that Mollepongo, as part of Azuay, included nearly all of Hacienda Tenguel.[6]

Even when a new company-supported commission was finally sent to Tenguel, the peasants' almost complete control at the local level quickly undermined its effectiveness. On November 17, General Manager Estrada wrote Dr. Cobo: "As you can see, these individuals are making fun of the authorities yet again. The Commission was not supported by [Civil Guards] and therefore was not respected. This makes it four the number of times they have made fun of the authorities—three earlier times when they promised the Intendente that they would not disturb our workers and each time they threatened them" (UFC 11/17/47). Members of a government commission designed to study a land conflict had arrived in Tenguel but were not allowed to enter the disputed sector because the peasants suggested they might damage the crops. This, as Llivichusca remembers, was an excuse to undermine a commission whose report they knew would not be in their favor. Frustrated by the fiasco, Cobo was simply perplexed: "At this time the situation is completely confused. . . . If you go to a Ministry one finds a communist or fascist. It is divided between socialists, who in this country are the same as communists, and conservatives, who are fascists and just as confusing as the communists" (UFC 11/19/47). The report resolved nothing.

By the end of March 1948, the company was faced with an impossible situation. The peasants were becoming more assertive both in terms of their actions on the land and their legal-bureaucratic maneuvers against the company. They had managed to subvert the most recent report, while initiating another—through the Board of Peasant Affairs—that would be authored by their own lawyer. From United Fruit's perspective, virtually every possible path had been tried and exhausted. The many faces of the Ministry of Social Welfare were hopeless; the Ministry of Government, while somewhat more sympathetic, had shown relatively little desire to become involved in the problem; the new president, whose "attitude on matters which imply responsibility . . . has been disappointing," certainly did not want to evict a group of peasants in favor of a foreign company (UFC 3/16/48); and although the U.S. embassy had not fully been utilized, the threat had been made.[7] The conflict was over, the peasants had won close to 3000 hectares of land, and the company was being slowly pushed out of direct production.[8]

CONCLUSION

Why was a major multinational unable to get the state to evict a small group of peasants? An easy answer would be that the Ecuadorian state was weak, that it lacked the resources to incorporate rural areas and establish the conditions necessary for a capitalist enterprise. Although this was to a certain extent true, such an explanation is unsatisfactory for two reasons. First, United Fruit was accustomed to installing infrastructure and developing entire regions on its own. The company's operations in parts of Central America often (though not always) depended on the "absence" of the state. Second, United Fruit's problems with the peasants began when it involved the state. It is the nature of the state's presence, not its absence, that needs explaining.

It was with the courts and the broader involvement of the state that a dispersed and unorganized group of peasants was transformed into a community and organization.[9] Without the conflict, the peasants may never have embraced the Law of Commune Organization, but once they did they were required to form a commune, a geopolitical body that was simultaneously an organization and a community. The formation of the commune, in turn, not only facilitated the peasants' own efforts to organize, physically uniting them on a single site and thus allowing them to increase their day-to-day control over the land, but gave them a legal presence before the state. This presence proved key as they and their allies pushed their case through a number of state ministries, offices, agencies, and institutions.

The ability of the peasants, as well as United Fruit, to successfully cultivate the state was shaped by a number of factors. To begin, the peasants proved remarkably effective in controlling the local level. They cultivated land, maintained close ties with local authorities, and destroyed the company's banana trees. Moreover, the central government's uneven and incomplete control over rural areas complicated the situation and frustrated United Fruit's own efforts. Once the conflict escalated, it would have taken a serious and sustained effort on the part of the state to evict the peasants. They were entrenched. Yet, it was not simply that the Ecuadorian state lacked the resources to evict a group of peasants on behalf of a foreign company. The state, or at least important sectors, also lacked the will. The political context was key. Peasants were not only able to contact labor organizations (most of whom had not existed ten years earlier), but could now find (and access) sympathetic sectors within the rapidly changing landscape of the Ecuadorian state. Velasco's nationalist-populist rhetoric, combined with the general instability of the central government during this period, opened up spaces for popular actors while at the same time serving to destabilize the political terrain that foreign corporations such as United Fruit were forced to navigate. By contacting allies and making sure that the central government did not *uniformly* support their eviction, the peasants were able to infuse their control at the local level with real meaning. Conversely, United Fruit confronted a state that remained a key and differentiated site through which conflict was played out, but one whose formal terrain could now be permeated, divided, and complicated by a much wider range of groups.

At the same time, I have also argued that there was more to the peasants' victory than the transfer of land from United Fruit to the Mollepongo Commune. The process through which the peasants were victorious served to increase the intensity of their dialogue with the state. As Llivichusca explained:

> After we won the land our conflict with the company was over. But our struggle with the state had just begun. It was not a violent conflict. Threats from the police and military have been rare. But we have struggled. We have struggled for potable water, roads, systems of irrigation, schools, credit to cultivate the land. . . . To get these resources requires resources. One needs to file petitions, make trips to [state offices in] Quito, hold meetings, meet with government officials. The struggle for the land was just the beginning. (J.L. 5/25/96)

It was, of course, not "the beginning." The peasants had had other encounters with the state prior to the conflict with United Fruit. But land conflicts, and particularly the formation of state-sanctioned peasant organizations (i.e., communes, cooperatives, and workers' associations), represented a key moment in peasant-state relationships because they organized and routinized the peasants' *formal* subordination to the state. This process, and the transition from formal to de facto subordination, would be dramatically intensified in the 1960s and 1970s as state resources increased and agrarian reform was implemented.

Although it is clear that the Mollepongo peasants entered into an increasingly intense and sustained dialogue with the state as a result of the conflict, it is less clear what impact this had on their organizations, communities, and subjectivities. On a simple level, the commune became increasingly dependent on the state. It was eventually turned into a client that was forever petitioning government branches for water, roads, and electricity. Once the peasants were organized into a commune—and thereby concentrated into a single population center that had a relatively clear and subordinate relationship to particular forms of state power— it was able to petition the state for a wide range of resources. That the community benefited from roads, water, schools, and electricity is clear. At the same time, many of these services also increased the peasants' dependence on the state and made it easier for certain forms to regulate, discipline, and watch the community.

The impact of this increasingly intense peasant-state dialogue is even less clear when we turn to the question of subjectivities. Quite clearly, we are not talking about a case where the state consciously tried to manipulate or promote certain beliefs and ideologies. Ideological consent was neither sought or given. Nevertheless, we could, in following Corrigan and Sayer, ask: Were the state's regulative, coercive, and sometimes enabling forms and agencies—its practices and routines—able to define certain kinds of subjects and identities while ruling out others (Roseberry 1994)? To be sure, the peasants did not suddenly adopt the identity of "comunero." Moreover, it seems clear that their understandings of both commune and comunero differed significantly from dominant groups. However, it did not always matter if the peasants shared the state's definitions. Rule was often accomplished in the absence of either consent or overt force. For the purposes of taxes, property boundaries, agrarian reform, and a multitude of other state practices, the peasants *were* now comuneros—and had to behave like ones when filing petitions or visiting state agencies—regardless of whether or not they adopted the identity in some deeper sense. In this way, it is important to distinguish between subjects and subjectivities; new subjects can be created even in cases where subjectivities remain relatively unchanged. The irony in this particular case was that the Ecuadorian state's ability to create subjects—

that is, to define the peasants as comuneros—did not come from its unity or coherence. The divisions within the organizational terrain of the Ecuadorian state simultaneously allowed the peasants to defeat United Fruit *and* facilitated their own incorporation (as subjects) into the nation-state.

The future implications of this contradictory process—through which peasant-workers participated in organizations that simultaneously furthered their struggles *and* facilitated their control by the state—will be explored in the second half of the book. As we will see, although peasants would continue to manipulate the fragmented lines of state power during the 1960s and 1970s, their increasingly clientelistic organizations became more and more subject to, and defined by, the bureaucratic logic of particular state institutions. First, however, we must finish tracing the evolving relationship between the emergence of peasant organizations and the dismantling of Hacienda Tenguel.

> One night in 1955 about twelve of us got together in La Esperanza in order to
> discuss what we were going to do. Most of us had just been laid off and had
> ninety days to leave our houses and Hacienda Tenguel. The others were not
> far behind and knew it was just a matter of time. Some talked about going to
> Guayaquil. No one really had a good idea. Then someone said, "Why don't
> we go start working over near the mountains?" Soon after, we went and took
> a look and decided to struggle for land and form a community in Shumiral.
> —Rafael León, founding member of the Colonia Agrícola Shumiral

The loss of land in Mollepongo meant little to United Fruit at a moment when production from Hacienda Tenguel was propelling Ecuador
to the top of banana world. The company had no serious problems with
its labor force in the early 1950s and production expanded throughout
much of the hacienda. For over ten years, from the late 1940s until the
late 1950s, the plantation was the largest single producer in Ecuador, employing over 2000 workers and exporting some 80,000 stems of bananas
a week at its peak. By the mid-1950s, however, the Panama Disease was affecting production levels and the multinational was beginning to explore
disease-free areas on or just outside the margins of Hacienda Tenguel. It
was at this point that the loss of land to the Mollepongo Commune took
on new meaning. In order to keep exports flowing in the face of devastation caused by the Panama Disease, the company had to either expand
its own production or contract with local producers. Both strategies were
adopted with limited success in the late 1950s.

Expanding production into disease-free areas essentially meant going
east toward the Andean foothills (because the property ran up against
the ocean to the west and large landowners to the north and south). Directly to the east, expansion was impossible due to the presence of the
Mollepongo Commune. Consequently, United Fruit turned to the southeast, extending the rail system, building roads, and constructing two new
towns from scratch. Hundred of workers were moved from older sections
of the hacienda into the zone of Brasil. Although United Fruit was able
to plant several hundred hectares in this area, it once again found itself

embroiled in a land conflict with a small group of peasants. Using methods that were conspicuously similar to those adopted in Mollepongo, the peasants of Brasil prevented the company from expanding its operations at a moment when the long-term survival of the overall enterprise required the development of new banana groves.

The combination of an expanding banana plague and a shrinking hacienda generated a number of ironies, but none was more devastating for the multinational than that of Shumiral, a community and peasant organization that was formed just to the northeast of Tenguel (or on the northern border of Mollepongo; see Map 1). Shumiral was not, as in the case of Mollepongo and Brasil, a community formed by smallholders who were trying to retain properties they had been working for years. Shumiral was imagined and developed by United Fruit's own workers—or, rather, ex-workers the company had been forced to lay off because production was down and expansion impossible. Unable to extend its cultivations into Mollepongo or Brasil, the multinational turned to the northeast section of Shumiral only to find its own ex-workers illegally occupying the land and building a community.[1]

The ensuing conflict, outlined in this chapter, was exceptionally important for a number of reasons. First, the laid-off workers consciously invaded an uncultivated portion of Hacienda Tenguel. Unlike the peasants in Mollepongo and Brasil, the ex-workers in Shumiral never justified their actions in terms of a legal claim to the land. Although the term "invasion" was not yet part of their political language, the ex-workers nonetheless inserted themselves into an emerging discourse surrounding agrarian reform, justifying what in essence was an invasion through the moral-nationalist argument that as Ecuadorian peasants they had the right to occupy uncultivated land owned by a foreign company. As one of the more open land invasions during the period immediately preceding agrarian reform, the conflict in Shumiral—and what it foreshadowed—posed a much greater symbolic threat to the company's enterprise. The invasion was a sign of things to come. Second, in 1960, after five years of struggle, the Colonia Agrícola Shumiral could claim victory against a major multinational. Forced to sell over 2500 hectares for a token price, the United Fruit Company was one step closer to abandoning direct production. Third, because it was orchestrated by a small group of ex-workers and a relentless lawyer, the victory in Shumiral provided workers at the core of the hacienda with a dramatic example of the possibilities opened up by organization and unity. No one had ever imagined that the company could be beaten by workers; Shumiral demonstrated otherwise. Encouraged by the example of Shumiral, workers in Tenguel would invade the heart of the hacienda less than two years later. Finally, as we will see more clearly in subsequent chapters, members of the Colonia Agrícola Shumiral, in alliance with *compañeros* from the Mollepongo Commune, continued to struggle long after their initial victories. Motivated by their own successes, the peasants and their descendants not only established alliances with sympathetic clergy and national-level popular organizations, but became regional-national leaders themselves. To a greater extent than in any other community, the *colonos* (settlers) of Shumiral developed a consciousness of themselves as peasants involved in a broader struggle against both the state and the agrarian oligarchy. By the mid-1970s, the very same leaders involved in the conflict with United Fruit formed UROCAL, a regional peasant organization that assisted other peasant groups in their struggles to obtain land and form communities. The formation of Shumiral, then, would not only provide a model and stimulus for the formation of other peasant communities and organizations, but represented the beginning of a broader process. Due to a variety of factors, including successful histories of union struggle, the disintegration of large haciendas, and the growing pressure for agrarian reform, groups of peasants began in the late 1960s to invade marginal sections of large haciendas and form independent communities.[2] Shumiral, as well as Mollepongo and Brasil, were early manifestations of a process that was just beginning to transform Ecuador on a national level.

WORKERS' SEARCH FOR LAND

Summoned by a friend who was living in Tenguel, Sergio Armijos arrived in La Esperanza on the eastern edge of the core of Hacienda Tenguel in 1957. What he found, however, was quite different from the fantasies fueled by his friend. Along with hundreds of other immigrants from the southern highlands, Armijos arrived with the hope of saving money and buying some land of his own. Both Hacienda Tenguel and the wages being paid were impressive, but there were no new hirings.

Sergio Armijos was not alone in his predicament. Stimulated by the spread of the Panama Disease, company layoffs had just recently begun in the La Esperanza section of the hacienda and discussion about the uncertain future occurred on a daily basis. Upon being laid off, most ex-workers found themselves with little savings and ninety days to pack up. They learned quickly that the houses and towns they had come to see as their own were simply rights they had acquired as workers. As ex-workers, they had to leave. It was under these circumstances that a Tenguel without United Fruit was first imagined. As Armijos explains:

> I told some friends that I was thinking of leaving because there was no work in the area. They asked me where I was going. I said maybe [the southern province of] El Oro. . . . But I really didn't know, I had no family in the coast. Others were also thinking of leaving. But by the time I arrived a group was already talking about creating a community near the mountains. (S.A. 1996)

The idea of forming a community on abandoned state lands (*terrenos baldios*) was first discussed in 1955, some two years prior to Armijos's arrival. That such talk emerged on the eastern edge of Hacienda Tenguel is hardly surprising. La Esperanza was close to uncultivated areas on the hacienda's fringe and workers in this section were in constant contact with the comuneros of Mollepongo.

The Mollepongo Commune was not, however, the only example to which the fired workers turned. Highland peasants had been slowly moving into the zone of Shumiral for at least a generation. Some came to the hacienda in order to work, while others occupied isolated sectors within or just outside the hacienda's ambiguous boundaries. Aniceto Sánchez and Don Orellena, for example, had been cultivating food crops in the zone for almost twenty years before the workers in La Esperanza thought about starting a community.

The idea to create a new community in Shumiral was given a strong impetus by a government official from the Ministry of Social Welfare. No one remembers exactly why the official came to the zone, but shortly after arriving he encouraged Aniceto Sánchez to try to become the legal owner of the vacant state lands on which he had been living for close to twenty years. Empowered by the advice, Sánchez went to La Esperanza to inform some of his friends and relatives who had been discussing the idea of moving to Shumiral. The first initiators, including Sánchez, the three León brothers, Hector Cardenas, Amadeo Zambrano, Don Ignacio, Alejandro Guaman, and others, then agreed that they should slowly pursue the matter and take the government official on as their advisor.

Their new advisor informed them that he would fix things by petitioning the National Institute of Colonization[3] and the Ministry of Social Welfare. Each worker was to be delivered fifty hectares of state land. After supposedly pushing the workers' cause through a variety of government channels, the official returned to La Esperanza and asked for money in order to facilitate the legal process. It was the first time their ally had requested money and the peasants had little reason to be distrustful. They were well aware that government palms had to be greased. Pooling their resources, the peasants sent the advisor off to Quito in order to terminate the legal process. He never returned.

That the deception was a setback goes without saying. The peasants had invested much of their money, time, and hopes with the "man from Quito." But all was not lost. The advisor's lies and false hopes had encouraged the peasants to possess the land. Three or four of their own were now living with Sánchez and a larger number had begun planting crops. Their legal cause had not been advanced, but they had begun to take physical possession of the zone. More important, the trip to Quito had not been a total loss and was in fact the turning point in their struggle. They had found Dr. Lautaro Gordillo, a middle-class Quiteño lawyer with ties to the CTE and experience in peasant land struggles and labor conflicts. He would become their next advisor and, in retrospect, a crucial key to their future success. Both Gordillo and his fearless confrontations with the North American giant have taken on heroic proportions in the narratives of the peasants. He was, by all accounts, completely straight with the peasants during five years of legal battles. He received virtually no compensation, insisting that his payment would be membership in the colonia. In addition, Gordillo had an undying belief that they would win. Such confidence, coming from a big-city lawyer, had an empowering impact on the colonia. "He didn't understand the word defeat," noted Rafael León (R.L. 1996).

Gordillo's most immediate and practical contribution, however, was *formal* organization. Although the workers had been organizing and holding meetings regularly, they continued to pursue their *legal* struggle on an individual basis. They provided mutual support toward the goal of obtaining individual titles to distinct plots of land. Gordillo immediately informed them that this was a losing strategy. Individual petitions would get them nowhere. They were, after all, just peasants. They had to form a legally constituted organization that would enable them to confront the company and give them a collective, coherent, and legal presence before the state.

It was just before, during, and after the legal formation of the Colonia Agrícola Shumiral that Sergio Armijos and workers in Tenguel began to hear about the ex-workers' struggle for land.[4] How was the location? Was it really vacant? Was there a chance of getting a plot? These were questions that ex-workers in and around La Esperanza and Tenguel began to ask themselves as Hacienda Tenguel declined. The land in Shumiral was less than ideal. Had it been of premium quality, the company would have cultivated it years before. Yet, because most workers were accustomed to the rocky soils of the southern highlands, the site seemed like paradise and it was rumored that the lands belonged to the state and not the company. Located on a river at the base of the mountains, there was plenty of unoccupied land. As Rafael León recounts: "We came to Tenguel to find work but this was only in order to earn money so that we could obtain our own land. This was the one idea we all shared: *la tierra*. Shumiral was our dream" (R.L. 1996). From the beginning, then, Shumiral—both as an idea and a collective struggle—was motivated by the shared goal of obtaining land.

The isolation and rugged nature of Shumiral worked to the ex-workers' advantage. Had they chosen a flatter, more accessible, area, they most certainly would have been evicted. By the time United Fruit officials realized that a group of ex-workers was possessing hacienda lands, the ex-workers had already cultivated significant sections of land and constructed the beginnings of a town. According to León, the first major blow to their campaign was taken in stride precisely because of the zone's relative isolation:

> Most of us knew the land belonged to the company. But when Dr. Gordillo informed us that it was certain that we were not on vacant state lands but on lands that belonged to the company we were devastated. How could we beat a company as powerful as [United Fruit]? The doctor said not to worry because he had other tactics. Later we sat down as a group and decided it did not matter who owned the land. It had been uncultivated and as peasants born in this country we had a right to a piece of land. The company was not using it and we had possessed and cultivated it. This was what was important. (R.L. 1996)

As the above quote suggests, the peasants had initially based their colonization of Shumiral on the premise that the land in question belonged to the state, was vacant, and thus could be legally colonized. Although most of the ex-workers knew that this was a fiction, the argument provided a dubious, but nonetheless legitimate, explanation for their actions—at a time when justifying the takeover of private property in terms of a "land invasion" would have been politically unacceptable. However, it is important to note that the legal claim was quickly abandoned in part because it was impossible to sustain (i.e. the land was not owned by the state), but also because of the fact that the argument that Ecuadorian peasants had the right to work uncultivated land owned by a foreign company was becoming increasingly compelling as agrarian reform was debated back and forth.

The company, however, was not impressed and although it could not depend on the state to evict squatters, neither could the colonos be sure that authorities would lend even ambiguous support to a group of ex-workers who had no legitimate claim to the land. Moreover, United Fruit had learned from its mistakes in Mollepongo. In the case of Shumiral, the company never even turned to state authorities, preferring instead to treat the conflict as an internal problem between the hacienda and its workers. It was difficult for company authorities to reach Shumiral, but the fact was that United Fruit remained the zone's principle economic and legal power on a day-to-day basis. Because of their isolation not only from Tenguel but from Guayaquil and Machala, the peasants were unable to get any physical support from regional popular organizations or sympathetic sectors within the state. Their main external ally, then, was Dr. Gordillo, a Quiteño lawyer who thrived on underdog cases.

As former United Fruit administrators insist, the company did in fact have plans for the zone. The sector was being divided up in order to be given to members of the hacienda's administration both as a reward for past work and as an incentive to stimulate local banana production. Experienced Ecuadorian administrators were to be given property at little or no cost in order to grow bananas which would then be sold to the company. The company, whose own enterprise was being threatened by the Panama Disease and an increasingly militant labor union, would extend the rail system further into the zone, but invest little of its own capital into the project. Or such was the plan.

When told by a company representative that the land belonged to United Fruit, the peasants feigned bewilderment and said that they would require proof. They had, after all, been told that the land belonged to the state. As the peasants freely admit, this was simply a tactic to buy time. Many had suspected, and Dr. Gordillo subsequently confirmed, that they were on company property. Dr. Gordillo encouraged Sergio Armijos, Rafael León, and the others to do whatever they could to make Shumiral look and function like a town. The more permanent their presence, the harder it would be to remove them. Buildings were constructed and production of food crops increased.

It became quickly apparent to United Fruit that its legal title to the land meant little to the peasants. Possession and use of the land was the key in a zone where the state did little to enforce legal property rights. As a result, the company stepped up the level of intimidation. Threats to bulldoze the town were accompanied by constant visits from the company police and occasional jailings. If they could catch the peasants, the police would imprison them on almost any pretext. Two members, for example, were jailed for supposedly stealing a banana tree and a third was incarcerated when he went to see why the first two had been jailed.

The colonos, according to León, were not moved: "One day they would come with an order to stop planting crops. So we would work on the town. Then they would say stop building the town. So we would go back to the crops. They would send police and we would hide or say that the leaders were in Quito. Or we would say that the land was in Azuay and that the police from Guayas had no authority" (R.L. 1996). Like their counterparts in Mollepongo, those from Shumiral became experts in playing one set of provincial authorities against another.[5] The resilience of the peasants, combined with their relative isolation from authorities, made threats and forms of intimidation only partially effective. New members were hard to recruit, but the peasants' resolve became stronger as they were harassed by the company's thugs.

With little support from the state, United Fruit recognized that it would be difficult to evict the peasants; sending the police only succeeded in forcing them into temporary hiding. Consequently, the company tried a new strategy. According to United Fruit's plan, the colonos simply had to sign rental contracts—thereby recognizing the company's legal control over the foothills—and pay a rather symbolic rent. In exchange, they would be given access to ten hectares for a period of five years and lent assistance in the production of bananas.

The plan nearly worked. The overwhelming majority of peasants signed, reasoning that the company, with all of its economic, political, and legal resources, could not be beaten by a bunch of unemployed workers and a Quiteño lawyer. It was, after all, the company's land. As Rafael León noted, "this just left the crazy ones" (R.L. 1996). Of the thirty or so families that originally formed the colonia, less than ten remained. The majority signed contracts and began to work the plots demarcated by the company. Needless to say, these plots conflicted with those that the colonia had assigned to its own members. Within a week, allies became enemies as the company transformed an emerging community into something resembling the Hatfields and McCoys.

The rental documents, later acquired by the colonia, remain a fascinating read as do the comments written by those who did not sign: "Señor Alvear . . . cut another 4 hectares of underbrush and grew pasture, making it 7 hectares of work destroyed by this man." "Señor Montaleza possessed the land of Julio Ochoa, a member of the colonia, in 1959 and prevented him from growing crops."[6] Others stole corn, destroyed crops, or put fences on the colonos' land. Clearly, the colonos were themselves involved in similar practices as the battle for possession intensified. Each group wanted land. Their goals, if not their strategies, were remarkably similar. The *arrendatarios* (tenants) had reasoned that they would have to wait for another opportunity in order to become legal owners. They signed five-year contracts which could be renewed only if both sides agreed. Any improvements they made to the land would not be reimbursed by the company and permanent crops other than bananas were expressly forbidden. In other words, the rental contracts were temporary arrangements to be terminated at the company's whim. Significantly, all bananas had to be sold to the company if and when the company so desired. United Fruit, which actively encouraged the arrendatarios to produce bananas, dictated both the terms of the contract and the sale.

It was not at all clear at the time that the arrendatarios were going to lose. As Sergio Armijos remembers:

> Don Aniceto brought us the news [of the rental arrangements] in La Esperanza and we had a meeting. But there were only five or six of us left. We had lost, someone said. I said no. I said I was going to live with Don Aniceto in his house and would not leave. I am entering and I am not going to leave. I was young then and with much passion. I said we are Ecuadorians. What is this a foreign country? So I said I would go and live in Shumiral and told each of the others to bring three or four friends and relatives to the next meeting. (S.A. 1996)

With the contracts signed, Aniceto Sánchez was the only member of the colonia still living in the zone and was effectively isolated. The others with houses had signed contracts. After a couple days of work, a number of the arrendatarios confronted Armijos and informed him that the land he was on belonged to United Fruit and was being rented. He was quite aware of this and told his accusers that if there was a problem he wanted to talk with the owner. "You should go and complain to the owner that the lands you have rented are occupied." Such bickering continued with the arrendatarios insisting that the colonia was a false hope. The land, they argued, belonged to United Fruit and the government was in no position to help them. But Armijos and the other colonos countered with arguments of their own, appealing to their counterparts both as peasants and Ecuadorian citizens; a few of the arrendatarios even (secretly) rejoined the colonia, keeping the organization up to date on the company's machinations. More importantly, within a week of the near defeat, the colonia had successfully grown to just over twenty members. The arrendatarios, in contrast, remained unorganized, depending on the company to enforce the rental contracts.

Exactly why United Fruit eventually gave in and abandoned the arrendatarios is unclear. One would like to attribute the colonia's victory entirely to the peasants' quite remarkable efforts. Their persistence clearly played a role. Dr. Gordillo proved more than a match for the company's lawyers and the remaining colonos were relentless. Yet the timing of the victory—April 29, 1960—suggests that other factors were also at work. Most of the original contracts were signed in 1957 when Hacienda Tenguel was still relatively strong. By 1960, however, the company must have known, given the deteriorating state of the hacienda, that it might not be in a position to renew the arrendatarios' contracts. United Fruit thus faced the possibility of having to confront two (now larger) groups of peasants, each of which possessed cultivated lands. Pressed by the colonos, an expanding disease, a militant union, and an unsupportive state, the company decided to sell the marginal section of Shumiral to the colonia. Actually, by the time Dr. Gordillo was done, United Fruit nearly gave the 2500 hectares away. Rafael León recounts the final episode as follows:

> The last meeting with the company was a real triumph. A bunch of gringos came here to Shumiral to negotiate. Yes, here. Our lawyer, Dr. Gordillo, wouldn't go to Tenguel. They all sat down and started talking. Dr. Gordillo never sat, he just paced. They talked for a bit and then Dr. Gordillo said he was leaving. He said he was a busy man with people waiting. Can you imagine? The gringos got real nervous. They wanted to end this matter and didn't like being in Shumiral. They would offer a price and he would reject it and say he was leaving. He said it was an insult that Ecuadorians were paying for our own land. Finally they agreed on a price and asked where they could write up the contract. Dr. Gordillo said we would have to go to Tenguel because we were only poor people here and didn't even have a typewriter. So we walked a bit and then got in the trucks with the gringos. Everyone came. The arrendatarios were following on their horses. That was a sight. We got to Tenguel and a gringo began to write up the agreement but Dr. Gordillo disagreed with every sentence. Finally they just gave him the typewriter and he typed it out in five minutes. The gringos signed and we had won. We left the offices and no one in Tenguel could believe us. They thought they had brought us here to put us in jail. And there we were leaving as landowners. That was a great day. (R. L. 1996)

The colonia's problems were far from over, but they would be of quite a different nature after April 29, 1960. Like the Mollepongo peasants, they did not have the resources to bring the land they won into production, and had to find additional members in order to purchase the 2500 hectares. The colonos were now landowners and faced a whole new set of problems surrounding production and the development of a community. Some of these problems, and the partial solutions developed by the peasants, will be the subject of later chapters.

For now, it should simply be pointed out that the colonos' long struggle with the company and the state had been an educational experience for both themselves and the workers in Tenguel. On the one hand, they could no longer be so easily deceived by state officials or crooked lawyers. Future attempts by the agrarian elite to intimidate the peasants would be seen in the context of earlier maneuvers on the part of a major multinational. The colonos had come to understand that the campesino struggle involved more than a piece of land. This understanding of a larger struggle would lead a number of the colonos to form a regional peasant organization in the 1970s. On the other hand, their victory, coming at the precise moment when the bulk of the labor force was being laid off, provided workers in Tenguel with both example and method. If ex-workers could defeat United Fruit and obtain marginal sections of the hacienda, what was stopping them from acquiring the core of the property as well? It is to this question, and the workers' answer, that we now turn.

6 The End of an Enclave

United Fruit had laid off almost the entire labor force by 1960. The workers were unemployed, threatened with eviction, and in a desperate state. They were also largely on their own. Labor activists from the CTE/FPTG lent encouragement and legal aid, sectors within the state made promises, and the victory in Shumiral provided a close-to-home example. Ultimately, however, it was the workers' own history of union struggle and organization that provided the basis from which they would confront both the company and the state—now more as peasants in search of land than as workers demanding better wages and working conditions. The present chapter examines the yearlong takeover of Hacienda Tenguel, paying particular attention to the local, regional, and national factors that not only forced the workers to invade the property in March 1962, but led the military to crush the invasion in July 1963.

"COMMUNIST AGITATORS"

It was on March 24, 1962, several days prior to the invasion of the hacienda, that the Ecuadorian public first became aware that all was not well on the country's most infamous banana plantation. "Five Communist Agitators were in Tenguel to Foment Violence," declared a journalist on the back pages of *El Universo,* one of the country's major dailies (*El Universo* 3/24/62: 23). According to the article, "Bolshevik agitators" were "causing trouble" and had "begun to organize" the workers, holding a protest and instructing the workers to invade the hacienda and expel United Fruit. Alluding directly to the growing discourse on agrarian reform, the article pointed out that although United Fruit had not been exploiting the land in a direct form for quite some time, the company had generously "delivered" the land to the ex-workers.

What makes this initial article so interesting is the routine way in which it, and subsequent accounts, systematically ignored and/or distorted this local history of hacienda decline and union activity. And Tenguel was not alone. Similar "disruptions" from various locales throughout Ecuador—haciendas, ports, factories, and cities—were reported with increasing frequency during the late 1950s and early 1960s. According to such reports, these disruptions were always instigated by "outsiders," most notably communists who had unproven, yet unquestioned, ties to Castro. The implicit message was that the average worker had been content prior to the arrival of outside agitators. Not only did outsiders put confusing ideas into the minds of the common folk, they provided organization. The two decades of union organizing in Tenguel was conveniently ignored: "the communists have begun to organize the workers" (ibid.).

This back page article also served as a warning. Several days later, ex-workers would invade and take control of one of the largest haciendas in the country. The invasion of Hacienda Tenguel, as well as the events that would follow, could be immediately distinguished from other similar protests along a number of lines.[1] It was the first full takeover of a major hacienda. The size, productivity, and foreign ownership of Tenguel only added to its importance. Tenguel immediately left the back pages and became the country's most urgent current event. Unlike strikes or isolated protests, the land invasion could not be easily resolved by the state. Increasing wages or firing a particularly oppressive foreman was not the answer. The conflict was not about wages, the labor code, or working conditions. It was first and foremost about the land. In this sense, the invasion of Hacienda Tenguel—foreshadowed by events in Mollepongo and Shumiral—signaled the gradual shift away from labor conflicts and the beginning of a period characterized by land struggles. It also represented the definitive end of enclave-style production, the beginning of agrarian reform, and the slow emergence of contract farming in Ecuador.

Although particularly intense in the agro-export heartland, similar land conflicts would take place throughout Ecuador in the 1960s and 1970s. They were both stimulated by, and gave life to, the movement for agrarian reform.[2] Tenguel, first as a "communist invasion" and then as the country's first agrarian reform project, occupied a central place in the initial set of agrarian reform debates. What did the invasion at Tenguel mean in terms of communism and agrarian reform? If workers were given land and agrarian reform implemented at Tenguel, would communism spread throughout Ecuador? Would a successful invasion only encourage other workers to take similar action? Did events in Tenguel signify the need for agrarian reform on a national level? Would a national agrarian reform—by addressing rural inequality and redistributing land—eliminate the allure of communism and the need for land invasions? If implemented, what would agrarian reform look like? Should workers be given land in individual plots? Should they be put into state-controlled cooperatives? Should the state simply take over the hacienda? These were the kinds of questions, and ideological boundaries, that were being raised in relation to events in Tenguel. It is important to remember that at the time of the invasion (1962) agrarian reform was only a debate. The first Agrarian Reform Law was not passed until 1964. The nation's elites used Tenguel, and frequently mislabeled it as "communist," in order to restrict the nature of the debate over agrarian reform. At the same time, local forces within Tenguel positioned themselves for a land struggle that would be shaped both by United Fruit's departure and a yet-to-be-determined reform project.

"ARMED WORKERS TAKE CONTROL OF HACIENDA TENGUEL"

The initial report regarding five communist agitators embodied the communist-paranoid lens through which the invasion itself would be viewed, debated, and eventually crushed.[3] When the actual invasion took place several days later, the first newspaper report continued in the same vein, noting that "well informed sources" confirmed that there was a plan to convert the zone of Tenguel into a communist outpost. Well-trained communist militants from Guayaquil, Quito, Cuba, and Russia had trained the ex-workers in the use of arms, dynamite, and gas bombs. Techniques of guerrilla warfare had also been taught. Red flags could be seen on many houses and adorned the few bridges that had not been dynamited. Immediately prior to the invasion, the police, sensing that something abnormal was going to happen, captured five individuals who had revolvers, gas, and Molotov cocktails. Arrested as revolutionaries, this captured group had been accompanied by two Cubans and a lawyer from Shumiral.

Upon taking control of the hacienda, the ex-workers reportedly shouted slogans—"Viva Cuba" and "Viva la Reforma Agraria"—as they shot their pistols wildly into the air and brandished Molotov cocktails. Despite the arrests and the best efforts of the police, the invasion succeeded. The list of casualties was extensive: the five police were injured in their heroic defense of the hacienda; the house of Don Julio Arguello, United Fruit's superintendent, was dynamited; three employees of the company were taken hostage (whereabouts "unknown"), and a woman was killed. As the news report explains:

> The workers, who lacked employment or economic resources, began to listen to the agitators of the extreme left and some of the leaders were converted who then began to agitate their compañeros into

believing that they could get the hacienda parceled out to them-selves. The atmosphere was ripe for communist propaganda and talk of agrarian reform.

The implicit message was that the government had dropped the ball and let dangerous conditions become worse. Some sort of intervention was necessary and if the government proved unwilling, the communist agi-tators would carry out agrarian reform on their own, Cuban terms. Most importantly, the article implied that the impoverished conditions which gave the communists their appeal were not isolated to Tenguel. The com-munists were coming and Tenguel was just the beginning.

Newspaper accounts probably tell us more about growing urban middle-class fears of communism and the peasantry than they do about the invasion of the hacienda. In this sense, what actually happened in Tenguel in the end of March will probably never be completely uncov-ered. Based on accounts by ex-workers, however, it seems clear that the actual events differed substantially from the newspaper reports. Since the mass firings had begun in 1959, the situation on the hacienda had be-come intolerable for the majority of ex-workers. Most were unemployed, had little access to the land, and, because they had been members of a union, were unable to find employment on neighboring haciendas.

Nevertheless, the workers' decision to invade came slowly and was de-layed by a wide range of factors. At various times during the two years prior to the invasion, most ex-workers hoped that United Fruit would either return or sell the hacienda to the state and/or workers. The latter hope was fueled by a number of factors and circumstances. By mid- to late 1961, the company was allowing the labor union, recently trans-formed into Cooperative Juan Quirumbay, to work part of the hacienda. Although insufficient to meet the ex-workers' basic needs, the agreement fueled the hope that the company would negotiate the sale of the ha-cienda with the cooperative. State-controlled agrarian reform was still several years away and the idea of a worker-owned and -managed ha-cienda did not seem unreasonable, nor did it fall outside the parame-ters of the ongoing debate over agrarian reform. In addition, Cooperative Juan Quirumbay had developed contacts with sympathetic state officials who were involved in negotiations with United Fruit over the sale of Ha-cienda Tenguel.

In short, the workers' grievances had been met by official and unoffi-cial statements that a meaningful land reform was about to occur and that the hacienda would be the centerpiece of the state's project. From the workers' perspective, there was no need to take action because the state was going to resolve the entire mess. The problem, however, was

that United Fruit was actively experimenting with a variety of arrangements in which the company itself would no longer be involved in direct
production. Each of these experiments directly threatened the workers'
access to land and/or employment.

First, the company turned the majority of the hacienda over to four
or five ex-administrators who worked the land with a drastically reduced
and poorly paid workforce. In a system that eerily resembled the form
of contracting that dominates the southern coast today, the administrators were essentially renting the land and then selling bananas back to
United Fruit. Second, there was a small minority of ex-workers who were
also renting small plots from United Fruit. Here, the tenant was little
more than a well-paid guard. The company would finance and organize
production, maintaining complete control over technical decisions. The
tenant, in turn, would oversee the laborers and maintain security. Third,
Gala, an eighty-man cooperative comprised of ex-workers and organized
by United Fruit, was renting about 3000 hectares of the most disease-
ridden sections of the hacienda. The company also organized a number
of other cooperatives in order to prevent the majority of ex-workers from
either gaining access to the land or retaining control over their houses.

Finally, and most importantly, United Fruit sold sections of the hacienda to four or five large capitalists who provided the ex-workers with
little employment and poor wages. While the sales represented a rather
small fraction of the hacienda, the workers feared that they represented a
sign of things to come. As national capitalists, the buyers did not face the
same constraints as United Fruit. They began to harass the workers and
train a private police force on Tenguel's soccer field. When direct intimidation failed they tried other tactics, including the placement of spies
in the cooperative's leadership and a smear campaign against Cooperative Juan Quirumbay (suggesting that the leaders were well connected to
Castro). Yet, it was their final ultimatum which provoked the invasion.
Two months before the invasion, local capitalists, tacitly supported by
the company, sectors within the state, as well as armed thugs, threatened
to remove the workers from the hacienda. They set the date of eviction
for March 30. That the workers invaded the hacienda just several days
prior to their scheduled departure was hardly a coincidence.

In order to navigate this constantly shifting terrain—characterized
by agrarian reform debates, state declarations, local thugs, and United
Fruit's machinations—the workers transformed their union into Cooperative Juan Quirumbay. Once fired, most members of the union
simply joined the cooperative. The name change was a strategic move
by the workers to place themselves within the context of agrarian re-

form. Cooperatives, as well as agricultural workers' associations, were to become the basic forms of state-sanctioned organizations through which peasant-workers acquired uncultivated land during the agrarian reform period. The difficulty was that the widespread formation of co-operatives would not occur until late 1960s, and particularly after 1972 when the oil boom made a more meaningful agrarian reform financially possible. Consequently, the process of forming a cooperative, which by 1970 would be etched on the minds of most peasants in Ecuador, was uncharted territory in the early 1960s.[4] As Jacinto Lozano pointed out: "For a short time both the union and [Cooperative] Quirumbay existed together but we knew that the future was in the cooperative. We were trying to encourage the government to buy the hacienda and deliver it to the workers. Few people knew what a cooperative was, but we felt that some sort of organization would show the state we could run the ha-cienda" (J.L. 6/17/95).

At the time of the invasion, the influence and organization of Co-operative Juan Quirumbay was indisputable. As the direct heir to the union, the cooperative had a membership of over 600 families, six times more than the five cooperatives supported by United Fruit. Juan Quirum-bay's strength grew as threats to the ex-workers' lives and homes in-creased. In response to the growing visibility of armed thugs, Coopera-tive Juan Quirumbay organized its own brigades and made appeals to student groups, unions, and political parties, any group with even re-motely democratic pretensions. The workers knew, however, that they stood little chance against the armed forces that were mounting against them. Their contact with the CTE/FPTG had been limited to a few trips to Guayaquil, and the few allies they had within the state had little in-fluence with the local police and military. In the end, the workers were largely on their own and concluded that a preemptive invasion was pref-erable to their own eviction.

THE TAKEOVER

As we saw in chapter three, the growing militancy of the workers, as well as the strength of both the union and Cooperative Juan Quirumbay, were rooted in the family and community. Men and women were joined in a confrontation against not only United Fruit but sectors within the state, neighboring landowners, and local police forces. As the situation became increasingly intense and the union-turned-cooperative came to represent not only the majority of workers but their families as well, the leaders of Cooperative Juan Quirumbay actively excluded women from key decisions. Women were counted on, in fact expected, to coordinate the cooking of food, the organization of rallies, and other activities necessary for the survival of the community and its political struggle. They were not, however, allowed to negotiate with company officials and members of the state, those public decisions that would determine their futures.

The women were also excluded from the invasion when it finally occurred during the night of March 26 and the morning of March 27. Although a military-like discipline was imposed, the overwhelming majority of male workers, some of whom were armed with machetes and shotguns, actively participated. Given the deteriorated state of the hacienda, an invasion essentially meant controlling the rather limited means of communication and transportation. The airstrip and access roads were blockaded and the radio-communicator was put under the control of loyal workers. The smaller hamlets surrounding the town of Tenguel were also secured. No one was allowed to enter, but administrators and others were free to leave. Key bridges were controlled, but not dynamited. Most importantly, no one was hurt or killed, the houses were not burned, and no women were raped. Nor does anyone remember shouting "Viva Cuba" or recall the presence of communists or outsiders of any kind.

Ironically, the men's decision to keep the invasion secret from their wives almost had disastrous consequences. Before being forced to flee to the town of Balao, the small police detachment arrested five members of Juan Quirumbay, including Adolfo Nieto and Segundo Lima, the cooperative's most important leaders. Fearing for their husbands' lives and ignorant as to what was happening, some of the women kidnapped a number of the hacienda's administrators, including Howard Johnson, a high-ranking United Fruit official who happened to be visiting the zone. Although the "hostages" were subsequently released, the kidnappings helped contribute to the very image of violent terrorists that the workers were consciously trying to avoid.

Nevertheless, once the hacienda was secured, the ex-workers immediately notified the government that they wanted to meet and find a solution to their problem. This was their central goal. In contrast to newspaper reports, they had no plans to parcel out the hacienda or form a communist outpost. They wanted to meet with the government and find a reasonable solution to the misery that had become their lives. There was one condition. The proposed meeting would not take place until the five arrested men—Segundo Lima, Adolfo Nieto, Manuel Valverde, José Zuñiga, and Ernesto Toalan—were released and returned to Tenguel.

Negotiations could not begin without Lima or Nieto, the leaders of Co-operative Juan Quirumbay.

The Arosemena government reacted quickly, if somewhat ambiguously, to the crisis. Guillermo Jaramillo Larrea, the Subsecretary of the Ministry of Social Welfare and Labor, led a commission comprised of other high-level state officials—Cesar Serrano Miranda, general director of Labor; Rene Moreno, director of Cooperatives of the Ministry of Development (Fomento); Daniel Leon Borja, director of the National Institute of Colonization; and economist Hernán Carrera Andrade, from the Ministry of Development—who were ready to negotiate a solution and bring a rapid end to an embarrassing situation. The state, however, was hardly unified with respect to the invasion or the broader issues of agrarian reform, popular uprising, and communism. A full-scale police invasion had not been ruled out, and the Ministry of Defense (which seemed to get all of its information from the newspapers) called for the violent eviction of the communist revolutionaries. The Jaramillo-led commission was stationed at Hacienda María Teresa to the south of Tenguel while police forces waited just to the north in the town of Balao. The state, as usual, was not of one mind.

Fortunately, sectors within the state that were sympathetic to the workers' plight initially prevailed and the commission was sent to Tenguel. Upon arrival, Subsecretary Jaramillo, himself a member of the socialist party, announced that the government was going to buy the hacienda and that United Fruit had forty-eight hours to leave town. The assistant manager of United Fruit's operations in Ecuador was put under house arrest, and the police who had arrested the five members of Juan Quirumbay were themselves placed in jail for mistreating the prisoners. In contrast, the five members of Juan Quirumbay were set free and the two leaders, Lima and Nieto, were present at Tenguel for the assembly between the ex-workers and the government delegation.

At the assembly, Lima and Nieto were the honored guests. Subsecretary Jaramillo began the assembly by saying that he had come on behalf of President Arosemena and was looking to restore peace in Tenguel. The government, he assured, wanted to resolve the problem quickly and deliver the hacienda to the workers. The other members of the government delegation gave similarly positive speeches, emphasizing that with the government in Tenguel (and the foreign company gone) the workers' problems would be solved quickly. The national director of Cooperatives, Dr. Rene Moreno, reaffirmed that the land would pass to the workers and that the system of cooperatives developed in Tenguel would be the model for all of Ecuador: "Agrarian reform was born in Tenguel," he emphatically shouted. With discipline and obedience, the government will solve the problem, "prosperity would return in a year," and "Tenguel will be turned into a paradise."

THE BACKLASH

The day after the government commission came to Tenguel, met with workers, and made all sorts of fantastic promises, an ideological assault began against both the cooperative and supportive state officials. Newspaper reports detailing the spread of communism in Ecuador increased after the invasion, and Tenguel was a central part of this discourse. Less than a week after the positive meeting with the government delegation and the apparent about-face on the part of the national press, *El Universo* reported that there were still "500 armed men in Tenguel" dedicated to robbery and other acts against persons and property. The article asserted that additional state intervention was necessary to root out the communist presence. Support for this claim was illustrated by the fact that members of Juan Quirumbay were instructing workers on Hacienda Villanueva to follow their example (which they would eventually do). The communist menace was spreading.

A subsequent editorial noted that "the expansion of disorder towards neighboring zones is on a level that such acts will quickly spread to the rest of the country." This threat was due to "the lack of good sense and the failure to apply legal norms on the part of the Ministry of Social Welfare after the workers had clearly committed outrages against the hacienda" and United Fruit. The author went on to suggest that this oversight on the part of the government should be corrected with "the severity that is required" and that a military contingent should be sent to take arms from the workers and root out "the clandestine agents of communism." This "repression" should be done quickly so that the "anarchist outbreak" does not spread beyond Villanueva to the country as a whole. In this particularly imaginative version of the domino theory, Tenguel and Villanueva were viewed as lost causes that should be repressed if the rest of the country was to be saved. Nor was such propaganda without its intended effects. On April 7, two days after the editorial, a military contingent was sent to Tenguel to make sure that people "were dedicated to agriculture" and nothing else. More significantly, Subsecretary Jaramillo became the ex-subsecretary, thereby ridding Juan Quirumbay of its most important government ally.

Although the ideological assault against the workers was largely a product of reporters, state officials, landed elites, and commentators living outside the zone, the workers themselves were intimately caught up in this discursive battle. Indeed, the battle, and the internal divisions it would exacerbate, began with the initial government commission led by Jaramillo. The national director of Cooperatives, Dr. Rene Moreno, had gone out of his way to stress that members of Cooperative Gala—the United Fruit–supported peasant organization that opposed the invasion —would no longer be favored over those of Cooperative Juan Quirumbay. In fact, Moreno publicly blamed members of Gala for the invasion and provoked a chorus of boos and hisses against its members. Unfortunately, this strategic move to place himself, the initial commission, and Juan Quirumbay on the right side of the communist fence served to exacerbate and solidify what at the time was a relatively minor division among the workers. As a result, once the tide began to turn against Juan Quirumbay and its allies within the state, Cooperative Gala returned the favor. Supported by local capitalists, Gala made continual and effective appeals to the press. They insisted that members of Juan Quirumbay continued to mistreat them and that the state was unduly favoring the "communist" cooperative. In addition, it was reported that Juan Quirumbay was "stealing" cattle from the zone's emerging capitalists—including Dr. Carlos Luis Plaza Dañin, José Aray Marín, and William Guerrero Parker—and was planning to appropriate the lands being worked by Cooperative Gala.[5]

Cooperative Gala's offensive, and particularly the way in which it was eaten up by the press, only encouraged others. In a commentary entitled "The Truth about Tenguel," a group of ex-workers and administrators who had been renting land from United Fruit prior to the invasion pointed out that the company had obeyed the labor code to the letter. United Fruit had paid severance to fired workers and delivered large sections of the hacienda to ex-administrators, capitalists, and ex-workers who had the economic resources to develop the land. Keeping in line with the external agitators theory and stepping up the attack on pro-worker forces within the government, the "united renters" go on to note that a major center of "international communism" existed in Tenguel due to "Doctor Jaramillo, ex-Subsecretary of Social Welfare, Doctor Rene Moreno, the current Director of Cooperatives, and Dr. Cobos Moscoso," a well-known "communist" lawyer and legal representative of Juan Quirumbay.

The most amazing feature of this public relations assault against the workers was its sustained nature. It lasted for well over a year after the invasion, continuing unabated until the military destroyed Cooperative Juan Quirumbay in July 1963. In fact, one of the most visible forms of this ideological attack came in the form of an editorial written one month before the military took power on the national level. Appearing well over a year after the invasion, the editorial speaks both to Tenguel's continued importance within agrarian reform debates and the impossibility of the workers' situation. The general point of the mean-spirited commentary was to poke fun at the workers while contributing to the assault against pro-reform forces within the state. Ironically titled, "An example of how we will make Ecuador into another Cuba: Tenguel," the article began by asking "how much ink and paper, how much Russian and Ecuadorian money, had been spent to organize and mobilize the workers against United Fruit and to attack the police and military that guarantee the security of property and people?" Saenz, the rather creative editorialist, noted that outsiders used "psychological methods" to gain control of the minds of the peasants and had them believing that they could get the land for free. He pointed out that the company did everything it could against the strikes fueled by communists and sympathetic government functionaries. Since the company's departure, the author continues, the government wasted endless amounts of money on the zone and the taxpayers have contracted an enormous debt—all in an effort to insure that another Cuba was not built in Ecuador. Despite these efforts, Saenz insisted that "Tenguel represents the most eloquent contradiction of the speech, already suffocating, of the wisemen of agrarian reform. . . . No one, not the political leaders, not the technical experts who have inspected the hacienda so many times, not the peasants, have wanted to transform the 17,000 hectares into minifundias or, according to the reformist lingo, 'family plots.'" But this was in fact what was happening. Another Cuba exists in Tenguel where two cooperatives have formed, reflecting the divergent ideas of the leaders: "One is managed by the Communist Party and the other, which pretends not to be communist, is run by agents of Castro. . . . The ideological controversy that separates Pekin from Moscow is being reproduced on a small scale in Tenguel."

PROPAGANDA IN PRACTICE

The ideological assault against popular forces throughout Ecuador, including Cooperative Juan Quirumbay, was linked to a nationwide transition in which conservative forces—led by the military and landed classes—began to repress populist sectors with increasing impunity. The shift was seen most conspicuously within the organizational terrain of the state, but was nonetheless visible throughout the political landscape between 1959 and 1963. In the middle of 1960, Velasco Ibarra, Ecuador's ultimate populist, was elected president for the fourth time on a wave of popular support. By the latter half of 1961, a little more than a year after his election, Velasco had managed to alienate virtually everyone and the country was in chaos. Demonstrations by students and workers were met by increasingly brutal repression from police and military forces as the streets of Guayaquil, and Quito became a battle ground that neither Velasco nor the Congress seemed able to control. Indeed, it was Velasco's fiery rhetoric, combined with his inability to control "the masses," that most worried the military. Not only was the entire country now opposed to the Velasco government, but, as Mary Martz explains, there was "increasing concern within and outside Ecuador that communism was growing in the country and that Velasco was doing nothing about it— that he appeared not to regard it as a threat" (Martz 1968). In an effort to avoid a full-scale military takeover, Velasco fled to Mexico in November 1961, leaving his vice president, Carlos Julio Arosemena Monroy, to pick up the pieces.[6]

From the very beginning of his presidency, however, Arosemena—who had made a very public trip to the USSR, declared himself sympathetic to Castro, and was widely believed to have left-wing sympathies—was under close scrutiny from the military and other conservative forces. Given the overall weakness of communist organizations in Ecuador, as well as the absence of a coherent social movement, there was virtually no possibility of Arosemena implementing anything but the mildest of social reforms. Indeed, his overtures to what constituted the left in Ecuador were an attempt to counterbalance the growing threat to his government posed by the right. Nevertheless, the communist label eventually stuck and served to paralyze an already weak government. Although Arosemena managed to remain in power for well over a year, the latter half of his presidency was essentially a transition to military rule. The military became increasingly brash in its attacks on peasant and labor organizations, laying the groundwork for a full-scale coup in July 1963, or a little more than a year after workers had invaded Tenguel.

The national shift from populism to militarism was not only seen in the intensity of the ideological assault against Cooperative Juan Quirumbay, but was played out in Tenguel in a number of quite concrete ways. The earliest and most visible sign of this shift was President Arosemena's firing of Subsecretary Jaramillo, the workers' most visible and powerful government ally. Portrayed as pro-communist and under attack on the national level, Arosemena was hardly in a position to support Jaramillo or anyone else who backed the "communist" invasion of Hacienda Tenguel. The removal from power of Jaramillo and other sympathetic state officials served to isolate the workers from the dominant producers of the invasion's history. Without the open and vocal support of at least some sectors within the state, the invasion was quickly mislabeled as communist. More importantly, the firing of Jaramillo signaled a decisive change not only in the discursive battle but in the ways in which national-level authorities would handle the situation in Tenguel.

On April 14, for example, only two weeks after the initial government delegation had left Tenguel, the minister of Social Welfare reaffirmed the government's commitment to buy the hacienda and apply a "colonization plan." In the brief interim, however, the emphases and priorities had shifted away from the politically popular toward the bureaucratically pragmatic. Rhetoric about delivering the hacienda to the workers was now replaced by a "colonization plan" that would "respect private property," "reestablish order on Hacienda Tenguel," and consider giving land to both cooperatives and private cultivators. From this point on, the related themes of private property, order, and increased production would remain unquestioned and serve as a driving force behind the agrarian reform program in Tenguel and Ecuador as a whole.

To confirm its renewed commitment to order and progress, the government sent a no-nonsense commission to Tenguel. This delegation was comprised of the minister of Development, the minister of Social Welfare, the chief executive of the Campaign for the Defense of Banana, and the general manager of Hacienda María Teresa, Carlos Cornejo Coronel. They, in conjunction with the manager of United Fruit's operations in Ecuador, had named a general administrator of Hacienda Tenguel. What is most interesting about this delegation is how different it was from the one initially sent to the hacienda after the invasion. In the place of sympathetic state officials with socialist leanings, the government was now sending a commission comprised of large capitalists and their allies.

During the next fifteen months, one state agency would mismanage the hacienda while a number of others would struggle over the long-term reform plan. Unfortunately, state announcements and inspections became increasingly meaningless as the number of plans multiplied beyond control (most of which contradicted each other). A declaration that the hacienda would be parceled out to a number of different cooperatives would be quickly followed by an announcement that the entire property would be worked through a single cooperative. As one worker recalls: "We quickly learned that the government was better at forming and sending groups of 'experts' to Tenguel than it was at solving our problems. They made plenty of promises but this did little to alleviate our immediate hunger or give us hope for the future" (V.M. 8/25/95). Contradictions between government agencies were routine and promises from one group of state officials were not a guarantee that something, or anything, was going to happen. Worse yet, cooperatives Gala and Juan Quirumbay routinely denounced state plans, each other, and anything that seemed to threaten their interests.

More importantly, not only were state "planners" a highly differentiated bunch who could not agree on what agrarian reform actually meant, but they had little control over more repressive sectors of the state. Many members of Juan Quirumbay were now prohibited from leaving their houses and the circulation of union and cooperative publications was forbidden. Tenguel was approaching martial law and the workers continued to spar with each other and local military forces. This uneasy balance, between competing cooperatives, an increasingly assertive police/military, and a variety of state agencies, existed for about six months from the end of 1962 until July 1963.

THE MILITARY COMES TO TOWN

The uneasy balance that characterized Tenguel in early 1963 was definitively broken when the government of President Arosemena was overthrown by a military junta headed by Rear Admiral Ramón Castro Jijón in July of the same year. To suggest that Tenguel itself was a motivating factor behind the military's takeover would be an exaggeration. Nonetheless, the central themes that were behind the military's actions—agrarian reform, communism, and state ineffectiveness—were also at the heart of the debate surrounding Tenguel. For many, and especially those in the military, Tenguel was one of the most conspicuous examples of state ineffectiveness leading to communism. More importantly, agrarian reform was the answer. As one of the key military figures involved in the takeover stated, "the principal motive [for the coup] was a feeling that the government [of Arosemena] had failed to take proper action against Communists and the extreme left and that it was unable or unwilling to put through a series of reforms" (Needler 1964: 2). The irony was, however, that not only was much of what was labeled communist not particularly revolutionary (in the sense of seriously threatening the broader social order), but that even relatively disruptive events such as those in Tenguel were largely isolated.

The military takeover of the Ecuadorian state was, to a certain extent, the intensification and expansion of a process of militarization that had been occurring in Tenguel for over a year. The junta's takeover on the national level led to the rapid and definitive shift in the balance of power at Tenguel. The military forces in Tenguel had been acting with increasing impunity during the past year but had been held in check by a weak set of alliances between popular forces and the civilian government. With the military government in power, these relationships were destroyed from both ends. The Communist Party and the CTE were immediately outlawed and the leaders of all the major left-wing groups were jailed. Many of those who were not imprisoned fled the country in fear. Sympathetic government officials at the national level were targeted and removed from their positions (Needler 1964). Whole ministries were often labeled as communist and rapidly dismantled.[7] On the other end, popular forces in Tenguel were either silenced or removed from the zone. This general repression was seen on a nationwide level for most of 1963 as local, regional, and national-level labor and popular organizations were targeted. Nowhere did it happen as quickly as in Tenguel. Four days after the military took power in Quito, a squadron entered Tenguel and arrested thirty of Juan Quirumbay's leaders. The arrests were violent. The leaders were beaten and placed in the United Fruit–built pool. As one town leader recalls:

> When the junta came to power the situation here changed quickly. When I heard of the arrests I went to see the Major. I asked him what had happened to the workers and where they were. He took me back behind the building and I saw the pool filled with men who had water up to their necks. They were surrounded by soldiers who had their guns aimed at the pool. He then asked if I had any questions. I said no. I didn't want to go in the pool. (S.Q. 7/95)

The arrested leaders were physically and brutally removed. Some spent close to a year in jail and all were forbidden to reenter the zone in the future. Other leaders were actively sought and forced to flee the zone permanently. Nor was the wave of terror limited to the leadership. The persecution on the part of the military was highly arbitrary and followed quite personalistic lines. As one ex-worker recalls:

> I arrived one afternoon in the train after working. I got there and saw the police but didn't know what was happening. I went to my house and my family was crying and the police were there going through our stuff. They said they were looking for communist literature and told me we had to leave the next day so we should get ready. Someone from the other cooperative had pointed me out. Why they picked some out and not others I don't know. I wasn't involved and didn't know anything about politics. I had worked for Juan Quirum-

bay but only on the land as a worker. Some were accused and others weren't.

That night when we were packing was awful. It was desperate. It wasn't just the women who were crying. We were from here, all of our family. I had only been to Guayaquil a couple of times and we had no family outside the zone. What were we to do?

The next day they dropped us off at the edge of the hacienda with all our stuff in the mud and told us to start walking. The people looked down on us and were told not to hire us. I don't know how we survived. (T.M. 5/18/96)

Many of those living in the hamlets surrounding the town of Tenguel first learned about the military junta with the arrival of armed forces on their doorsteps. Such was the end of Cooperative Juan Quirumbay. Even today former leaders insist they cannot return to the zone. Members of the opposing federation of cooperatives were not persecuted, but popular organizations ceased to exist as the military took over. One need not be "communist" to be under suspicion; organization was cause enough for persecution.

The period of military rule in Tenguel, from July 1963 until the middle of 1964, was characterized by a martial law that was simultaneously systematic and unpredictable. Local military forces enjoyed a new freedom that the junta's takeover at the national level permitted. Tengueleños were afraid to leave their homes and were forbidden to do so during certain hours. Groups of more than two or three persons were immediately harassed as the military moved off the newly constructed base, which was located in the town of Tenguel on the exact site where United Fruit used to house its administration, and into the streets. Even the most politically inactive were questioned about past events and organizations. A wide range of actions on the part of the military seemed to be only indirectly aimed at eliminating "communism" and peasant organizations. As Jacinto Lozano remembered: "One time I was walking to the center plaza and I saw the Major enter with a group of troops. There were people selling things, you know, french fries, clothes, just like today. He suddenly blows a whistle and tells everyone they have ten seconds to clear the plaza. After only five seconds he starts shooting his pistol wildly. It was the strangest thing I have ever seen. People were grabbing their fries and running in every direction" (J.L. 7/95). Such actions not only worked to eliminate existing organizations from the zone, but instilled enough fear to cripple popular organization for years to come.

CONCLUSION

Peasants in Mollepongo, Shumiral, and Brasil, followed by workers in Tenguel, invaded portions of United Fruit's Hacienda Tenguel and helped bring an end to enclave production in Ecuador. With remarkable speed and uniformity, foreign-owned companies were forced out of direct production throughout the coast in the early 1960s (Larrea 1987).

It is important to stress that these invasions, both individually and collectively, mattered. By making it impossible for foreign companies to cultivate bananas, they shaped the path that capitalism would take in the southern coast. At the same time, it is crucial that we not idealize either the invasions or their impact. If the first half of this book examined how peasants and workers severed the relations of domination and exploitation based on a particular system of capital accumulation, the second half outlines how, in an equally struggle-filled process, new forms of domination and exploitation emerged. Indeed, the beginning of this process was under way even before the invasions were complete. The workers, as we have seen, defeated United Fruit only to be crushed by their own government. In the case of the peasants, whose location on marginal lands afforded them slightly more autonomy, the process was significantly different, though equally ironic. Several years after peasants had secured victories (and land) in Mollepongo, Brasil, and Shumiral, United Fruit extended contracts and credit to the invaders-turned-landowners in order to encourage them to produce bananas. Despite years of struggle and remarkable victories, the comuneros of Mollepongo and the colonos of Shumiral became tenants of United Fruit, producing bananas for their old foe. The implementation of this system of contracts—a strategy which had been forced on United Fruit by the peasants themselves—would be cut short by the 1962 invasion and then resurrected in a radically different form in the mid-1970s. Nevertheless, it was representative of the range of production and marketing problems that all peasant-workers would face on acquiring a small plot of marginal land.

The point—made even more clear in the second half of this book— is that to stop the historical narrative at just the moment when subordinate groups have achieved some long-sought-after goal is not only populist, and dangerously so, but bad history. It is to replace processes with events. The profoundly *political* events outlined in the first half of this dissertation—including United Fruit's uneven entrance into Ecuador; the purchase of Hacienda Tenguel in 1934; the buying out of the tenants in the mid-1930s; the court case against Victor Velez in 1938; the peasants' forced signing of rental contracts in 1940; the ongoing conflicts between the company, the state, independent peasants, and an increasingly militant workers' union; the Mollepongo Commune's victory in 1955; the Colonia Agrícola Shumiral's victory in 1960; the workers' invasion in 1962; and both the military's destruction of Cooperative Juan Quirumbay and the tentative emergence of contract farming—have been at the core of a single process of capitalist transformation.

To suggest that this process has been contingent because it was so political is not to argue that any and all outcomes were possible. United Fruit's size insured that a number of strategies could be implemented in a variety of locales. Setbacks in one location did not mean the company would suddenly collapse. Nevertheless, an increasingly organized class of peasants and workers, as well as an unpredictable state, insured that the company's intentions and actions would be continually frustrated. Multinational corporations held most of the cards, but they could not always decide how and when they would be played. Both the state and popular groups had a dramatic impact on United Fruit's actions and the particular path that the Ecuadorian banana industry would take. They were relations of production that formed through (and helped propel) a series of struggles that not only made foreign-owned plantations untenable in Ecuador and Central America, but were part of the contradictions and incoherencies of an ever-changing system of capitalist accumulation.

PART TWO The Emergence of
Contract Farming

■ ■ ■ Introduction to Part Two

The first part of this book examined the emergence, management, and contestation of a process of capital accumulation that was characterized by direct agricultural production on the part a large multinational corporation. Although the 1962 workers' invasion represented the definitive end of enclave-style production at Tenguel, the process of dismantling spanned several decades, transformed numerous spaces, and involved a wide range of differentiated actors, institutions, agencies, and organizations. Nor was this process isolated to the zone of Tenguel-Balao or even the southern coast. It occurred with surprising speed and uniformity throughout Ecuador's coast during the early 1960s. Immediately after the invasion at Tenguel, United Fruit abandoned production on its other haciendas and eventually stopped exporting from Ecuador altogether in the mid-1960s. All foreign-owned plantations experienced similar problems with labor unions, peasants, agricultural diseases, and the Ecuadorian state during this period. Swedish, German, Panamanian, Chilean, and American-owned plantations were rapidly dismantled (Larrea 1987). As the call for agrarian reform grew louder, it became clear that the political climate was not going to become more receptive to multinationals. The foreign-owned banana enclave was thus relegated to Ecuador's past.

This leads to a series of questions that guide the second half of this book and the analysis of the period from 1964 until 1995. What characterized the emerging process of accumulation? How and by whom was contract production and marketing developed? In what ways were the relationships between peasant-workers, capital, and the state reworked? As we will see, the political-economic process through which contract farming emerged was extremely complicated, involving agrarian reform, the transformation of banana production, military repression, and the rise of capitalist planters. It also included the emergence and decline of a regional peasant movement that requires us to expand the geographic scope of our analysis to include a much larger portion of the southern coast. Restructuring was not, as the term often seems to imply, a predetermined process driven solely by the strategies of multinational corporations.

BANANAS AND CRISIS

During the 1950s, Ecuador quickly became the largest banana producer and exporter in the world. Foreign-owned plantations, which dotted the coast prior to the mid-1960s, led this expansion by opening credit, expertise, and the market to Ecuadorian planters. In this sense, it was ultimately domestic producers, particularly those possessing less than 100 hectares, who transformed much of the coastal region into a sea of green trees, planting bananas from the northern province of Esmeraldas to the southern province of El Oro. Ecuadorians produced most of the country's bananas and no single exporter controlled more than one quarter of banana exports during the 1950s and 1960s (Larrea 1992: 169–78).[1] The relative absence of multinationals from direct production did not, however, make the Ecuadorian banana industry more independent. It simply made domestic producers more vulnerable. During the boom period (pre-1965), such vulnerability was only rarely exposed. Producers did not have formal contracts with exporters, but an expanding world market provided relative security.

Although the vulnerability of the Ecuadorian banana industry was evident from the outset, the full implications of the country's second-class status as a reserve supplier—one which multinationals turned to only after they had sold bananas from their own plantations—were not completely apparent until 1965. Beginning in 1965 and continuing into the early 1970s, both United Fruit and Standard Fruit began to increase exports from their plantations in Central America. They more than doubled their exports to Europe and cut significantly into Ecuador's share of the U.S. market.[2] This dramatic increase in production on foreign-owned plantations in Central America was aided by a new banana variety that allowed multinationals to produce more bananas on less land, reduced the relative production costs for highly capitalized producers, and undermined the position of marginal countries such as Ecuador. Producing and selling more of its own bananas, and frustrated by growing problems with labor, disease, and the Ecuadorian state, United Fruit stopped exporting bananas from Ecuador in 1965 (Larrea 1987d: 74). The "golden" years of the banana boom were over and Ecuador's banana industry plunged into a crisis that would last through the mid-1970s when Standard Fruit (Dole) transplanted a new system of contract farming to Ecuador.

A NEW BANANA

At almost the same time as Ecuador was being pushed out of the U.S. market and the country's banana industry was going into crisis, multinationals began to replace the Gros Michel variety of banana with the Cavendish (LaBarge 1959). The switch transformed the banana industry on global, national, and regional levels. The Cavendish was not simply resistant to the Panama Disease. It could produce up to four times more fruit and be cultivated on the same piece of land for an indefinite period of time. Banana production was no longer a semimigratory enterprise that required large quantities of reserve land.[3]

Once the new strain was introduced, the production of bananas became a capital-intensive enterprise. With the Cavendish, everything must be done quickly and with considerably more care. The fruit must be carefully and quickly taken from the tree, to the processing facility, and onto refrigerated ships. The Cavendish is more fragile and needs a costly system of cables for transporting the stems within the plantation. Once off the production site, the fragile fruit requires well-maintained roads in order to move quickly and gently to ocean ports. In addition, although the strain is resistant to the Panama Disease, it is highly susceptible to other diseases and therefore requires the constant application of fertilizers and pesticides. The Cavendish also demands a regular supply of water that leaves little room for error. Too much water damages the crop and not enough can drastically reduce output. Primary and secondary canals, equipped with a mechanized system for pumping large quantities of water, must be well maintained in order to allow for constant irrigation and drainage. Quite simply, the Cavendish requires technology, expertise, and access to chemicals and fertilizers. Where the Gros Michel needed large quantities of land, the Cavendish requires high-quality land and expensive inputs (Larrea 1987, 1992; Sylva 1987: 123–27).[4]

Exactly what the ideal producer would come to look like was far from clear when the Cavendish achieved dominance in the late 1960s. On a global level, multinationals were ideally situated. Because they possessed both capital and land, foreign companies were able to reduce their relative production costs in comparison to other producers (Larrea 1987c: 57). The rapidity with which both United Fruit and Standard Fruit switched to the Cavendish helps explain the rise in production on their own Central American plantations during the late 1960s and early 1970s. However, due to a variety of reasons, including the increasingly complicated nature of direct production, multinationals continued to depend on, as well as exploit, domestic producers in places like Ecuador.

With the switch in variety, it became immediately clear that the importance of peasant producers would be reduced. The Cavendish requires a level of investment well beyond the reach of most smallholders. Systems of canals and transportation make little sense on plots of only five or ten hectares; a contiguous holding of *at least* twenty hectares was and is essential. Furthermore, although producers did not need large quantities of reserve land, they did need access to technology, expertise, chemicals, fertilizers, and markets. It was the multinationals' monopoly over these factors—and not land—that not only allowed companies such as Chiquita (United Fruit) and Dole to rework their domination over the industry, but allowed foreign companies to dictate *who* would produce bananas.

It was in this context that multinationals began to establish contracts with relatively large landowners. The contractual relationships varied, but "associate producers" in Ecuador had to own at least fifty hectares of high-quality land. Most planters resided in urban centers such as Machala and Guayaquil, descending on rural zones of the southern coast in search of investment opportunities opened up by the Cavendish and the new system of contract production. Some had their own capital and could develop the type of plantation demanded by the new strain and multinational exporters. Most, however, could not establish a modern plantation even if they owned the land. Multinationals extended credit to finance the building of canals and systems of transport, the purchasing of chemicals, and the employment of wage labor necessary to develop an efficient capitalist enterprise. They also extended the technical advice needed for starting and maintaining high-quality plantations. Domestic landowners then paid the multinational through (future) production. Contracting with associate producers allowed multinationals to control virtually every aspect of the production process without assuming any of the risks.

Although this new form of contracting differed along a number of lines from earlier forms, it was the rapidity and extent to which it came to dominate the industry that truly distinguished the (new) system of associate producers.[5] Domestic planters with formal and informal contracts had always supplied multinationals with an important portion of their exports. Up until the late 1960s, however, it was multinationals and their plantations that defined how and where bananas would be produced. With the Cavendish, once a plantation was established, it could, with the continued help of multinationals, be managed by the same domestic capitalist for an indefinite period of time. Many smaller producers held on, but most were now forced to sell through a maze of middlemen and found it increasingly difficult to gain a secure and profitable access to the market (or key inputs). Production became the privilege of a small minority.

In Ecuador, the only thing that was immediately clear when the Cavendish variety was introduced was that the southern coast would continue to be an important site of production. The southern portion of the Guayas Province (including Tenguel-Balao) and much of the province of El Oro became *the* place where bananas were produced and exported. Because the new strain was so much more productive, the amount of land under (banana) cultivation in Ecuador was cut in half and became concentrated in the southern coast where better roads, land, and access to ports proved decisive (Larrea 1987). Nevertheless, although it was clear that the southern coast would continue to occupy a central place within the banana industry, the process of creating a class of contract producers was exceptionally protracted. Much like the process through which foreign-owned plantations were dismantled, contract farming emerged through a conflict-laden period in which multinationals held many, but not all, of the cards. Before a class of relatively large and efficient producers could be created and controlled by multinationals, domestic entrepreneurs had to possess the right kind of property. This process—of reworking property patterns and creating the conditions for the emergence of a modernizing agricultural bourgeoisie—took place through agrarian reform and a decades-long struggle for land. It is this struggle that the second half of the book outlines.

AGRARIAN REFORM

The first Ecuadorian agrarian reform (1964–1968), much like the second (1970–1976), was an attempt by sectors within the state and dominant classes to achieve short- and long-term political stability while modernizing agriculture and increasing production. Although elites differed over how political stability and agricultural modernization would be achieved (and what they would look like), these twin goals drove both agrarian reforms. Ideally, capitalist farmers would work high-quality land while peasants brought marginal properties into cultivation. A state-organized class of agricultural laborers would be turned into landowning peasants, production would increase, and the growing urban middle class would receive a steady supply of cheap food. Or so was the plan.[6]

Although the military government of Castro Jijón (1963–1966) was responsible for enacting the first serious piece of legislation (1964), the first agrarian reform was quite limited. Because the military squashed peasant organizations in places like Tenguel, the 1964 Agrarian Reform Law was formed through debate between the military and factions of landlords. The final version was inspired by the Ecuadorian Commission for the Alliance for Progress (Saad 1987: 139). The law's rather conservative focus was on expropriating uncultivated land and abolishing archaic forms of land tenancy. As Howard Handelman notes, this modernizing process was well under way before the first agrarian reform was passed:

> By virtually any criterion . . . the 1964 law was weak. The more feudalistic types of landlord-tenant relations it prohibited were already being abandoned in much of the inter-Andean plain and were not of consequence for most of the coast. For the most part, the basic structure of land tenancy was kept intact. Given the great political influence of the most capitalistic landowners and the weakness of peasant organizations, such an outcome was not surprising. Indeed, the agrarian reform clearly demonstrated the ability of major banana and sugar growers and of the modern Andean dairy farmers to protect their interests. Such reforms as were actually implemented sacrificed the most inefficient and politically ineffective landlords— the southern Andean hacendados and coastal cocoa growers—to the winds of change. (Handelman 1980: 8)

In both the first and second reforms, the actual pieces of legislation were less important than the balance of forces struggling over how and to what extent state bureaucracies would be formed and the various laws and projects implemented. In contrast to the first reform in which the military actively repressed popular groups (thereby insuring a quite limited reform), the implementation of the second reform was propelled by a nationalist-reformist military government that for a short period of time actively encouraged popular groups to fight for and enact the post-1970 series of agrarian reform laws.

In other words, whereas the emergence of agrarian reform in 1964 served to temporarily squash the political activity of rural popular classes, the agrarian reform legislation of the early 1970s stimulated peasant invasions and struggles. This key difference was due in large part to the quite different contexts in which the two reforms were enmeshed. The oil boom of the early 1970s made a more serious reform possible. Oil money not only financed the second reform but provided the reformist military government of Rodríguez Lara (1972–1976) with a source of income that was relatively independent from landed classes.

In addition, the Rodríguez Lara government recognized that the implementation of a serious reform and the modernization of agriculture depended on the participation and organization of the peasantry. Large landowners did not automatically become efficient capitalist producers. Sometimes they had to be pushed by both the government and peasant-workers. Not surprisingly, the military quickly clamped down on the peasantry once political activity had served its modernizing purpose. Yet, at particular places and in specific moments, this brief space provided peasants with the room to organize, seek allies, and confront land-lords. Such space did not allow the majority of peasants to benefit from an agrarian reform that they were forced to implement themselves. In most places, landlords, supported by the military and sectors within the state, were simply too powerful for peasant groups. Yet, when peasants were well organized, able to acquire allies in key places, and confronted a weak landlord, they could and did acquire significant quantities of land. That they then had no resources to work the land is one of the principal legacies of agrarian reform.

PEASANT, STATE, AND CAPITAL AFTER 1965

Agrarian reform was not simply a struggle in which groups of peasant-workers were more or less successful in acquiring land. It was also a process through which the relationships between peasant-workers, the Ecuadorian state, and domestic and foreign capitalists were transformed in ways that would far outlive the implementation of agrarian reform. The most visible part of this transformation involved a redistribution of land in which (1) foreign capitalists lost or sold their land and pulled out of direct production, (2) domestic banana planters acquired the most fertile sections of the southern coast and contracted with foreign exporters, (3) a landowning peasantry grew in size but struggled to retain their small plots of land, and (4) a younger generation of workers found themselves working on banana plantations without labor unions, job security, or decent wages. The second half of this book traces this complicated process in considerable detail, but it is worth outlining the broader contours of class struggle at the outset. What types of changes were transforming the political-economic landscape during the period covered in the second half of the book? In what ways did the internal composition, goals, orientation, and effectiveness of peasant-worker organizations change?

Despite the dramatic proliferation of popular organizations in the southern coast, several factors turned the tide against peasant-workers during the 1960s and 1970s, making it increasingly difficult for them to negotiate the fragmented lines of state power with the same efficacy as they had in the 1930s and 1940s. To begin, the state expanded rapidly and exponentially during the oil boom of the 1970s, providing the Rodríguez Lara government with an independent source of income from which to implement agrarian reform. State expansion did not, of course, necessarily mean that the Ecuadorian state was any more coherent than in the past. Although IERAC, the Instituto Ecuatoriano de Reforma Agraria y Colonización, had the most formal and direct control over agrarian reform, there was a wide range of differentiated state sectors that intervened in rural areas in contradictory ways (including the Ministry of Agriculture, local police, and the military to name only a few). As we will see, even IERAC itself was not unified, but was rather one of the many sites where struggles for control over land, resources, and profits took place.

Nevertheless, state expansion, and the implementation of agrarian reform, did succeed in channeling and routinizing rural class conflict in such a way that consistently (if not always purposely) favored an emerging, domestic, agrarian bourgeoisie. Peasants now found themselves engaged in a series of conflicts with domestic capitalists who, in response to the opportunities opened up by the banana boom, aggressively sought to acquire and develop the most fertile sections of the southern coast. Not only could domestic planters count on an expanding state to open up the lines of credit and access roads needed to develop the region, but they could frequently depend on local police and military forces to aid them in their battles with peasant "squatters." Local authorities were "local" in a way that they had not been in the 1930s and 1940s. They were physically present in rural hamlets with greater consistency, in larger numbers, and almost always under the control of large landowners. On the national level, the military government of Rodríguez Lara encouraged the peasantry to organize and promote the regime's attempt to implement reform. Although this powerful rhetoric served to stimulate popular organizing, it did not translate into local military support for peasant-workers. In the southern coast, the police and military consistently came down on the side of plantation owners (who, in contrast to the 1930s and 1940s, were now aggressively moving into the region). The "good old days," when Victor Velez and the Mollepongo Commune could garner the support of local authorities by simply paying a visit to the teniente, were now largely a thing of the past. This was especially true in Tenguel where a military outpost, located on what used to be United Fruit's administrative compound, became the site from which military forces repressed peasant-workers on behalf of local landowners. The importance of the military, and the increased role it played in 1960s and 1970s, will become abundantly clear in the following chapters.

In addition, Rodríguez Lara's outspoken support for agrarian reform succeeded in producing a powerful counterforce that the peasantry of the 1930s and 1940s never faced: a unified elite. The growing power (or at least visibility) of populist forces, first under the guise of Velasco and then in the more threatening form of Assad Bucaram and the Concentración de Fuerza Populares (CFP),[7] succeeded in uniting the dominant classes and bringing the military government of Rodríguez Lara to power in 1972. With Rodríguez Lara, however, Ecuadorian elites got more than they had bargained for—a government whose moderate reforms were potentially more threatening than the populism it was intended to replace. As Catherine M. Conaghan notes: "Joining in the industrial bourgeoisie's fierce opposition to the regime were the traditional landowning classes and commercial groups of the dominant classes. This unified coalition was primarily responsible for the demise of reformism and the replacement of Rodríguez Lara by a more conservative military triumvarate in January 1976" (Conaghan 1988: 76). She continues:

> What one finds most impressive is the rapidity with which the reformist project fizzled and fell flat. Dominant-class lobbying efforts were comprehensive and effective, defusing the project at the implementation level . . . and sometimes even as policy was being formulated (demonstrated in the tepid character of the agrarian reform proposal). Decrees were enacted that had no support in the business community, provoking endless streams of criticism from dominant-class organizations. . . . In the face of such concerted resistance from the privileged and the powerful, the regime [of Rodríguez Lara] could do nothing but retreat—making itself and its aspirations for change more vulnerable with every step backward. . . . Major policy initiatives by the regime were met by unbending opposition from the private sector expressed in the press and other public forums. These public confrontations were similar to those in neighboring Peru between business and the Velasco Alvarado regime. But in contrast to the Peruvian case, private-sector opposition to reformism in Ecuador was generally effective, often resulting in embarrassing policy reversals by the regime . . . or a quiet abandonment of policy implementation (such as . . . agrarian reform). (98, 105)

Peasant-workers of the late 1960s and 1970s thus confronted (1) a relatively unified elite on the national level, (2) an emerging landowning class in the southern coast that was aggressively appropriating the region's highest-quality land, and (3) local police/military forces that actively repressed popular organizations. This was a very different situation from the one faced by our protagonists in Mollepongo, Shumiral, and Tenguel in the 1930s, 1940s, and 1950s.

Worse yet, the growing power of dominant classes was not matched by an equally dramatic increase in the strength of *national*-level peasant and labor organizations. The Communist Party, and its trade union organization the CTE, represented the most coherent form of national popular organization in Ecuador at the time. But the party itself was extremely small, and even the CTE had well under 50,000 members in the early 1970s (at the height of popular organizing in Ecuador). Moreover, the CTE, like populist organizations in general, was an extremely fluid "organization" that was based on "fragile networks that constantly dissolved and reassembled on the basis of clientelism" (Conaghan 1988: 100). As Conaghan sums up:

> Organizations such as trade unions and peasant associations represented only a small portion of the labor force. The average level of unionization . . . hovered around 16 percent in the 1970s. Within this reduced group of the unionized, over half were members of independent unions not affiliated with any of the national trade union confederations. Moreover, political rivalries inside trade union ranks further divided the movement. . . . In addition to the Communist CTE, two other confederations vied for power: the Confederación Ecuatoriana de Organizaciones Clasistas (CEDOC) and the Confederación Ecuatoriana de Organizaciones Sindicales Libres (CEOSL). (Conaghan 1988: 100–101)

National peasant organizations were not only plagued by the same sorts of problems as labor,[8] but had the added difficulties of even fewer resources and less history. FENOC, the Federación Nacional de Organizaciones Campesinas, was the strongest national peasant organization operating in the southern coast during the 1970s. Yet, it had almost no sustained physical presence in the zone. Moreover, the anticommunist paranoia that served dominant groups so well in the early 1960s continued to be a much repeated justification for crushing local struggles in the 1970s. Elites in Ecuador had seen what populism and more radical movements could do in places like Chile, Cuba, and Nicaragua. As a result, a "siege mentality took hold of these new capitalists. Holding the line against communism became an all enveloping strategy, allowing no room for even the mildest of adjustments" (Conaghan 1988: 11).

The relative absence of strong national-level popular organizations had two related consequences. First, the Rodríguez Lara government could not count on popular groups to counter dominant-class opposition to reforms. Second, local peasant-worker organizations were left largely on their own when facing landowners and police-military forces. To be sure, as the second half of the book outlines, local organizations proliferated in the southern coast and continued to depend on national organizations for legal advice and moral support. When they were not in jail or in hiding, advisors from the CTE/FPTG were now joined by allies from CEDOC and FENOC, providing local peasant organizations with crucial information and meaningful access to state agencies. The greater number of national organizations did not, however, translate into on-the-ground support for peasants involved in local struggles in the southern coast. Local organizations, including cooperatives, communes, colonias, and workers' associations, would eventually come together to form a regional organization. But peasant-workers remained largely on their own as they struggled for land against an increasingly powerful class of Ecuadorian plantation owners who could now depend on the fairly consistent support of key sectors within a greatly expanded state.

In this sense, the 1960s and 1970s were characterized by the proliferation of local peasant-worker struggles and organizations—due in part to Rodríguez Lara's support for reform, ongoing land pressures, and a history of organizing in the southern coast—at the same time as it was defined by growing opposition from an increasingly unified and powerful coalition of landed and commercial elites, industrial bourgeoisie, and various sectors within the state. This protracted struggle, which in the southern coast was eventually "won" by an emerging class of domestic plantation owners, had a powerful impact on the nature, orientation, and internal composition of local peasant-worker organizations. In the time period covered in the first half of the book, peasant-workers formed organizations that were legally recognized by the state and designed to confront the region's capitalists in a struggle for the land. Although the formation of state-sanctioned organizations provided peasant-workers with a powerful weapon against landlords, it also paved the way for greater state intervention into community affairs. The formation of a commune, for example, not only provided peasants with a legally recognized form of organization through which they could confront landlords, but formally subordinated their community and political organization to the state. The long-term implications of this subordination were far from clear in the 1940s and 1950s. At the time, the intensified and formalized relationship between the state and rural peoples often benefited, even empowered, the latter. State-recognized forms of organization such as the Mollepongo Commune, the Colonia Agrícola Shumiral, and Cooperative Juan Quirumbay were the vehicles through which peasants organized, confronted landlords, and, depending on the balance of forces, acquired land. The formation of communes and colonias did not, except in a formal sense, necessarily subordinate the peasantry to the state or dramatically increase the state's control over rural peoples. In the southern coast, these forms of organization served to locate rural communities on the state's geopolitical map. The Ecuadorian state, prior to the 1960s, simply did not have the resources to turn peasant organizations into the mechanism for managing rural landscapes and peoples.

Nevertheless, the organization and mapping of peasant sectors was an important step in the uneven and incomplete process through which peasant-workers have been incorporated by the state. This conflict—*over whether peasant-worker organizations would be the vehicles through which rural peoples struggled for justice or the method by which they were co-opted by the state*—would intensify with agrarian reform during the 1960s and 1970s. The struggle would never be definitely resolved one way or the other, but the trend was clear and peasant-workers were on the losing end.

In order to participate in agrarian reform (the only game in town), peasants had to organize themselves into state-sanctioned organizations, follow a particular set of procedures, and work through a defined set of state institutions. The Ecuadorian state never "controlled" cooperatives and workers' associations,[9] but it did set an agrarian reform agenda that peasant-worker organizations were required to follow. During the first part of the second agrarian reform, from about 1970 to 1975, this agenda was by no means clearly defined. Sectors within and outside the state continued to battle over the meaning and implementation of agrarian reform. As a result, although peasant-workers saw their organizations become increasingly dependent on, and shaped by, the bureaucratic logic of particular state institutions, they were nonetheless able to use their organizations to push forth a fairly radical set of political demands that included the invasion and redistribution of private property.

However, once those demands were removed from the political agenda by the military triumvirate that replaced the Rodríguez Lara government in 1976, the implications of this broader process became increasingly transparent. The triumvirate prohibited land invasions and agrarian reform, redefining the development agenda in such a way that rapidly intensified the process through which state-sanctioned and increasingly clientelistic peasant organizations became the vehicles through which rural peoples and their political demands were routinized, incorporated, and co-opted by the state. What the second half of the book essentially outlines, aside from the rise of contract farming, is the transformation of peasant-worker organizations and communities from land invaders battling with hacendados to state clients struggling with various agencies and bureaucracies for the resources needed to work the land. In so doing, it is suggested that this shift in peasant-state relations, and the reorientation of peasant organizations in general, has benefited domestic and foreign capitalists. They not only control a profitable system of contract farming but dominate an agrarian landscape characterized by popular organizations that no longer confront the very class that controls the region's wealth. Put bluntly (and a bit simplistically), if the first half of the book demonstrated how popular organizations transformed a particular system of production (based on foreign-owned plantations), the second half outlines the opposite: namely, how a new system of production, backed by the state, transformed popular organizations and struggles.

The second half of the book consists of four chapters. Chapter seven examines the agrarian reform project in Tenguel after the military took over the hacienda and implemented the first agrarian reform law in 1964. The project at Tenguel was the most important in the country during the 1960s and is a particularly interestingly place from which to view the political process through which peasant beneficiaries of agrarian reform first won and then lost land to an emerging class of capitalist planters. Chapters eight and nine, in turn, examine the reform process in marginal areas located near Shumiral and Mollepongo in the Andean foothills. Once the military relinquished power in 1966, landless peasants in these areas began to reorganize, invade marginal haciendas, and push for a more meaningful reform. Tracing the emergence, transformation, and decline of a regional peasant movement, these chapters pay close attention to the quite different types of struggles through which factions of capital, the state, and peasant groups entered into and transformed marginal zones to the east of Tenguel. Finally, chapter ten explores the current system of contract farming and its relationship to popular organizing among a new generation of plantation workers.

7   From Workers to Peasants and Back Again: Agrarian Reform at the Core of an Enclave

Agrarian reform, both in Tenguel and the southern coast as a whole, was a process of struggle through which peasant organizations were ultimately weakened, a modernizing agrarian bourgeoisie emerged, and the groundwork for a multinational-controlled system of contracting laid. In the case of Tenguel, the state's newly created agrarian reform institute, IERAC, appropriated Hacienda Tenguel and delivered thousands of hectares of extremely fertile land to the ex-workers during the mid-1960s. Then, during the course of the next decade, the process of agrarian reform succeeded in dispossessing the majority of ex-workers and delivering their land to an emerging class of capitalist planters and shrimp growers. Workers became peasants only to become workers again. This economic "modernization" of agriculture was a profoundly political process that was orchestrated with remarkably little coherence. Agrarian reform was a series of interconnected class struggles whose outcomes varied considerably depending on locale. At the core of a former enclave, Tengueleños were dispossessed *through* agrarian reform, a truly bizarre process that included the betrayal of state officials, the trickery of local capitalists, and the complicity of military forces.[1]

A PLAN?

It was with the military junta headed by Rear Admiral Castro Jijón (1963–1966) that agrarian reform was finally implemented, allowing the ex-workers to secure relatively direct access to the land. The project in Tenguel was the country's first and a central part of the military's larger goal of carrying out a nationwide reform. It was, as state officials repeatedly asserted, a model for the entire country. The debate that had consumed Tenguel for the previous three years now ended, or was at least transformed. The shape of reform in Tenguel would no longer be decided in the nation's newspapers, but by state bureaucrats working within the communist-paranoid parameters set up by the military. That the peasants themselves might have a role in developing the plan was never considered. To the contrary, the military's resolve—and its lack of hesitation regarding violent means—was decisive in imposing reform in Tenguel.

Although the implementation of a nationwide reform distinguished the military dictatorship from past governments, its understanding of reform did not represent a dramatic break. To be sure, the use of force reached a new level. The political situation was forcefully resolved and a military base permanently established where United Fruit's administration was once housed. Cooperative Juan Quirumbay, in fact all popular organizations, were destroyed and "agitators" were not allowed to join the (state-sponsored) cooperatives. With respect to the actual plan, however, the military essentially picked up where the previous government had left off—with additional studies and delegations directed toward implementing a system of cooperatives.

According to IERAC's key study, "The Plan of the Resettlement Project of Hacienda Tenguel,"[2] the zone's infrastructure remained impressive despite the fact that the property had deteriorated considerably during the past five years. There were virtually no banana trees, but 1000 hectares of cacao remained, and 1400 hectares of pasture covered the property. Equipment, roads, rail, buildings, as well as the port were all deteriorating, but not beyond repair. There were over fifty kilometers of primary drainage canals, and secondary canals covered 4500 hectares of the hacienda's coastal plain. Potable water had become somewhat less reliable, but United Fruit's system of electricity was still functioning. The schools, hospital, church, theater, and stores were largely abandoned, but in relatively good condition (IERAC 1964; OAS 1968).

The infrastructure, then, was both extensive and functional. More importantly, IERAC, or least the officials formulating the agrarian reform project, were in awe of United Fruit's enterprise. Such perceptions were important in two ways. First, it seems clear that the agency underestimated the resources needed to renovate, maintain, and run the hacienda. Railroads and machinery, as well as systems of electricity and water, were not easily repaired without parts from the United States. Second, within the boundaries of a cooperative-based agrarian reform, IERAC was determined to run the hacienda like the company. This desire would both shape and plague the project from the beginning. For better or worse, IERAC was not United Fruit.

Although IERAC officials were not as impressed with the human resources as they were with the company-built infrastructure, they were nonetheless hopeful. During the year in which they had been conducting the study and running the hacienda, IERAC officials had "educated" the workers with respect to the cultivation of food crops. As a result, the workers had begun producing corn, beans, and rice on close to 500 hectares. In addition, a series of self-help programs designed to create a sense of responsibility and community had achieved limited success. IERAC had even given the ex-workers classes on how to administer the hacienda in a collective form (IERAC 1964). Tengueleños, not surprisingly, have quite distinct memories of these projects:

> When IERAC came they started organizing us to produce short-term crops. This was before the cooperatives. But many of the experts from IERAC were from the sierra and thought they knew everything and that we did not know how to grow anything but bananas. I am from the sierra too but you cannot grow things in the same form. The soil and climate are different here. Some didn't even know the names of the fruits we have here. We had been growing crops for several years just in order to survive. We just needed resources.
>
> We joined [the state's] projects because they had some resources. Not many, but some. Also they told us we had to participate if we wanted land. So we joined and they paid us sometimes. Some of the crafty ones—there always are some—joined in order to get in good with IERAC people. But I joined because there was little alternative. (M.V. 8/19/95)

IERAC's attempts to develop leaders, a sense of community, and a collective orientation were motivated by a number of perceptions on the part of state officials, not least of which was the belief that Tengueleños had been so dependent on United Fruit that they had not developed their own leaders or leadership skills. But, as one ex-worker ironically notes, there are other possible interpretations:

> When IERAC first came to form cooperatives few people wanted to join, let alone be President or Secretary. Past leaders were now in jail and we did not know that IERAC would last for thirty years. We had been hearing about the cooperatives for years. IERAC was just the next jefe. Few wanted to join and most had fear about participating too much. (J.I. 7/2/95)

Most Tengueleños remember the IERAC officials who lived in Tenguel during the initial stages of the reform project (1965–1970) with considerable fondness and respect. Because the project was something of a model for the entire nation, Tenguel received some of IERAC's best and most committed employees. The first people assigned to Tenguel not only believed in IERAC and agrarian reform, but were politically committed to the peasantry. Unfortunately, such commitment was not enough to overcome the lack of resources. Moreover, as IERAC and agrarian reform came under attack on the national level, and the project in Tenguel collapsed in the mid-1970s, a new set of IERAC officials began to facilitate the dismantling of the cooperatives. They increasingly sided with local capitalists who coveted the cooperatives' lands. In this sense, the support received by Tengueleños during the initial stages of the project was truly unique. It was not sufficient and did not last long enough for the project to actually succeed, but such support was unheard of in most parts of Ecuador. As we will see in the next two chapters, peasants living in marginal areas such as Shumiral and Mollepongo almost never encountered IERAC officials in their communities. Few even remember the names of the bureaucrats they dealt with in Guayaquil and Quito. In contrast, for better or worse, Tengueleños had a series of quite different IERAC officials who lived (or were supposed to live) in Tenguel, monitoring the cooperatives, sending reports to Quito, and determining how land and resources would be distributed.

Despite a number of problems in Tenguel, IERAC developed a plan for four relatively large cooperatives.[3] According to the plan (IERAC 1964), each cooperative would have 160 members and work 1600 hectares of land. Families would have a one-hectare plot to cultivate food crops and the rest would be exploited collectively. Every hectare was accounted for. Each cooperative would collectively cultivate short-term food crops as well as cacao, plantains, citrus fruits, and avocados. One-quarter of each cooperative would also be devoted to pasture and the development of cattle herds. Costs for seeds, labor, chemicals and the resources for developing a cattle herd were all outlined. Local markets were examined, construction costs were included, and a detailed credit plan was elaborated that would allow the cooperatives to pay for the project. IERAC would control the technical, financial, and administrative aspects of the five-year-long project while maintaining the basic infrastructure (IERAC 1964).

A number of important themes ran through the report, which would reemerge as a radically different project was finally implemented. First, the four cooperatives were to receive only 6400 of the close to 19,000 hectares that IERAC had appropriated/bought from United Fruit.[4] Although IERAC was only "delivering" one-third of the former hacienda, the workers had to pay not only for the land but for the houses and infrastructure as well as the cost of the project (including IERAC's study). Moreover, despite the fact that workers who had left the zone during the early 1960s were now returning in order to acquire land and participate in the reform project, Tenguel had suffered a significant population decline during United Fruit's prolonged departure, the military invasion, and the state's subsequent mismanagement of the property (i.e. the 1960s). This out-migration, which ultimately cut the population almost in half (to under 1000 families), would continue until about 1970 and place considerable financial burden and debt on the families who decided to stick it out and participate in the project.

Second, although there were to be four distinct cooperatives, the emphasis was on maintaining the unity of the hacienda by coordinating all activities, from production to commercialization. According to the plan, "the cooperative form will maintain the territorial unity of Hacienda Tenguel" toward the goal of conserving infrastructural works (IERAC 1964: 138). The cooperatives, "utilizing the collective work method developed by United Fruit,"[5] would process products in common and the "union of cooperatives" would control commercialization and communal services (IERAC 1964: 137–45; OAS 1968: 5).

Third, profits from production would theoretically allow the cooperatives to pay for the project. The problem, however, was that IERAC lacked its own resources to begin the project and was forced to look for other funding sources. After the proposal was rejected by the Interamerican Development Bank, IERAC was left implementing a plan it could not finance, let alone manage. Without resources to renovate the infrastructure, the idea of maintaining the scale of the hacienda became a fantasy —but one that IERAC nonetheless entertained. To make matters worse, the project's budget was reduced even further when agrarian reform and IERAC came under attack on the national level.

COOPERATIVE FORMATION AND INTERNAL ORGANIZATION

Due largely to a lack of funding, the actual project varied dramatically from IERAC's initial plan. In the place of four large and equally sized cooperatives, twelve cooperatives of radically different sizes and compositions emerged. Two of them, San Rafael and La Esperanza, roughly resembled the cooperatives originally proposed by IERAC. They had over 100 members and 1000 hectares each. A third large cooperative, San Francisco, was in the works but was modified radically when a group of agronomists from Israel became involved; they immediately divided it into three more manageable cooperatives (San Francisco, Israel, and Fauller). The remaining cooperatives, ranging in size from just 16 to over 100 members, formed for a variety of motives and did not resemble the cooperatives originally designed by IERAC (see Table 3). Each had its own composition and forms of internal organization and decision making.

Table 3   Cooperatives: Number of Members and Land Distribution

		NUMBER OF HECTARES	
Name	Members	Family/Individual	Communal
San Francisco	45	180	270
La Esperanza	70	32	1174
Fauller	50	200	
Cotopaxi	39	390	0
Chimborazo	30	300	0
Balarezo	20	300	19
Ferroviarios	28		
San Rafael	133	333	1305
Pagua	79	790	0
Pasaje (Palo Prieto)	16	240	0
Israel (military)	44	132	540

Source: OAS 1968

Some had formal governing boards, while others were more informally directed, and at least one, Pagua, was simply "without organization" (OAS 1968: 34). In 1967, only eight of the cooperatives were found to be functioning. Relationships with IERAC differed substantially and were shaped by the timing of the cooperative's formation, individual leaders, and the internal makeup of the organization.

Within these parameters, the peasants had relative freedom in shaping the composition of the cooperatives. As a result, membership tended to reflect preexisting divisions and antagonisms. Ex–railroad workers formed one cooperative, the ex-field bosses another, and so on. Even the old division between Juan Quirumbay and Gala played itself out within the context of cooperative formation. Complicated by differences in age, education, occupational orientation, and agricultural experience, these divisions not only weakened attempts to unify the cooperatives but served to complicate and politicize the relationship between IERAC officials and particular cooperatives.[6]

LAND DISTRIBUTION AND PRODUCTIVE ORGANIZATION, 1964–1968

Despite numerous problems, the cooperatives—in different sizes, shapes, and internal forms—began to function, both as organizations and productive units, in the mid- to late 1960s. Although most cooperatives were given ten hectares for each member, the division between *communal land* and *individual plots* varied dramatically. In fact, four cooperatives had no communal land, leading one to wonder what made them cooperatives.

Regardless of form, production levels were disappointing. Members were unable to plant even half of their individual holdings due to a lack of resources and poor access to markets. Rice had been cultivated, but the climate turned out to be unfavorable. Output from bean production was low and although members in San Rafael had planted some cacao, the trees were not yet producing. Only corn seemed to be marginally profitable (OAS 1968).

Output from communal holdings was even worse. Collectively, cooperatives San Francisco, La Esperanza, San Rafael, and Israel had over 3000 hectares of communal land. Only 780 were planted with crops, over one-third remained uncultivated, and the rest was in pasture. The communal lands tended to be of poorer quality and therefore required more capital and labor to be made productive. The cooperatives lacked the resources to turn semi-inundated savanna into productive pasture or banana groves (OAS 1968). As we will see, the inability of cooperatives to bring large tracts of their holdings into production made these lands particularly vulnerable to local capitalists.

The 1968 evaluation of the reform project in Tenguel emphasized that "worker mentality" and hostility toward the cooperative method would ultimately prevent the project from having success (OAS 1968: 27). To support this interpretation, the evaluation noted that many members preferred the security of a fixed salary and three-quarters wanted a private company to take over the hacienda. Less than one quarter of the cooperative members declared a preference for the cooperative method; most wanted individual plots. Similarly, the report noted that many members displayed paternalistic attitudes toward IERAC officials.

There is undoubtedly a degree of accuracy in the evaluation's explanation for the project's status (in 1967–1968) and future potential. There is no doubt that cooperative members were hostile toward IERAC and the project. This was due in large part to a fact that the evaluation failed to emphasize. As one former cooperative member noted: "There was no project. IERAC made many promises but nothing happened. It helped us with the bureaucratic procedures to form cooperatives. But it did not help us become cooperatives in a more profound sense" (R.L. 8/95).

It is within this context that a "lack of cooperative spirit" and "paternalism" must be understood. When asked in late 1967 whether they wanted a company to replace IERAC, the answer was obvious. The workers pointed out that with United Fruit the pay had been considerably better, the work well organized, and social services more consistent. By 1967, only 6 percent of the members believed that the cooperative method was a better way of organizing the hacienda. Given the circumstances, it is surprising the figure was so high. How could workers not have had a negative view of the cooperative method?

Similarly, the lack of any real resources undoubtedly encouraged workers to seek patron-client relationships.[7] By the time IERAC arrived, the workers' own organizations had been destroyed, they were completely dependent on the state, and had virtually no role in decision making. A weekly food ration was necessary to keep the workers alive and the zone's limited employment opportunities almost all emanated from IERAC. Thus, when the state-controlled cooperatives began to operate, some workers embraced paternalistic relationships with state officials rather than investing their energies in the development of cooperatives. The unsuccessful history of state intervention taught them this much. IERAC could not finance, develop, or administer an agrarian reform project, but it could provide protection for the lucky few. State jobs, available to those with the right connections, were critical to short-term survival and even provided a small minority of clients with the necessary resources to put their newly acquired properties into production.

CAPITAL RETURNS: SCENE ONE

IERAC, the peasants, and the independent evaluation all agreed that the prospects for the medium to long-term survival of the cooperatives were dismal. From IERAC's perspective, the project—no longer a model for the country—was a money drain on an overburdened state agency. According to IERAC's own evaluation of the project, the program was far from a failure in that it resolved "the social problem" and distributed lands, but the lack of resources meant that much of what had been gained politically could be lost in the near future.

Thus, in August 1967 a government commission, including representatives from IERAC, the National Board of the Banana, and the Ministry of Agriculture went to Tenguel in order to hear a "joint" proposal put forth by Carlos Cornejo and the cooperatives.[8] Carlos Cornejo was the owner of Hacienda María Teresa just to the south and had acquired part of Tenguel during the early 1960s. He had also been a member of one of the key government commissions sent to Tenguel just after the worker invasion. The objective of the present commission was to carry out a study and determine the feasibility of his proposal.

The proposal, essentially put forth by Cornejo (who would receive a generous salary), was to form the Compañia Anónima Empresa Repobladora del Banano (hereafter Repobladora), a company designed to replant the zone with slightly over 1000 hectares of the Cavendish variety.

IERAC would finance the project through a loan that would come from the Hannover Trust Bank in the United States, pass through a variety of government bureaucracies, and then eventually make its way to the Repobladora. Hiring cooperative members as wage-laborers, the Repobladora would plant the zone and then manage production and commercialization for seven years, or the amount of time it would take the cooperatives to pay off the loan. The cooperatives would thus be on firm financial ground when they received the banana plantations from the Repobladora. It is important to note that although the state was facilitating and administering the loan, it was the cooperatives that were assuming the risk. The cooperatives—that is, the workers—never saw the money or controlled its destiny, but it was their loan (IERAC 1967; Contrato 1966).

The program had an undeniable appeal. From the workers' perspective, it was a chance to receive consistent employment, something they had not enjoyed since the time of the company. Over one-third of the cooperative members were employed full-time on neighboring haciendas, and it was estimated that each of the 850 families could contribute two full-time wage laborers to the project. As one worker concluded:

> Carlos Cornejo and the Repobladora provided the expertise and the money. Without them we could never have gotten the loan. Who would loan peasants money? He made the purchases, the investments, all the decisions, and we provided the land and labor. We needed jobs. The land was still ours, but he controlled it. It was a good arrangement for everyone. (E.P. 8/19/95)

Although the cooperative members had to give up control over the best sections of their land for an extended period, these very same lands would be returned to them with productive banana plantations and modern processing facilities.

From IERAC's perspective, the proposal represented a way out of a project that, by 1968, was destined to fail. IERAC could obtain its central objectives of political stability and increased productivity while relinquishing the majority of its technical, administrative, and financial responsibilities. The agency's role would be reduced to oversight, a productive export crop would be planted, and Tengueleños would receive a consistent source of income. It seemed like an ideal alliance between private capital, the state, and the peasantry. And yes, as both IERAC and the Repobladora noted, it was to be a model for the entire country (IERAC 1967).

It was not at all clear in the beginning that the project was destined to fail. The land was ideal for the new variety of banana, the system of irrigation needed only be renovated, and the zone was home to the most experienced workforce in the country. In fact, the project started off with a bang. The Cavendish was planted and within a short period of time hundreds of hectares of high-quality banana trees were in place. The Oversight Committee, comprised of members from both IERAC and the cooperatives, inspected each work and authorized the release of funds to the Repobladora (Comité de Vigilancia). Juan Moreno, IERAC's representative in Tenguel, maintained a close watch over the Repobladora, insuring that works were completed prior to the release of funds. His inspections were themselves subject to the close scrutiny of cooperative members and outside officials, including the national director of Agrarian Reform (A.B. 8/95).

Exactly what went wrong after the first year remains unclear.[9] Irresponsibility on the part of IERAC and dishonesty on the part of Repobladora officials played a role—at least this is what the military court determined (Tribunales Especiales n.d.; Contraloria General 1973). Carlos Cornejo and Otto Von Buchwald, president and chief of the Empresa Repobladora, informed the court that they managed everything with honesty, completed the said works, and only received money that was legally authorized by IERAC and the Oversight Committee. They insisted that the problems were the result of IERAC and the cooperatives. The Repobladora and its leaders were the victims. IERAC, they argued, lost the funds belonging to the program by diverting them to a reform project on Hacienda Villanueva. The cooperatives, for their part, had illegally taken control of the plantations in October 1969, thereby prohibiting the Repobladora from completing the contract (Tribunales Especiales n.d.; Contraloria General 1973).

In the end, the excuses and explanations of the various participants are less important than the final outcome.[10] Cornejo and Von Buchwald were convicted of siphoning money from the project, with the former fleeing to Canada and the latter spending the better part of two years in jail. Several officials from IERAC were also held responsible, lost their jobs, and, in some cases, spent a short period of time in jail (Tribunales Especiales n.d.; Contraloria General 1973). More importantly, the cooperatives were left with a half-done project. Six hundred seventy-five of the over 1000 hectares had been planted and some basic infrastructure was installed. But most of the work necessary for the commercialization and processing of bananas had not been completed.

The main consequence of the fiasco was that the cooperatives were now left with increased debt and little means of paying it. The original plan had the Repobladora repaying the debt after the trees had begun to generate an income. The loan would be paid pack with future production. Since the project had only lasted a year, the trees had produced little and the Repobladora had not yet paid back any of the loan. The irony of the situation was not lost on cooperative members:

> Sure, we had some wonderful bananas. They were young and healthy and were just beginning to produce. But we should have had these without the debt. Also, everything else would have been built in order to handle the processing of the fruit. The project was only half done. The worst thing is that we did not just assume the debt for the banana but for the administration costs and everything else. We assumed the debt for the salaries of Cornejo and the others. This was on top of the debt we owed to IERAC for the houses and the land. And now we had all this debt and could not finish the project. And if we could not finish the project how could we pay the debt? (T.I. 7/22/95)

In short, the Repobladora robbed the cooperatives, IERAC allowed it to happen, and the peasants were left to clean up. They were now paying two debts, both to the state. One was for the initial loan to buy the houses and land from a major multinational. The other was for one of the nation's most prominent capitalists and for a project that the cooperatives underwrote, but did not shape, manage, or oversee.

CAPITAL RETURNS: SCENE TWO

Once the Repobladora project failed, IERAC became even less inclined to commit resources to Tenguel and the cooperatives experienced a variety of events and calamities that both signaled and induced their impending collapse. Notwithstanding variation in both the pace and intensity of the collapse, the cooperatives followed a remarkably similar pattern of decline. Internal disorganization and corruption, accompanied by increased invasions by local capitalists, led to the large-scale sale and/or parcelization of communal holdings by the mid- to late 1970s.

In general, the sale of communal lands by individual cooperative members was encouraged by a number of factors, including both the poverty of the peasants and the eagerness of local capitalists to purchase high-quality land. Moreover, by the 1970s, IERAC did nothing to invalidate the illegal sale of communal lands, especially when it involved the transfer of land from struggling cooperatives to "efficient" capitalists. The individual sale of communal holdings was generally followed by the collective sale of land by the cooperatives themselves. These sales usually occurred in two ways. First, with the idea of paying off debt, a cooperative would collectively decide to sell off communal lands that it had been unable to cultivate. By ending the debt the members effectively ended the cooperative (which by 1970 was exactly what they were trying to do). The second method of sale involved pressure from landlords. A local hacendado with a bordering property would slowly expand his sphere of control and make various investments on the cooperative's land. Once caught, the hacendado would feign ignorance with respect to the boundaries, beg forgiveness, and then generously offer to leave the lands—provided the cooperative reimburse him for the investments made. Unable to pay, the cooperatives would have to sell.

Once the communal holdings were invaded, sold off, or divided, the cooperatives ceased to exist in any meaningful sense and members began the legal process of obtaining individual titles to lands they had been independently working for years. Many peasants were left with no land, virtually all lost a portion of their holdings, and a class of local capitalists slowly gained control of Tenguel's most fertile sections. To capture the political nature of this general process, the state's role, and the variation that occurred among the various cooperatives, we will now turn to the invasions of Cooperatives San Rafael and Fauller by neighboring capitalists.

The Invasion of Cooperative San Rafael

Created in 1965 with around 150 members and 1600 hectares of land, Cooperative San Rafael was struggling to survive when the Repobladora project was introduced in late 1967. Despite inheriting much of United Fruit's cacao plantation and cattle herd, the cooperative lacked the resources to begin the production of even food crops. According to one ex-member:

> We were relieved when the Repobladora came. We had nothing but the land. We were not advancing, just surviving. We had no resources and the cooperative had trouble running. It was too big. The Repobladora was to leave us with bananas. We would also have less debt. Of course it did not work as planned and today we no longer have the land. Much of the banana you see here we planted, first for the Repobladora and later for the rich. (P.Q. 12/26/95)

What makes San Rafael's post-Repobladora history so interesting is that the cooperative lost its communal lands in almost every conceivable way. The most memorable, however, involved a conflict with a group of capitalists who were masquerading as a cooperative. At the very end of 1968, when problems with the Repobladora were just emerging, San Rafael decided to rent 400 hectares of its communal land to Cooperativa Bananera de Producción y Mercadeo "Oro Cavendish." San Rafael did not have the resources to plant the sector, and by renting the land hoped to acquire capital and pay off some debt. At the beginning of 1972, however, "Cooperative" Oro Cavendish stopped paying rent, refused to leave, and made a move to gain legal ownership of the land.[11]

That Oro Cavendish was technically a "cooperative" speaks to the ambiguities and contradictions inherent in agrarian reform. Oro Cavendish had less than ten members and all were relatives of two interrelated and quite wealthy families (IERAC 2.117). In short, Oro Cavendish was a well-capitalized company hiding behind the cloak of agrarian reform. Led by Emilio Cordova, Oro Cavendish began the legal maneuver by arguing that Cooperative San Rafael had betrayed the "principles of co-operativismo" and broken the Agrarian Reform Law. San Rafael had not obtained authorization from IERAC to rent the lands and thus had violated a basic tenant of agrarian reform: The land should belong to those who work it. To support its argument, Oro Cavendish carried out an inspection of the lands in question. Not surprisingly, each of the tenants passed their own inspection. Emilio Cordova, for example, possessed an eighty-hectare plantation that was in excellent condition and equipped with canals and the necessary infrastructure required for the efficient production of bananas. Fabian Cordova, Eduardo Cordova, David Cordova, and Cesar Gonzalo Cordova had smaller plantations, but they were all in excellent condition and completely cultivated with the Cavendish. They continued to note that prior to the rental arrangement all of the land in question had been uncultivated. In contrast, they pointed out that all of Cooperative San Rafael's banana trees were uncared for and in poor condition (IERAC 2.117).

IERAC, after noting that Oro Cavendish's exports served "the best interests of the country," carried out its own study of Cooperative San Rafael. The study began by pointing out that San Rafael's processing facilities were in poor condition. The peasant cooperative had about 200 hectares of banana, most of which was on individual holdings of between two and eight hectares (i.e. too small to be efficient). Diseases were devastating the trees because the cooperatives could not afford the necessary chemicals. There were forty hectares of new trees which lacked maintenance; the seventy hectares left from the Repobladora needed cleaning and protector bags. The cooperative also had 275 hectares of cacao; all the trees were over twenty-five years old and half were more than fifty years old. The basic conclusion, as the IERAC-authored report stressed, was that all of the cooperative's lands, both communal and individual, needed work and were poorly maintained. In addition, there were 350 hectares of savanna that the cooperative was not using because it was inundated during the winter. This last observation was made in order to demonstrate a pattern. The cooperative was not cultivating a large portion of its land—land that could, as Oro Cavendish had demonstrated, be made productive with considerable investment from a capitalist (IERAC 2.117).

The most interesting fact about these studies, and the IERAC one in particular, was that they were conducted in the first place. The condition of the lands being rented was irrelevant to a rental agreement that was exceptionally clear—Oro Cavendish, as the tenant, had no claim to the land. The condition of San Rafael's land was even less relevant. The ownership of this land was not in question and had nothing to do with the issue at hand: the rental of a quite distinct section. Nonetheless, the fact that the studies were carried out, and carried out in the way they were, suggested that it was around the condition of the lands that the issue would be settled. IERAC did everything it could to develop the contrast: a highly efficient producer of exportable bananas versus an inefficient, negligent cooperative incapable of maintaining banana and cacao trees that had been handed to them. That an agrarian reform might benefit small producers was not as important as the level of production and export earnings generated. The modernization of Ecuadorian agriculture would be furthered by transferring the lands to a capitalist company. Finally, and perhaps most interestingly, the studies, and IERAC's in particular, were unconcerned with the history of San Rafael or IERAC's own role in shaping the financial and productive status of the cooperative (IERAC 2.117).

Cooperative San Rafael immediately questioned the validity of the inspections, noting that the tenants were businessmen with the capability of hiring wage laborers and were only masquerading as members of a cooperative. The capitalists, they suggested, had initiated the rental arrangement with every intention of breaking it. Worse yet, IERAC officials had assisted them in carrying out this deception. Given the frequency with which this tactic was used, San Rafael's argument holds considerable weight. Knowing that the agrarian reform law prohibited beneficiaries from renting out their lands, capitalists often initiated rental arrangements with cooperatives. Then, prior to the termination of the contract, they would petition to have the land returned to the state and distributed to themselves—as the "true" direct producer of the lands in question. That Oro Cavendish did this with the knowledge and even assistance of IERAC officials is likely. Indeed, IERAC officials were well aware of the arrangement and did little to advise San Rafael of its mistake (IERAC 2.117).

San Rafael's arguments, however, did little to help its cause. It was capitalists that IERAC was looking for. The damage was done and in August 1972 San Rafael was forced by IERAC to discuss the sale of the lands in question. With the papers just about signed, representatives of Oro Cavendish did not show up for a key meeting with the executive director of IERAC. Tired of expensive trips to Quito, Cooperative San Rafael interpreted this as a delaying tactic and threatened to invade its *own* land. Oro Cavendish, in turn, responded with its own letters and actions. Writing to IERAC, Emilio Cordova stated that some of San Rafael's members, notably Jacinto Lozano, had "unionist tendencies" and that the leaders had been acting without the permission of the rank-and-file. A month later, the president of San Rafael sent a telegram to IERAC stating that the members had decided not to cede the land to Oro Cavendish. Cooperative San Rafael was taking possession of the land. The next day Cordova went to the military encampment in Tenguel and garnered the support of armed forces. Any attempt on the part of San Rafael to take back its *own* land would be met by the army. The cooperative's tactic had failed completely. The state appropriated 401 hectares from Cooperative San Rafael and redistributed it to "Cooperative" Oro Cavendish. Cooperative San Rafael received nothing and lost over one-quarter of its land to local capitalists (IERAC 2.117). Agrarian reform was thus complete.

The Invasion of Cooperative Fauller

Troubled since its formation, Cooperative Fauller was one of the most indebted cooperatives after the Repobladora failed—an event that seemed to exacerbate internal squabbles within all of the cooperatives.[12] The cooperative thus entered the state's rice project with the hope of acquiring resources to cultivate crops and pay off some of its debt. Ecuadorian rice production had ceased to meet domestic consumption needs and the state was forced to subsidize rice imports. Such subsidies had a devastating impact on export-import ratios and put an immense strain on state spending. The state therefore began to promote domestic rice production.[13]

As part of this broader program, the Ministry of Agriculture began a rice project in Tenguel that was skeptically embraced by a number of the cooperatives. As a member recalls: "We wanted to grow banana. This zone is for banana we said. We told [the Ministry] that rice had not been profitable when IERAC first had us plant it [in 1964–1965]. The climate is not good. But they said we would be helping the country with rice. And they wouldn't give us a loan for banana, only rice" (S.U. 10/11/95). According to IERAC experts, the zone was ideal for rice and in August 1973 the agency sent a letter to the National Bank of Development in order to facilitate a loan.[14] The duration of the project was so short and its failure so rapid that most of the peasants would have forgotten the project entirely had it not left the cooperatives with their third state-induced debt.

The failure of the rice project, the illegal sale of communal lands, and Cooperative Fauller's financial turmoil were exacerbated by an assault on the cooperative by both IERAC and local hacendados. In November 1974, after two years of infighting, Cooperative Fauller's manager was finally expelled. A month later, IERAC's representative in Tenguel, José Arbenz, issued a report to the regional office in Guayaquil on the status of the cooperative. It essentially concluded that Fauller was made up of a bunch of uneducated and illiterate peasants who were disorganized from day one. Short on specifics, Arbenz's report stated that the cooperative possessed uncultivated lands that should be immediately reappropriated and distributed to those more worthy of agrarian reform (MAG-Fauller).

Two weeks later the motivation behind the report was revealed. Arbenz, who was the opportunistic type of IERAC official that continually sided with large capitalists, not only thought the land should be given to a more competent producer but had located a worthy candidate. On January 15, 1975, Fauller was forced to call an emergency assembly to discuss the invasion of cooperative lands by the Maldonado brothers, a pair of emerging capitalists from Machala who currently own some of the zone's largest banana haciendas. In this particular case, the Maldonado brothers had begun to clear, cultivate, and fence the cooperative's property. Cooperative Fauller, fearing that IERAC was going to appropriate their uncultivated lands, sold over one-quarter of the communal holdings to the invaders (MAG-Fauller).

Variations between the particular cooperatives notwithstanding, this story would be repeated numerous times from the mid-1970s until the early 1980s.[15] The blunder with the Empresa Repobladora had come full circle. Lacking capital as well as employment, the cooperatives had entered the Repobladora program with encouragement from IERAC and the hope of employment, paying their debt, and receiving new banana plantations. The project resulted in more debt, leading both the cooperatives and individual members to rent or sell part of their holdings. The destructive search for capital also forced the cooperatives to embrace a state rice project that few would have entered had they been able to acquire resources from any other source. In the end, Cooperative Fauller, along with the other cooperatives, was forced to sell land its members had planted as wage laborers in order to pay debt(s) it had received little or no benefit from.[16] Worse yet, these sales generally involved the cooperatives' best lands and were facilitated by IERAC. Large capitalists have since developed these lands into some of the zone's most profitable shrimp farms and banana haciendas.

AGRARIAN REFORM AND INDIVIDUAL MEMBERS

The history of the cooperatives is, of course, somewhat distinct from the history of individual members. Whereas each of the twelve cooperatives followed a remarkably similar pattern, individual members entered, participated in, and left the cooperatives with different sets of resources. Nonetheless, processes of differentiation must be placed in perspective. Together, the least successful cooperatives—Fauller, Palo Prieto, Ferroviarios, and Ganadera—began with approximately 140 members and 2500 hectares of land. If we exclude the one ex-member who accumulated 200 hectares, there are about twenty former members who still own land. Together, they possess around 100 hectares. In other words, ex-cooperative members currently possess less than 3 percent of the cooperatives' former lands.

Even in cooperatives where a higher percentage of the lands remained in the hands of individual members, a conspicuous fact remains: the cooperatives, as well as the individuals in them, lost the overwhelming majority of their lands to capitalists from outside the zone such as the Maldonado brothers. In Tenguel, agrarian reform, the failure of the cooperatives, the pauperization of cooperative members, and the reemergence of an agro-elite went hand in hand. By the mid-1970s, the overwhelming majority (over 90 percent) of cooperative members were in one of two *relatively* similar positions. They either had a portion of their individual holdings or no land at all. Many had been forced to sell part or all of their individual lands in order to pay off debt. Very few had more than five hectares.[17] In short, processes of differentiation took place among cooperative members, but within very narrow boundaries and within the context of the collective loss of land to more capitalized producers.

Even in the case of one of the most successful cooperatives, San Rafael, this process can be seen in sharp relief. Like the other cooperatives, San Rafael lost a large portion of its communal holdings to capitalists from outside Tenguel, including the notorious Oro Cavendish. However, despite invasion, state betrayal, and the loss of communal holdings, members of San Rafael were among the zone's most successful in holding on to *individual* lands. In 1986, when the cooperative's debts had been paid and land titles delivered to individual members, approximately 70 percent of the original members (or descendants) still had some hold on the land. Close to one-third possessed no land and over 600 hectares had been lost. But a significant majority still had access to the land.[18] More importantly, the 70 percent who possessed land in 1986 had managed to retain 60 percent of the cooperative's 1600 hectares. Collectively, they owned nearly 1000 hectares. And, on average, each smallholder still possessed slightly over eight hectares, a significant quantity in a zone as productive as Tenguel.[19]

However, the fragmentation of holdings is nothing short of astounding. Although the average ex-member (who still owned any land) possessed slightly over eight hectares in 1986, this land was divided (on average) among *four* separate plots. Such fragmentation was, in large part, the legacy of a cooperative system that tried to ensure that individual members receive similar quality land by dividing it into a maze of family, individual, and communal plots. As a result, the 100-plus members who still had cooperative lands in 1986 possessed over 400 distinct plots, and only 11 of these plots were greater than ten hectares! It is not uncommon for a peasant to own five hectares on five separate plots.[20]

Despite the maze of small plots, capitalists have continued to acquire cooperative lands since 1986. Once an agreement to sell a number of smallholdings is reached with a particular landlord, the pressure on one or two holdouts can be intense. A conservative estimate suggests that less than half of the former members currently possess any land (down from 70 percent), collectively owning about 40 percent of the San Rafael's 1600 hectares (down from 60 percent).[21] When combined with capital, the smallholdings of numerous peasants make for a profitable plantation. By themselves and without capital, small plots of two to three hectares make for a precarious existence in an agro-export zone dominated by medium to large plantations.

Individual Histories: Struggling to Survive
Despite a certain uniformity of experience among individual members, significant processes of differentiation have occurred. Differences are due not only to the quantity of land owned by a particular family, but the size, quality, and location of particular plots, as well as a family's ability to put their lands into production (which in turn depends on family size, ages, and access to externally generated sources of income). If a norm exists, however, it is the smallholding of between four and six hectares,

planted overwhelmingly with cacao and to a lesser extent low-labor food crops; most peasants are forced to leave a portion of their land uncultivated due to a lack of resources. In addition to a wide variety of personal factors, individual variations within this norm can be partly attributed to the histories of particular cooperatives as well as their composition at the time of formation. Members of Fauller, for example, are generally worse off than their counterparts in San Rafael and San Francisco.

Salomon Urbano, Manuel Arteaga, and Samuel Neira were all members in Cooperative Fauller and, despite having lost their communal holdings, have managed to hold on to their individual plots. Each owns four hectares. Having been pushed out of banana production in the early 1980s, Arteaga and Neira have all of their land in cacao. Because of its low labor requirements, cacao allows men in their seventies to generate an income and remain agriculturally active. Urbano, in contrast, still has a portion of his land devoted to banana. Like the others, however, he has been trying to switch to cacao. "Banana just doesn't pay for the small guy. The middlemen take all the profit. With all the costs, I am not making a profit and have been trying to switch to cacao. It doesn't produce all year but is less work; that is better for someone my age. The problem is it is expensive to start the trees" (S.U. 6/10/95).

In the case of Cooperative Fauller, Urbano, Arteaga, and Neira represent the success stories. Few ex-members have any land and no one has more than eight hectares. In contrast, the average ex-member of cooperatives San Rafael, Israel, San Francisco, and Esperanza has done slightly better. Jacinto Lozano, a key leader from the invasion until the present day, currently owns six hectares. Virtually all of it is planted with cacao which he and his son work. Owning six as opposed to four hectares, combined with the fact that he has been able to bring all of his land into production, allows for a slightly higher standard of living than his counterparts in Fauller. He is, for example, in a better position to help his children explore nonagricultural alternatives.

This general move away from agriculture is a universal desire among an aging generation of smallholders and their children. As peasants who have devoted their entire lives to agriculture, this seemingly inevitable trend is only reluctantly accepted. Most landholders derive considerable satisfaction from the fact that they have been able to retain their plots, however small. As a former United Fruit worker and cooperative member explains:

> I have never sold my land because I always wanted my children to have something here. Others sold for many reasons, but not me. But I know the future here is not good. I never was able to get an education

and so I live as best as I can. But my children, I always encouraged to study so they could leave and get something better. It is sad, but this is our situation. There is no security here. The small producer cannot survive. But I won't sell. If one of my children can't study, what will they do? We need the land even though it does not provide. (J.C. 6/30/95)

In contrast to their parents, most sons, daughters, and, especially grand-children have few regrets or moments of indecision. They never envisioned a future based on land ownership. The irony, however, is that both the older generation (who stress the need for land despite its inadequacy) and the younger generation (who see no future in the land) are at once correct and incorrect. Although the future of the younger generation cannot possibly be rooted in the land, the alternatives are equally illusory. The access to capital, education, and/or connections that success outside of agriculture requires is not available to the majority of young people in the zone. It is the paucity and illusory nature of alternative options that gives the older generation's argument regarding the necessity of land ownership its strength. They, like their sons and daughters, realize that several hectares of cacao offer little in the way of a future. Yet, they correctly question the younger generation's readiness to embrace the "easy money" that wage labor provides. Few of their daughters are able to move beyond low-paying clerical jobs; and their sons, who earn about five dollars a day working on banana plantations, rarely acquire enough capital to pursue their entrepreneurial dreams. At the same time, the sons and daughters have little choice but to explore these empty opportunities. The most urgent question facing much of the southern coast today is what will happen to the next generation.

CONCLUSION

The elimination or transformation of popular organizations—indeed, the *failure* of the cooperatives—was a key component of the long process of agrarian reform through which an agrarian bourgeoisie emerged and the basis for contract farming was established. After agreeing not to participate in political organizations, Tengueleños, who had once developed some of the most militant popular organizations in Ecuador, were forced into state-controlled cooperatives in the late 1960s. These cooperatives, for all their problems, not only succeeded in shaping the nature of popular organization in the zone, but determined the form that demands and conflicts would take and the avenues through which they would be channeled. More broadly, the creation, structure, and goals of cooperatives, communes, and workers' associations came increasingly under the control of the state. Popular organizations no longer turned to the state in the hope of moderating capital's excesses, but made appeals for land and resources. Such appeals had to be channeled through certain types of legally constituted organizations and follow particular sets of bureaucratic procedures. The relationships between popular organizations and state forms was becoming increasingly intimate and, above all, clientelistic; Tenguel was the beginning of a broader trend that was strengthened by the second agrarian reform and an oil boom that greatly expanded state power and bureaucracy.

This broad shift in the nature of popular organization and struggle has left a number of frustrating and ironic legacies. Both in the struggle to acquire land and in the struggle to work it, peasant-workers demanded something quite radical: autonomy. The various struggles examined throughout this study were motivated by the desire of peasant-workers to be independent and autonomous. As an owner of land, one would be autonomous from both capital and the state. Or so it seemed. Upon acquiring a piece of land, smallholders found themselves immediately overwhelmed by state forms, a complex system of middlemen, and an agrarian landscape that was increasingly hostile to small producers. Yet, not only was "autonomy" (even in the most partial and unsatisfying sense) largely unattainable, but the struggle to work the land and remain independent from local haciendas and traders forced peasants to become increasingly dependent on the state.

The preceding narrative brought this general process into sharp relief. Well aware that the state's reform project was not going to succeed, Tengueleños tried to develop a certain degree of autonomy from both IERAC and the cooperatives. The struggle for autonomy came in a variety of forms, including wage labor on local haciendas, the development of small businesses, and the production of crops outside of the reform project. Yet, there were few alternative sources of capital beyond the state's agrarian reform project; and capital was precisely what the peasants needed in order to develop their properties and achieve a degree of independence. In their search for capital, Tengueleños, both as individuals and as cooperatives, were thrown back at the state. They entered a variety of state-controlled institutions and programs, including the cooperatives themselves, the project with the Empresa Repobladora, and the rice program, all with the hope of acquiring capital and becoming independent smallholders. This irony—that to become autonomous from the state they had to first embrace it—is not lost on the majority of Tengueleños. To become free from (or at least less dependent on) the state (and capital), they had to become enmeshed in its very essence—in its organizations, procedures, programs, projects, and bureaucracies. Because the state was and is their only source of capital, peasants had to become its clients if they wanted the resources to cultivate their land and acquire even limited independence from wage labor and state programs. This unsuccessful state path to independence has not only left them in debt, landless, and more dependent on a state that has been withdrawing resources from rural areas since the 1980s, but has also weakened their organizations and left them more vulnerable to capital, in all its forms.

The next two chapters examine the different ways in which a similar set of processes—including the struggle for land and resources, agrarian reform, the formation of popular organizations, and growing state power—unfolded in the marginal foothills just to the east of Tenguel during the second stage of agrarian reform in the late 1960s and early 1970s. As we will see, the marginal nature of the lands involved gave the peasants more room to maneuver and allowed them to tap into more sympathetic sectors within the Ecuadorian state. At the same time, such "autonomy" presumed and reinforced a state of geo-economic marginality that could not be easily overcome.

8 From Struggles to Movement: The Expansion of Protest and Community Formation

When the military government of Castro Jijón assumed power in July 1963 it took armed forces less than a week to destroy Juan Quirumbay and remove the cooperative's leaders from Tenguel. A week after the first wave of repression destroyed popular organizations in Tenguel, the military went to Shumiral and Mollepongo, spreading its message of fear and expanding its sphere of control. If Tenguel was seen as the center of communism in the southern coast, Shumiral was an important outpost. Military repression was less intense in marginal areas of the Andean foothills such as Shumiral, but its impact was nonetheless felt. The peasants, their communities, and their organizations were rooted in the land and could not be eliminated. But from 1963 until 1966 when the military government was removed from power, the political links between the Colonia Agrícola Shumiral, the Mollepongo Commune, and outside groups were virtually eliminated as popular organizing was paralyzed in the zone.

When the military finally relinquished power in 1966, the transition to democracy was slow and uneven, and it abruptly ended in 1972 when the military government of General Rodríguez Lara came to power. Nevertheless, the brief and uneven return to democracy between 1966 and 1972 was sufficient to allow for the slow reemergence and strengthening of popular political organizations and activity.[1] While Tengueleños were immersed in the country's largest agrarian reform project, independent peasants in the marginal foothills to the east were beginning to clamor for a second agrarian reform. These clamorings are the subject of this chapter. Starting from individual conflicts and organizations, this chapter traces the slow emergence of a region-wide movement for the land that dates back to the United Fruit period, is intimately tied to the conflicts in Shumiral and Mollepongo, and ultimately culminates in the formation of UROCAL, a regional peasant organization, in 1976.

LA FLORIDA: THE PEASANTRY'S FIRST STEPS

With its own production under attack from workers, peasants, and the Panama Disease, United Fruit began to encourage local producers to cultivate bananas in the mid- to late 1950s. Credit, technical advice, and a guaranteed market were among the incentives used by the company in order to encourage production beyond the boundaries of its own property. By 1960, company representatives recognized that Hacienda Tenguel was finished as a site of production. If the hacienda continued to exist, it would function more as a port or marketing center. Costs would be kept to a minimum. Rail systems would facilitate the transportation of fruit from outlying areas, but little else would be invested and direct production would be abandoned.

In practice, United Fruit would buy bananas from just about anyone, including peasants in Mollepongo and Shumiral who had invaded the hacienda. Due to a number of factors, however, including property patterns, the peasantry's own intransigence, and the fruit's suitability to large-scale production, forming relationships with smallholders was difficult. As one of United Fruit's ex-administrators outlined:

> As the Panama Disease spread it became clear that we would run out of new lands. The company could only own so much land. We had to look for other producers. We looked to the uncultivated lands near the mountains. The land was not as good but it was open and not affected by the disease. We built roads and extended the train. This was the best way. Now we simply gave the landowners money and they hired the workers. It was cheaper and we did not have to deal with unions. It was good for everyone.
>
> Yes, we tried to work with peasants as well. But it was complicated. It was easier to lend a lot of credit to a large landowner than give a little credit to a lot of peasants. Some produced bananas, others would plant a little banana, a little cacao, and some corn. Others would just disappear. It was complicated. (C.G. 1/4/96)

It was within this context that United Fruit established relations with large haciendas directly north of Shumiral in the region of La Florida at the base of the Andes. Dry, rocky, and lacking infrastructure, this sector was less than ideal. In terms of land quality and geography, La Florida was quite similar to Shumiral, Brasil, and Mollepongo. In fact, it was and is the most isolated of these zones. La Florida's major advantage was that it possessed an extensive tract of uncultivated forest owned by a small number of families who had planted cacao during the early decades of the century. Most had returned to Guayaquil after the collapse of cacao production in the 1920s, and all were looking for opportunities to bring their land back into production. Thus, by establishing contracts with a number of absentee landowners, United Fruit was able to control a relatively large and disease-free zone. Despite the existence of quite distinct properties, including Haciendas Mirador, Santa Rosa, Guatemala, and Adelina, the arrangements varied little from property to property. The company approached the expansion into La Florida as a single enterprise. United Fruit installed the basic infrastructure, including railroads, canals, and roads, allowing La Florida's landowners to begin planting in the late 1950s. By the middle of 1960, then, La Florida was part of the region-wide banana boom that was unevenly consuming much of Ecuador's coastal plain and extending the limits of cultivation, road-building, and settlement into frontier zones that had not been brought into production during the cacao boom several decades earlier.[2]

Unlike the rest of Ecuador's coast, however, La Florida's boom ended as quickly as it began. The sector had just been planted when the workers invaded Hacienda Tenguel and United Fruit pulled out of the region in 1962. Local capitalists in La Florida were left with banana plantations they could not maintain and products they could not market. The workers, in turn, were fired and went in search of other opportunities, one of which—land invasions—was caught up in broader processes of agricultural restructuring and agrarian reform. Indeed, United Fruit's rapid entrance and departure from La Florida was one of the key reasons why, only a few years later, the zone became home to some of the first land invasions associated with the second agrarian reform. If United Fruit's brief presence made La Florida more accessible, its rapid departure created a conspicuously abandoned zone that seemed ripe for agrarian reform. Once United Fruit pulled out, the zone became home to a rare combination of accessible and largely unoccupied land. As a result, when the military dictatorship relinquished power and democracy tentatively returned to Ecuador in the late 1960s, La Florida became a key site where peasants tested the political waters and began to clamor for a second reform. To understand this process, we now turn briefly to one of the major landholdings in the zone.

Hacienda Adelina

After signing a contract to produce bananas for United Fruit in 1960, Don Arturo Moncada, the owner of La Florida's most isolated property, Hacienda Adelina, immediately subcontracted to *contratistas* or *sembradores*. In reality, it was sembradores such as Luis Andrade who planted the hacienda for United Fruit. Despite subsequent confusion, the arrangement between Moncada, an absentee landlord living in Guayaquil, and Andrade was fairly straightforward. According to the contract, Andrade was to plant bananas on several hundred hectares of land. After the trees began to produce (eight to twelve months), the plantation would return to Moncada who would then begin selling bananas to United Fruit. This process was to be repeated by Andrade and other sembradores until Hacienda Adelina was completely planted. Beginning in 1961, Andrade planted several hundred hectares and within a short period of time employed a workforce of close to 100 men.

Andrade, and even Moncada himself, were little more than company middlemen. United Fruit gave money to Moncada, the owner, who then gave money to Andrade, the sembrador, who then paid the workers. That Moncada and Andrade each received a cut is self-evident. Yet, as the company's departure in 1962 would make abundantly clear, the plantation was completely dependent on United Fruit for credit, chemicals, and basic machinery. The fruit could not be sold or even moved without the company. United Fruit's monopoly over capital and marketing insured its de facto control over production. More importantly, such arrangements allowed the company to reduce its wage bill, eliminate labor problems altogether, and maintain high levels of exports in the face of its own problems at Hacienda Tenguel.

In March 1962, a little over a year after the first banana trees began to produce in La Florida, Cooperative Juan Quirumbay invaded Hacienda Tenguel, United Fruit pulled out, and La Florida was reconverted into an economic backwater. New plantings were halted and the workers were laid off. The firing process was reminiscent of the very contract out of which it was born. The company cut off the owner, Moncada, who cut off the sembrador, Andrade, who then fired the workers. In short, United Fruit was gone.

With slight variations, the history of Hacienda Adelina was repeated on the three other major holdings in La Florida. United Fruit located the owners in the late 1950s, installed the necessary infrastructure, and planted a significant portion of the zone by 1961 (over 1000 hectares).[3] And, when the company pulled out, all of the haciendas were devastated. Losses varied from hacienda to hacienda, but each were left in a similar situation—no workers, no market, and no way of moving an export product they were now producing in large quantities. After brief attempts to salvage their investments, the landowners retired to Guayaquil and the zone once again assumed its marginal status.

Although the zone would remain marginal, it would never again be unpopulated or uncultivated. La Florida's short flirtation with banana production served to attract landless peasants from both the highlands and the coast. By the late 1960s, all of the zone's haciendas were under attack by peasants. On the one hand, there were groups of peasants from the highlands who proceeded to occupy uncultivated lands in a largely unorganized and unplanned way. Some were squatters who had been tolerated and used as a source of labor during the zone's brief banana boom. Others had been pushed into La Florida due to land pressures in the highlands. Both of these groups should be seen more as frontier settlers than as land invaders; neither made formal claims to the land they occupied. On the other hand, they were joined by plantation workers from the coast who were forming organizations and invading uncultivated land in La Florida and elsewhere. These land occupations involved the formation of legally constituted organizations, were almost always planned, and were carried out under the rubric of agrarian reform. If the former group was part of a decades-long process in which land pressures pushed highland peasants down the western slopes of the Andes, the latter belonged to a plantation labor force who now seized the opportunity to acquire land—an opportunity that prior struggles, the banana boom, and agrarian reform all helped make possible.

Although all of La Florida's haciendas would be dismantled by peasant invasions, the process was particularly protracted in the case of Hacienda Adelina. The owner, Arturo Moncada, was not only left with more bananas than he could eat when United Fruit departed, but had acquired a considerable debt. More significantly, much of what he owed belonged to Andrade. From Andrade's perspective, it mattered little that United Fruit had pulled out. He had completed the overwhelming majority of a contract he had signed with Moncada, not the company. The two men thus began a legal battle that lasted the better part of fifteen years—a battle that neither would win.

It was during this period of relative decline that landless peasants from both the sierra and the coast descended on Hacienda Adelina and other uncultivated properties that were owned by vulnerable landlords. Andrade had decided to sell small sections of the property to anyone who would occupy and cultivate the land. His motives for selling property he did not own were twofold. First, he and his sons needed capital to develop the land they occupied. Second, they could not possibly work the entire hacienda. The presence of smallholders, who also served as temporary wage laborers, only strengthened their hand against Moncada (who neither worked nor possessed a single hectare). What the Andrades did not count on, however, was a second agrarian reform that was aimed at weak "landowners" such as themselves. Their possession of the land was no more legitimate than the peasants to whom they were selling small plots. Neither group had legal title.

Wanting out of the whole mess, the Andrades tried to sell the hacienda to a third party. It was their second attempt to sell a hacienda that they did not own that led the peasants to form Cooperative Lucha Campesina. Prior to this common threat, there had been little to bring the peasants together. As with the settlement of other haciendas in La Florida, the peasants arrived family by family and settled onto their respective farms. It was only with the possibility of losing their plots that the smallholders came together, eventually deciding to form a cooperative and a community.

Although the peasants purchased their plots from Andrade in the late 1960s and early 1970s, the legal formation of Cooperative Lucha Campesina occurred at the height of agrarian reform's second major thrust. When marginal lands belonging to weak hacendados were involved, IERAC could lend considerable help to landless groups of *organized* peasants. The peasants of Adelina represented a perfect case for agrarian reform and, by all accounts, IERAC was fully supportive. The problem, however, was that IERAC had no day-to-day presence in zones such as La Florida and therefore had no real influence with local authorities. No one remembers exactly how many times the police and military came to Adelina, but a significant percentage, including all of the main leaders, suffered beatings and arrests. One leader was arrested on three separate occasions:

> The Andrades would send the police from Balao or Tenguel in order to arrest and scare us. I had a receipt saying I had bought the land but the police came and took me anyway. The lawyer got me out, and IERAC said not to worry, that the police were just trying to scare me. But I was the one getting beat up and taken to jail. One time IERAC sent an order from Guayaquil to the police in Balao telling them that this was a problem of IERAC and that they should stay out. So the Andrades sent the police from Tenguel. We just had to suffer and wait while the bureaucratic procedures were pushed forward. (A.S. 5/96)

In the end, IERAC expropriated the hacienda and everyone was left poorer. The peasants spent a small fortune fighting for their cause and ended up with no more land than they had originally bought. On top of everything, they had to repurchase their plots from the state. As one member of Lucha Campesina sarcastically noted: "I spent a fortune trying to defend land that I had bought so that I could buy it again" (J.R. 5/96). Few failed to note the ambiguities of the agrarian reform process:

> Without IERAC and agrarian reform we would have lost the land. The police supported the owners and IERAC was our only hope. But how slow they were! And we kept having to pay for this and that, the law-

yers, the trips to Cuenca and Guayaquil. . . . And we really weren't asking for anything that wasn't already ours. It wasn't like the invasions that some cooperatives carried out in order to get new lands for their members. We had the land. The problem [of agrarian reform] was that after the struggle with IERAC we were left too poor to work the same land we had owned for almost 20 years. We were worse off than when we had begun. Is this agrarian reform? (J.M. 5/96)

All of the peasant land invasions of La Florida shared a number of commonalities. Because they occurred on marginal properties with weak landowners, including Haciendas Adelina, Mirador, Santa Rosa, and Guatemala, they received tentative support from the state, particularly IERAC. Due to the change in banana variety, the zone had no potential of becoming an efficient producer of exports and was thus ideal for reform. With a little state assistance, workers could be turned into peasants and uncultivated land brought into production. The marginal nature of the zone was only reinforced by the loose hold that the various landowners had over their respective properties.[4]

In this sense, it is not entirely surprising that the invasions in La Florida were among the first in the southern coast associated with the second agrarian reform. The struggles began at a time—1968—when peasant groups were just beginning to test the political space opened up by the transition away from military rule. Mass mobilization was not necessary, considered, or even possible. Agrarian reform was barely on the table and the popular means of enacting it remained relatively restricted. Large-scale land invasions, which became possible during the second wave of peasant struggles in the mid-1970s, were avoided. Confrontations with any but the weakest of landlords were dangerous. IERAC would intervene on behalf of peasants, but only in cases where the opposition was minimal or nonexistent.

This is not to suggest that the application of agrarian reform in La Florida was inevitable. Peasants had to demand the intervention of IERAC, a state institution whose explicit goals and objectives had potentially radical implications for land redistribution in rural areas, but which nonetheless lacked the resources to provide peasants with a consistent, sustained, and locally visible ally on a day-to-day basis. To a much greater extent than in the past, a sector of the state was both physically present (if inconsistently) in rural areas and, in some cases, relatively sympathetic to the peasantry (remembering too that IERAC had many faces). Yet, with the exception of "model" reform projects such as Tenguel, IERAC officials were entrenched in underfunded, understaffed, and overworked offices in major regional centers such as Guayaquil, Machala, and Naranjal. Working on hundreds of disputes that covered thousands of hect-ares, IERAC officials could only rarely (if ever) visit a place like La Florida, much less control the actions of local landlords, police, and military forces (who, like IERAC, now had better access to the peasantry than in the past). As a result, peasants had to form organizations and communi-ties, search for allies, and send their representatives to what seemed like an endless number of (often faceless) state offices and agencies. As we will see, this process involved numerous contradictions, including a legacy of incomplete victories and a growing dependence on a small number of leaders. Yet, the invasions in La Florida nonetheless represented the peas-antry's first political steps after the return to democracy. Together with peasants in Shumiral and Mollepongo, the peasant organizations formed in La Florida in the late 1960s—including Cooperative Lucha Campesina (Hacienda Adelina), Cooperative Rio Balao (Hacienda Guatemala), and particularly the Association of Independent Agricultural Workers of Balao (ATAIB, composed of Haciendas Mirador and Santa Rosa)—pro-vided the backbone of the emerging regional movement. As part of a growing call for agrarian justice, they were a resource on which subse-quent groups of peasants would organize and enact the second agrarian reform.

THE SECOND WAVE OF LAND INVASIONS, 1973–1976

In February 1972, the "reformist" military government of General Rodrí-guez Lara overthrew Velasco Ibarra. One of the military's principal justi-fications for ending democratic rule was the need to implement a second agrarian reform in order to modernize agriculture and redistribute land in a more equitable fashion. As a result, peasant organizations prolifer-ated during the year and a half of intense debate between the military coup in 1972 and the ratification of the Second Agrarian Reform Law in October 1973. Upon passage of the law, both the military dictatorship and popular organizations called on the country's peasantry to organize and support the government's struggle to implement a meaningful re-form. This increased external support for local land struggles was one of the key differences between the first and second reforms. It is within this context that the southern coast emerged as *one* of the key centers of peas-ant political activity in early 1970s.[5]

Luz y Guia
Although it seems unlikely that the founders of Cooperative Luz y Guia were aware of it at the time, they chose the name of their organiza-tion with remarkable foresight. The cooperative became something of

a "light and guide" for the region as a whole in the early 1970s. Building on the foundation constructed by those in Shumiral, Mollepongo, and La Florida, Cooperative Luz y Guia's intervention was decisive in several ways. First, it was one of the first real *invasions* to occur after the military dictatorship relinquished power in 1966. Second, it occurred on the marginal lands of one of the most powerful landowners in the region. Finally, the Luz y Guia invasion of Hacienda Balao Chico was the largest during this period both in terms of participants and the quantity of land involved. Taking place in the early 1970s, Luz y Guia not only helped stimulate the second wave of agrarian reform in the southern coast, but reinvigorated the method through which other peasant groups would struggle for land and community within the confines of the state's halfhearted reform.[6]

It was in the summer of 1970 that Silvio Chavez first began planting corn just to the north of La Florida, or in what at the time was the far eastern section of Hacienda Balao Chico (see Map 2). There were no roads and the entire area was covered with dense forest, but the soil was productive and the rivers provided an excellent source of natural irrigation. The area was also attractive because it was close to a number of peasant cooperatives that had either acquired, or were in the process of acquiring, fairly large tracts of land.

After hacienda guards cut his crops and forced him from the land, Chavez and some similarly situated friends immediately went to Eloy Alfaro, a peasant community and cooperative located just to the southeast, in order to ask Gonzalo Flores how they could form a cooperative.[7] Flores, a schoolteacher, was initially skeptical. Hacienda Balao Chico was an extremely large (over 20,000 hectares), productive, and functioning banana hacienda that was owned and operated by the Compañía Frutera, a Chilean multinational that along with United Fruit had dominated Tenguel-Balao's geopolitical landscape since the banana boom began in the 1940s. As Chavez's own eviction demonstrated, the Compañía Frutera could and would destroy crops and evict squatters. Chavez and friends were not dealing with a group of weak landowners as in La Florida. Nonetheless, Flores was encouraging when Chavez appeared at his door. "I knew it would be hard. The company had security all over. But there was so much land that was not being used and the peasants need land. There was much talk of agrarian reform because of Rodríguez Lara, so I said let's do it and joined" (G.F. 7/96).

Within a month of this first meeting, the peasants formed a cooperative with nineteen members, most of whom had worked for either United Fruit or the Compañía Frutera. Cooperative Luz y Guia quickly acquired more members, and in July 1973 invaded marginal sections of Hacienda

Balao Chico. Unfortunately, the hacienda was prepared and three days later a police contingent of close to 100 armed men arrived at the site. Unarmed and unprepared, the peasants were violently and rapidly evicted. The owners of Balao Chico had their own police and the tacit support of local military forces. The peasants, it seemed, had invaded the wrong hacienda.

Members of Luz y Guia were discouraged, but the failed invasion did not break their resolve or their organization. The cooperative's families went to Guayaquil in order to acquire new members and outside support. That such a move was possible, even imagined, speaks to the rapidity with which the zone had been integrated into the nation-state over the last twenty years. The banana boom had not only brought the southern coast physically closer to the rest of Ecuador, in the form of a highway extending south from Guayaquil to Machala, but had also integrated the zone politically and imaginatively as well. National labor and even peasant organizations were still based in urban areas; but in many cases they now had two decades of experience and, more importantly, were the first places that peasants turned to when searching for legal and political allies. To be sure, the case of Cooperative Luz y Guia is somewhat extreme. Most local peasant organizations sent one or two representatives in order to contact the CTE/FPTG, obtain a lawyer, and push their case along. Luz y Guia brought the whole community. Setting up camp in a park located in the middle of Guayaquil, they began to establish contacts with student groups, labor organizations, and sympathetic lawyers. *El Universo* published articles about the cooperative's plight and the organization's leaders made a variety of appeals on local radio and television stations. The attention facilitated contacts with labor organizations and outside groups, including the FPTG and a number of skilled and dedicated lawyers/advisors. In addition to helping the cooperative navigate the maze of bureaucratic procedures, these contacts succeeded in uncovering important information about the disputed lands. According to at least some legal documents, the land in question did not even belong to Hacienda Balao Chico. The Chilean multinational, it seems, had been somewhat creative with the boundary markers.

Luz y Guia's move to Guayaquil and the resulting public attention served to attract additional members. By August 1973, or slightly over a month after the peasants had been violently evicted, the cooperative's numbers swelled to several hundred. Including families and outside supporters, Cooperative Luz y Guia could now depend on close to 1000 individuals for the second invasion of Hacienda Balao Chico. The peasants decided it was crucial to create a permanent presence on the disputed land within as short a period of time as possible. They resolved to enter the isolated zone with two weeks worth of food and the tools and materials necessary for building houses and other buildings. If a cooperative member wanted a piece of land, both he and his family had to remain in the zone for the first two weeks. Anyone who left during this initial period gave up their rights to the land. There would be no free riders. It is hard to grasp what this organizing effort involved. Even today, years after access roads have been built, the trip to Luz y Guia is over an hour from the Guayaquil-Machala highway and involves crossing numerous rivers. This is by truck. In September 1973, the men, women, and children of Luz y Guia walked for hours with their animals, guns, and the materials necessary to build a community.

Confident in their numbers and empowered by the fact that the lands might not have a legal owner, the cooperative sought to establish a visible presence. As Gonzalo Flores remembers: "We were not invading uncultivated lands of a hacienda [as in the first time]. We had a legal organization and had made a legal claim based on the fact that it had been abandoned. We were not hiding" (G.F. 7/96). The families of Luz y Guia, along with students, labor groups, and peasant-workers from neighboring cooperatives and haciendas, then marched to the town's future site. Within days, houses were constructed, schools were built, and temporary cooking and eating facilities were feeding anywhere from 500 to 1000 people. Working collectively, the peasants cleared and cultivated large sections of land. In contrast to the first invasion, armed peasants were on guard twenty-four hours a day. Every man, woman, and child knew exactly what to do if and when the police came (S.C. 7/96).

The police's arrival came as no surprise. By the time the police contingent of 200 men arrived, Gonzalo Flores already had his school operating and the town was beginning to look more and more like a community. As he notes,

> The police arrived at the pueblo in the early afternoon. Our guards notified everyone and followed the police up to Luz y Guia. The leaders came out to talk with the police. The rest of the people were not hiding but were surrounding the town. The police announced that we had exactly one hour to leave. Hearing this, we laughed, and someone said that *the police* had ten minutes to leave. The people slowly came out and the whole town was surrounding them. Many of the men were holding guns but there was no violence. We talked with them for awhile, trying to explain our situation, and the police just slowly backed out. They never returned except to talk. They knew we were armed and well organized. (G.F. 7/96)

It was the peasants' confidence, born more from past failures, a strengthened organization, and outside support than from their increased numbers, which intimidated both the police and the hacienda's owners. After the first few weeks, the only boundary problem that Luz y Guia had was with two other peasant cooperatives that had begun to make similar claims. Peasants throughout the coast, now sensing the political opening created by the military government's push for a second reform, were more assertive and at times became entangled with one another as the struggle for land intensified.

After the invasion, student and labor groups continued to maintain contacts with Cooperative Luz y Guia, but the mundane activities of building a community and cultivating lands were left to the peasants. In general, outside groups played a key and positive role in Luz y Guia's successful struggle for the land. It was, for example, during the invasion that Padre Hernán Rodas and his small group of Spanish activists made their first definitive appearance on the political scene. As we will see below, it was out of such struggles, and Rodas's participation in them, that UROCAL, a regional peasant organization, emerged and began to play a key role in assisting peasants in a wide range of political conflicts and challenges. Yet, UROCAL was still a couple of years from forming, and Padre Hernán had just arrived on the scene. As one former member of Luz y Guia remembers:

> There were *so* many groups from the outside, political groups, student groups, reporters, state officials. . . . We could not tell whom to trust. Some [outsiders] just wanted land. Others had their political agendas. Some would help for a little bit and then leave. Most would not stay for long. At this time, Padre Hernán was just one among many [outside groups]. He had just gotten to the zone and we did not know what he was about. Why was a priest involved? We had not seen a priest like him before. Sure, he eventually proved himself and was here for years, working alongside us. But in the beginning he was just one among many. (M.O. 2/95)

Throughout the period, Luz y Guia, or more accurately its leadership, remained closely linked with quite militant and radical labor groups from Guayaquil. Links with Leninist groups were key in giving Luz y Guia its military-like discipline and undoubtedly played a role in its success. The radical views and practices were, however, largely out of place with the majority of the cooperative's membership and served to isolate Luz y Guia from region-wide efforts to organize the peasantry, particularly UROCAL and Padre Hernán's group. Cooperative Luz y Guia lent support to particular peasant and worker struggles, and a number of UROCAL's leaders came from the cooperative, but the organization was unable to extend and maintain its influence on a broader level. As a result, although Luz y Guia provided a key stimulant to peasant political activity, the center of peasant struggle shifted back to its earlier place of origin— Shumiral/Mollepongo.

Luz y Guia's political problems were complicated by internal troubles. Despite definitive control over more than 4000 hectares of land and the support of lawyers and a number of IERAC officials, the process of legalizing the land was long and painful, involving sustained conflicts with neighboring cooperatives and IERAC's bureaucracy. Padre Hernán's group helped establish boundaries, and Luz y Guia's strength and size allowed the cooperative to protect its claim, but collective forms of production quickly broke down as the members scrambled to obtain their ten hectares.

Adding to the confusion was the fact that many of the members who had joined during the organization's stay in Guayaquil were not peasants in any sense of the word. Not only did a portion of Luz y Guia's new members already own land, but at least a few were employees of IERAC. Agrarian reform involved many things, including class struggle, shifting property relations, and the mobilization of peasantries, but it was also a business that sustained an entire class of more or less crooked lawyers, activists, organizers, and state bureaucrats. In exchange for their support, some IERAC officials based in Guayaquil were promised ten hectares of land. Not only did this type of "member" not contribute to the building of the community or the cultivation of lands, but quickly sold his or her plot as soon as the boundaries were drawn and the lands legalized.

Nevertheless, it is difficult to overestimate the brief importance that Luz y Guia had on the zone. By adopting and strengthening a tradition that "began" in Shumiral-Mollepongo, but which had been largely dormant during the first military dictatorship (1963–1966), Luz y Guia not only reinvigorated the form of struggle that came to characterize the southern coast's second agrarian reform (community formation through invasion), but provided the groundwork for establishing links between often isolated conflicts. Luz y Guia's struggle, and the wide range of connections that it involved (including students, labor, priests, state officials, and peasant groups), represented the first steps toward a broader regional movement. If these steps, and the relationships which they embodied, were hesitant, ambiguous, and filled with contradictions, so too was the embryonic movement that emerged several years later.

Workers' Association Santa Martha

The victory in Luz y Guia represented a key moment in the regional expression of peasant organizing and political activity. Peasants throughout the zone followed the events closely and word of the victory spread rapidly. The victory, moreover, coincided with the debate and passage of the Second Agrarian Reform Law in October 1973. By the time members of Luz y Guia were consolidating their hold over 4000 hectares, peasants throughout the coast were involved in land struggles and the push for a more meaningful reform. Such mobilization, at least for a moment, received tentative support from sectors within the military government as well as peasant and labor organizations. In the zone of Tenguel-Balao, strong organizations already existed in Shumiral, Mollepongo (La Independencia), and La Florida by the time Decreto 1001 was passed in 1970.[8] In the early 1970s, numerous cooperatives, workers' associations, and communes emerged and strengthened this organizational base, including Luz y Guia, Santa Martha, Rio Gala, San Miguel del Azuay, Hermano Miguel, Lucha Campesina, and Unión y Progreso. And this does not include dozens of other organizations that were formed throughout the southern coast during this intense period of organizing and land invasions.

The struggle at Luz y Guia also signaled the growing strength, importance, and diversity of regional actors such as Padre Hernán, the Spanish activists, and national-level labor organizations. Peasants sought out these actors as they attempted to form organizations and strengthen political relationships among themselves. The following chapter explores these *regional* relationships in some detail. However, before doing so, the next two sections examine key conflicts in Santa Martha and Rio Gala. These conflicts not only give us a local sense of what was happening on the regional level, but help us understand how regional relationships and actors were formed through local conflicts.

In December 1973, while members of Luz y Guia were still celebrating their victory and the Rodríguez Lara government was inaugurating the Second Agrarian Reform Law, a smaller land struggle began within a short distance from where the Mollepongo Commune had once confronted United Fruit some twenty years earlier. Several kilometers to the east of La Independencia (the community formed by the comuneros of Mollepongo), a group of landless peasants began to stake out a claim in what would become the community, peasant organization, and zone of Santa Martha (see Map 2). Santa Martha's struggle would have none of the publicity or notoriety of Luz y Guia. The Santa Martha Workers' Association never reached many more than twenty members. Its conflict was not with a major multinational, but with a group of small-time capitalists from Machala led by Jorge Camayo and, unfortunately, the Colonia Agrícola Shumiral. The land in question was not several thousand hectares, but several hundred. In the sense that the confrontation was smaller, more local, and considerably more bitter, Santa Martha's struggle was quite typical of the conflicts that occurred during the wave of popular political activity that accompanied the second agrarian reform. As the military crushed one invasion, or landed elites and peasants resolved a particular conflict, another struggle would emerge several kilometers away. Relatively small base organizations such as Santa Martha came to form the backbone of UROCAL, but they rarely provided the regional peasant organization's leaders. No one from Santa Martha would ascend to regional or national level prominence. As the 1970s turned into the 1980s, they would be lucky to hold onto the land that took them nearly ten years to acquire.

Like many of Hacienda Tenguel's agricultural laborers, Segundo Bermeo was a recent immigrant from the southern highlands. As one of the last workers to be let go by United Fruit in the early 1960s, Bermeo had worked for the company for close to seven years before his firing forced him to find employment on a smaller hacienda in Balao. Because his new job paid poorly and offered little security, Bermeo decided to pursue the dream that had brought him to the zone in the first place—a piece of land. As he recounts:

> I wanted to form a cooperative on lands that had been donated by [United Fruit] to the state. See, I knew the company had donated some lands to the government in 1936 and this land should have been distributed to the poor. It was not to be sold. One just had to occupy the land and work it. I knew that the Colonia [Agrícola Shumiral] had appropriated some of this [donated] land. I discovered this error because when the company sold the land to the Colonia I was there. I discovered where the boundaries of the Colonia were and what part belonged to the state. (S.B. 5/5/96)

As a result of Bermeo's knowledge, about twenty friends and family formed pre-cooperative Santa Martha in December 1973 and began to settle the vacant state lands located between the Colonia Agrícola Shumiral and the Mollepongo Commune. By early 1974, or just months after the second agrarian reform law had been passed, the organization was pushing its claim in the IERAC offices in Cuenca.

Despite the relative isolation and marginal utility of the chosen site, the pre-cooperative—now transformed into a workers' association[9]—ran into immediate problems with the Colonia Agrícola Shumiral and several capitalists from Machala who had bought part of the Colonia's 2500 hectares. The problem revolved around ambiguous boundaries dating back to the time of United Fruit. The site chosen by the peasants was, depending on perspective, either vacant lands that had been donated to the state by United Fruit or uncultivated lands belonging to the Colonia Agrícola Shumiral. If the matter had been that simple, however, it probably would have been resolved by a land sale between the Colonia and the Santa Martha Worker's Association. This was not to be. The majority of the disputed section had been sold by the Colonia to a group of investors led by Jorge Camayo, a relatively small businessman from Machala who was looking to invest in agriculture.

The Santa Martha Workers' Association thus found itself embroiled in two disputes, one with the Colonia, and another with Camayo. The dispute with the peasants of Shumiral never turned violent but cacao trees and other crops were cut as tensions rose. The slow escalation of the conflict brought the decisive intervention of Padre Hernán, who was just getting a foothold in the zone. One member of Santa Martha remembers Padre Hernán's involvement as follows:

> The conflict with the Colonia was becoming very serious. Those from Shumiral did not know the boundaries and intervened, saying the land belonged to them. This was not true and we had the land titles. But then Sergio Armijos [who belonged to the Colonia Agrícola Shumiral] came here with Padre Hernán and we explained the situation. We did not know Padre Hernán at this point. I asked him what a priest was doing involved in a land struggle. We did not trust him. Only later did we learn what kind of man Padre Hernán is. He quickly realized that we [from Santa Martha] were right and that this struggle between the poor helped no one. After that the Colonia and Padre Hernán supported us in our struggle, largely because of Señor Armijos who cleared up everything and brought the Padre. (N.B. 5/12/96)

The conflict with the capitalists would not be resolved so easily. From the perspective of the capitalists in Machala, Padre Hernán's presence, as well as the involvement of national peasant-labor organizations such as CEDOC and FENOC, only confirmed what they already knew: the peasants were communists. The conflict intensified. Although the peasants, with the help of Padre Hernán and outside peasant organizations, had developed allies within IERAC, they were unable to resolve the conflict in their favor. More to the point, the capitalists had their own allies within the agrarian reform institute *and* the military. As one member of Santa Martha relates:

> IERAC even sent the police and put us in prison; but we continued because we were well organized. The military was sent by the rich and persecuted us. IERAC would file a report and the governor would send the military to evict us or take us to prison. They beat me and took me to prison three times. Once I was taken to Tenguel by the military. This was during the time of the military junta. I was also taken to Milagro and Guayaquil. It was when we went to prison that we affiliated with CEDOC and got some support. They helped us get out of jail. Another time I was going to IERAC in Cuenca and the military caught me and took me to Tenguel. They said we were guerrillas and communists and that we had lots of arms. They said Padre Hernán was a communist. Lies. (E.B. 5/5/96)

The conflict continued in this form for several years, with members of Santa Martha, assisted by Padre Hernán's group, UROCAL, and national-level peasant organizations, trying to work the land and push their cause through IERAC while being harassed by the military and police. As one member recalls, it took the death of a friend to finally end the conflict:

> The *ricos* from Machala hired some professional killers and murdered one of our compañeros, Romero. This was in 1976 or 1977, before the floods. When this happened IERAC intervened. They took a piece of the land we had been working and left us with less land than we wanted. (J.S. 5/8/96)

The conflict in Santa Martha was quite typical in a number of respects. For one, it was a small conflict involving little land and few participants, with at least part of it involving confrontations between peasants themselves. Moreover, the confrontation emerged from, depended on, and created a wide range of relationships and alliances. Twenty landless peasants, most of whom had worked for United Fruit, began a quest for land that placed them in conflict with a neighboring Colonia, a group of capitalists, and the state's agrarian reform agency. The conflict with those from Shumiral subsequently turned into an alliance between a workers' association, a colonia agrícola, and a politically committed group of Catholic activists, an alliance which itself was simultaneously caught up in, and helped generate, a regional peasant organization. Along the way, this small group of twenty peasants was also brought into contact with the most important peasant organizations in the country. Indeed, by the mid-1970s, peasants were no longer turning to *labor* organizations such as the CTE/FPTG, but could now depend on the support of national *peasant* organizations such as FENOC.[10] Although these contacts provided no on-the-ground support at the local level, they nonetheless helped peasants maneuver through state offices and gave them a sense that they were not alone in their struggle.

This particular victory was, however, shallow from a variety of perspectives. Not only did they lose a friend and receive considerably less land than they wanted, but the peasants of Santa Martha, like so many involved in similar struggles during this period, were left in an extremely weak position from which to work the land and build a community. This, in short, was and is the legacy of agrarian reform and the process of capitalist transformation in which it was enmeshed.

Cooperative Rio Gala and the Invasion of Hacienda Rio Blanco
Leonardo, Felipe, and Angel Guaman grew up on Hacienda Rio Blanco in the northern part of Tenguel-Shumiral. Their father had worked for United Fruit before being laid off in the early 1960s. Like most of the ex-workers, he remained in the zone, desperately looking for some sort of stable employment. Ironically, his journey led him back to the hacienda, or that section—Rio Blanco—that had fallen into the hands of Aray Marin, a well-connected capitalist from Guayaquil who first appeared in the southern coast during the time of United Fruit. The Guaman family lived and worked on the hacienda until the mid-1970s when, according to Leonardo, they had had enough:

> We had worked on the hacienda all our lives and had nothing to show for it. Agrarian reform started . . . and we realized that despite our work we really received few benefits from the hacienda. We asked Aray Marin for a piece of land that was not being used. We said we were peasants and needed some land for our future. He said no and a bit later decided he wanted to evict us from the hacienda. This is when we went to talk with the Vasquezes in Shumiral and united with them to invade some of the land. We went to Shumiral because we were alone and they knew about these things. There was Padre Hernán and some Spanish people who helped us a lot. They put us in contact with Fernando Gutíerrez, a lawyer from CEDOC. (L.G. 1/28/96)

By the time the Guaman brothers went to Shumiral, UROCAL was within months of forming and all of the key organizers were already working with Padre Hernán and his group of Spanish activists. Some from this group, including Sergio Armijos, Juan Ochoa, and José Llivichusca, had worked for and later confronted United Fruit in the 1950s. As founders of the Colonia Agrícola Shumiral and the Mollepongo Commune, they were no strangers to political conflict and peasant organization. At the same time, there was also a younger, post–United Fruit generation of leaders, including Joaquin Vásquez, Julio Coyago, and David Romero, that provided a key force behind UROCAL. In their twenties, they identified with and were influenced by Padre Hernán and the Spanish activists. As a group, Padre Hernán, the Spanish, and the younger generation of local peasant-activists were strongly influenced by the revolutionary ideas that were circulating in Ecuador, Spain, and the world at large during the late 1960s and early 1970s. Those that were not committed to a broader socialist revolution were at least dedicated to the political struggle that was emerging in their part of the world. More importantly, this younger generation was forced to take up the same struggle for land—albeit in an entirely different political-economic context—that their parents had begun over twenty years earlier.

Arriving in Shumiral, then, Leonardo, Felipe, and Angel Guaman were not only impressed with the organizational efforts of Sergio Armijos and others from the Colonia Agrícola Shumiral, but encountered a younger generation who were politically committed to region-wide organizing. In this sense, the Guamans, as well as other peasants who organized after the passage of the second agrarian reform law, could now count on the support of a regional network of organizers that had emerged from earlier struggles. Peasant struggles beginning after 1973 benefited from an almost institutionalized and formulaic method of creating organizations, invading marginal lands, and pushing through agrarian reform. Peasants now knew the procedures for forming cooperatives and workers' associations, or at the very least were able to quickly contact an emerging group of professional activists who could guide them through the process. Land invasions were anything but routine, but they did follow a fairly predictable pattern after 1973. This did not insure that all peasants in all places would be successful, but it did, at least for a moment, alter the balance of forces.

After seeking out the assistance of those in Shumiral, the Guamans quickly formed pre-cooperative Rio Gala and planned to occupy an uncultivated section of Hacienda Rio Blanco. Despite a strong organization, apparent support from the agrarian reform law, and outside help from Padre Hernán's group and national-level peasant organizations, the invasion did not go as planned. The fifteen members of Rio Gala petitioned IERAC to have approximately 250 hectares adjudicated to the peasant organization. While sympathetic lawyers and members of Padre Hernán's team were pushing the claim forward, the pre-cooperative began to collectively cultivate a small portion of the disputed property. They planted as much as possible, but were also working for wages on local haciendas. Due to constant harassment from hacienda police and their relatively small numbers, they were unable to establish a permanent presence in the zone. Hacienda authorities cut or burned crops as soon as they were planted and the local police continually harassed the cooperative.

This continued for some time until it appeared as though IERAC was going to adjudicate seventy hectares to the cooperative. However, just as this claim was about to go through, Aray Marin sold the disputed section to Francisco Brito, a local hacendado with extremely close ties to both military forces in Tenguel and IERAC officials (who began to file dubious reports that undermined the peasants' claims). The jailings and humiliations sent the organization into crisis by late 1975. As one member described in one of the popular political newspapers that were emerging during this period of heightened conflict:

> Those of us from Rio Gala have been working since the past year on virgin mountains of Hacienda Rio Blanco. José Aray Marín and Francisco Brito . . . ordered their workers to destroy our crops. [They] work with the support of the military and police [and] also robbed our wood and burned the communal house. Without a single official order they took to prison our president and compañero Guaman and later beat them and took them to the military base in Tenguel. During the . . . fiesta in Shumiral a truck of people with hired guns arrived and police came to provoke.
>
> We have had two inspections by IERAC, one more false than the other. We know clearly that they are in favor of the patron. Finally, in the last week the major [of the military base] in Tenguel ordered that all the members of the association present themselves, in the case that we do not he will send a detachment to capture everyone. (TURIPAC 3/1975)

Another account at roughly the same time recalls similar events:

> This time they took ten of us to jail. On Monday we were working and trying to save our crops that they had destroyed when two military detachments with guns forced us onto the highway. Some of them beat us in a car and others made us walk on our knees on the highway for almost half of a kilometer. When we arrived to the crossing they made us put our heads in the rocks with our hands behind and kicked us. As before, they took us without a single order, without an official paper. The order came from the landlords who are

friends of the heads of the [military] detachment in Tenguel; with
their money they got a false report from IERAC; [paid officials] to
lose our petitions in the offices of IERAC in Guayaquil; and pay the
police to mistreat us. We were accused as invaders and terrorists, all
on the word of landlords who also said the town of Shumiral was full
of communists. A list was made of dangerous communists including
Padre Hernán and his group. (TURIPAC 8/75)

Despite the peasants' determination, IERAC forced them into an unfavorable agreement. They received only the twenty-five hectares that they
had managed to cultivate. The majority of the seventy hectares (already
much less than the original petition) was sold to Brito who had physically occupied the property and made clear that any attempt to acquire
the remaining land would be met with continued violence. All and all, it
took Cooperative Rio Gala close to ten years to become the legal owner
of twenty-five hectares.

   The peasants' partial success was accompanied by a number of ironies.
Most conspicuously, none of the three Guaman brothers—who were
born on the land, initiated the struggle, and suffered its violent consequences—currently own any of the land. In their fifties and sixties, they
continue to work for wages on local haciendas. In addition, Brito himself no longer owns the land. Most of the disputed property currently
belongs to a mining company owned by Juan Baidal, a man who ranks
among Ecuador's wealthiest, owning extensive shrimp, cattle, banana,
and mining interests in the southern coast. Ironically, Baidal is among a
rare breed of capitalists who actually owns a home in the zone, moving
between Guayaquil, Quito, Miami, and an estate in Tenguel that he built
on land acquired from one of the peasant cooperatives—that is, on land
that quickly passed through the hands of United Fruit's ex-workers on
the way to one of Ecuador's largest capitalists. This was agrarian reform.

CONCLUSION

During both the 1950s and the 1970s, successful land invasions always
involved the formation of communities. What passed for a community
in the 1950s, however, was not what passed for one in the 1970s. A number of the colonos brought their families to Shumiral during the initial
stages of the Colonia's struggle in the 1950s, but most lived outside the
zone for years, working for wages on local haciendas while raising their
families in relatively well-established towns such as Tenguel. This limited presence in Shumiral was possible because the zone was so isolated;
neither United Fruit, local police, nor the peasants could easily get to the

area and thus a claim to the land could be made through the cultivation of crops and the acquisition of a dedicated lawyer. In contrast, by 1970, a successful land occupation required the full and immediate participation of every cooperative member and their families. At least initially, participation meant temporarily leaving one's job and permanently settling in a densely forested zone that had no roads or basic infrastructure. Although most new communities in the early 1970s formed in isolated areas, the southern coast as a whole was, after the banana boom, relatively well connected by a growing system of roads. This made it easier for peasants to mobilize themselves, but it also made it more difficult to sneak onto land or hide from authorities.

This broad change had an important impact on the internal makeup of peasant organizations. In 1970, peasant organizations were still run by middle-aged men, a fact that is true to the present day. But the process of invasion demanded the full participation of the entire family, and particularly women. Quite clearly, women also played a key role in the formation of communities during the 1950s. It could hardly be otherwise. But it was quite often the case that they were shielded from direct confrontations with authorities and remained outside the disputed territory while the men began to cultivate crops (but lived with their families elsewhere). Regardless of how they supported the struggle in other ways, women's absence from these key moments and places only served to justify their formal exclusion from leadership bodies.

By 1970, things were much more complicated. The changed nature of land invasions forced women into more prominent roles. Quite often, this simply meant extending familiar roles onto new terrain. In Luz y Guia, women were still cooking and cleaning, but they did so collectively as police planes flew over the emerging community and a makeshift kitchen was feeding close to 1000 people. In other words, the same tasks that they had always performed took on new meaning and heightened importance once those jobs were placed in the middle of the invasion process itself. "Women's work" became central to the initial period of land invasion. Cooking meals, cleaning clothes, establishing schools, and clearing land were what an invasion was about.

After 1970 it is hard to find a land invasion in the southern coast in which women were not sent to confront police forces at some time or another. When a national newspaper reported in 1976 that the "women of [Santa Martha] had managed to stop" the [police] destruction of houses and the repression of their husbands, it would have surprised no one (*El Nacional* 10/16/76: 6). Women's role in confronting armed thugs had become a standard part of peasant strategies by the early 1970s. It was widely believed, and to a certain extent true, that women would not receive the same brutal repression as men. Moreover, the presence of women, much like the existence of churches and schools, served to legitimate a community. Men who invaded a hacienda and simply cultivated crops were easily labeled as squatters or communists. An invasion with women, children, schools, and churches suggested the permanence and history of a community. As a result, women were often the first line of defense. It is only with an understanding of the range of places that women occupied in the initial stages of land invasions that we will be able to make sense of the unprecedented (though contradictory) roles that they began to play as the process of community formation continued in the mid-1970s.

The range of outside contacts and alliances that characterized the conflicts at Luz y Guia, Santa Martha, and Rio Gala also distinguished them from the land invasions of the 1950s. In the case of Luz y Guia, which involved a cooperative of several hundred members, this should hardly be surprising. But the much smaller conflicts in Santa Martha and Rio Gala also illustrate the extent to which the political-economic landscape had been transformed in the 1950s and 1960s. The peasant organizations involved in these conflicts had only about twenty members, but were nonetheless connected to a range of state officials and bureaucracies, not to mention religious groups, lawyers, and national-level peasant organizations.

It is equally important to note that each of the outside groups were involved in a much wider range of relationships than their earlier counterparts. As we will see in chapter nine, the early 1970s was characterized by the countrywide emergence of "regional" actors such as Padre Hernán and UROCAL, individuals and entities who were busy establishing connections with other regional actors, national bureaucracies, and international organizations. It was the intensity and nature of these contacts between and among local organizations and regional actors that both gave the movement its strength and contributed to its eventual dismantling.

Indeed, as we look more closely at the broader development of the regional movement, it is important to keep the surge of popular organizing during this period in perspective. It is undeniable that popular political relationships, both among peasants and between peasants and outside allies, were being expanded and strengthened during this period. In most cases, however, peasant relationships with outside allies remained instrumental, allowing numerous cooperatives and workers' associations to take better advantage of existing opportunities and gain access to state bureaucracies and resources. It was only in a very limited way that alliances between local cooperatives and national organizations such as CEDOC and FENOC strengthened the peasantry's collective capacity to exert political pressure on the state and *expand* the range of opportunities open to them. For most peasants, CEDOC and FENOC were faceless (and largely urban) entities whose political projects were less important than their capacity to provide legal aid or access to state bureaucracies.

More importantly, almost without exception, the most powerful landlords in the southern coast, particularly those located in fertile sections near towns like Tenguel and Balao, managed to defeat peasants (or avoid conflict altogether) as they consolidated their hold over the zone's best lands, modernized their holdings, and developed exceptionally profitable banana plantations and shrimp pools. In other words, as we continue to examine the expansion of popular political activity in the marginal zones of La Florida, Luz y Guia, and Shumiral, it is important to remember that it was during this same period that peasants in and around Tenguel were being rapidly dispossessed by regional power brokers such as Juan Baidal and the Maldonado brothers.

9 The Reconstitution of State, Capital,
and Popular Struggle

From the end of 1973, when the Luz y Guia invasion took place and the second agrarian reform law was passed, until the end of 1976, when the military dictatorship of Rodríguez Lara relinquished power and agrarian reform was effectively ended, land invasions covered the entire southern coast. The first part of this chapter examines how and to what extent the numerous struggles that dotted the southern coast in the mid-seventies coalesced into a regional movement. This analysis takes place through a discussion of two sets of "regional actors" that emerged in this period: (1) the Grupo Pucara (GP), a group of Spanish-Catholic activists led by Padre Hernán Rodas, and (2) UROCAL, a regional union of local peasant organizations. As we will see, it was no coincidence that these two groups—the most successful attempts to organize on a regional level— arose in Shumiral-Mollepongo, home of the region's most stable land-owning peasantry and some of the oldest peasant organizations. Nor was it coincidence that these groups emerged when they did. Although the development of regional organizations such as the GP and UROCAL cannot necessarily be equated with the cohesion of a movement, the emergence of these actors was indicative of the surge in popular organizing during this period (1973–1976).

The second part of the chapter also focuses on the GP and UROCAL but within the context of the regional movement's *decline*. The formal constitution of UROCAL in 1976 reflected and coincided with two key changes that transformed the political economy of the southern coast, including the nature, orientation, and effectiveness of popular organizing. First, the Rodríguez Lara government was replaced by a military triumvirate that ended agrarian reform, repressed peasant land invasions, and implemented a quite different model of rural "development." Second, at almost the exact same moment, Dole Fruit began a new system of contract farming that was made possible by agrarian reform, subsequent political repression, and a relatively stable landscape that was and is characterized by large producers of bananas, semi-proletarianized producers of cacao, and a large class of landless plantation workers.

BUILDING A REGIONAL MOVEMENT

As friends and detractors like to insist, Padre Hernán was "not just a priest."[1] For a twenty-year period, between the early 1970s and late 1980s, Hernán Rodas and his group of Spanish activists were a major inspirational, economic, organizational, and educational force behind both the formation of peasant organizations and the broader political-economic development of the zone. He arrived at a time when the struggle for land was gaining momentum (1972) and departed during a period when state development projects had begun to lose their steam (late 1980s). Regardless of shifts in the political economy, Padre Hernán was, as an organizer, educator, manager of state funds, and international fundraiser, at the center of organizational activity within the zone for a period of twenty years.

In the beginning of 1973, Padre Hernán announced that a group of Catholic activists from Spain, including experts in agronomy, social work, medicine, sociology, and education, would arrive in the coastal zone later in the year. Numbering less than ten, the GP was comprised of young, well-educated activists who had been deeply influenced by liberation theology and "1960s" political activism. Padre Hernán, who was born in the highland city of Cuenca, first began making trips to coastal sections of the largely highland province of Azuay in the early 1970s. By this time he was not only a Catholic priest, but had also spent considerable time in Madrid where he obtained a Ph.D. in sociology, made contacts with activists, and deepened his knowledge of left-wing politics. In Ecuador, the GP would be working in a number of parishes in the coast and highlands of Azuay, concentrating their efforts on education and the promotion of popular organizations.

The GP arrived when the Luz y Guia invasion was reaching its culmination and the group was immediately thrust into the conflict. Less than two weeks after the invasion, Padre Hernán was delivering masses and doing baptisms in Luz y Guia in order to support the struggle and give the emerging community a certain legitimacy. Although its involvement was generally embraced by the cooperative's rank and file, the GP came into conflict with landlords, military forces, left-wing militants, and even some of the cooperative's leadership. On the one hand, left-wing militants clashed with the Catholic activists both on methods and ideology. Questions concerning the relative value of certain strands of socialism and the necessity of violence were cause for heated debate during this period. On the other hand, the GP, and Padre Hernán in particular, were quickly labeled communists by the region's dominant classes. For some, they were not communist enough, for others they were communist by definition (C 115710, 1974; C 115811, 1976; C 116711, n.d.; Sistematización de la Experiencia Investigativa de CECCA, 1990).

What separated the GP from national-level political parties and peasant-labor organizations was that the religious activists were tireless organizers who lived and worked in peasant communities—on a range of problems from education and the raising of political consciousness to the organization of work teams and the construction of housing. As locals, their understanding of the problems confronted by the zone's inhabitants allowed the GP to promote popular forms of local organization. As outsiders, they were crucial conduits of information, contacts, and financial resources. They were the first group that consciously occupied the ambiguous space between different peasant communities within the region, and between local peasant organizations and outside groups.

During the same period when they were getting their feet wet in Luz y Guia, members of the GP quickly established links with peasant organizations such as the ATAIB, Rio Balao, Lucha Campesina, Eloy Alfaro, Brasil, Santa Martha, Rio Gala, 29 de Febrero, 29 de Abril, and the Colonia Agrícola Shumiral. They were also key factors at San Miguel de Azuay, Hermano Miguel, and Unión y Progreso, all key struggles for the land that took place in the early 1970s as land conflicts were becoming a region-wide phenomenon. The GP established its home base in Shumiral, and in alliance with key leaders from Mollepongo, La Florida, and Shumiral, began to link together and support local peasant organizations (ibid.; *Diagnostica Zona Baja*).

It should be stressed, however, that just as we cannot equate the presence of regional actors and region-wide conflict with the emergence of a cohesive movement, it would be a mistake to place too much importance on Padre Hernán and the GP. Many of the struggles for land took place *before* the arrival of Padre Hernán's group. Peasant organizations in La Florida, Rio Balao, Shumiral, Mollepongo, Brasil, and Luz y Guia were already formed and, in some cases, had long histories of struggle and organization before some of the Spanish activists had even been born. Many of the peasants involved in Shumiral and Mollepongo in the 1940s and 1950s began helping groups in La Florida and Santa Martha before the arrival of regional actors. Links between an experienced group of peasant organizers and semi-organized groups of landless peasants were well established before Padre Hernán had ever visited the zone. Social, cultural, economic, and political ties dating back to the time of the company linked local organizations and their members before attempts were made at formally constituting a regional organization.

At the same time, the importance of the intervention by the GP should not be underestimated. Although peasants often had *local* organizations before they approached outside allies with quite specific and relatively well-defined needs, it was the GP, along with a group of local peasant leaders, that created a formal *regional* organization. This regional organization, UROCAL, served to solidify and strengthen preexisting links between small groups of already organized peasants and workers. The organizations in Shumiral, Mollepongo, Santa Martha, and La Florida were by no means isolated from each other prior to the arrival of regional actors. Before Padre Hernán and his group, however, there was no formally organized method of linking these distinct struggles—of sharing information, of soliciting state and nongovernmental agencies for resources, of confronting IERAC, landlords, and the military.

Quite obviously, Padre Hernán and the GP did not come to the zone with a regional organization intact and ready to be implemented. Nor did the group itself become anything resembling a regional peasant organization. The GP worked to strengthen local peasant organizations and leaders, the relationships between those organizations, and the connections they had with outside groups. In so doing, they, along with a number of peasant leaders who were involved in the same sorts of things, began to see the need for a regional peasant organization that would serve to strengthen and coordinate the myriad cooperatives, communes, and workers' associations that were emerging around the struggle for land. This is, in short, what led to the formation of UROCAL.

UROCAL

The formation of UROCAL, the Regional Union of Peasant Organizations of the Southern Coast, represented both the consolidation of the regional movement and a broad shift in its orientation and makeup. On the one hand, UROCAL was the product of popular political activity dating back to the 1940s and, more recently, an alliance between peasant leaders and Catholic activists in the zone of Shumiral-Mollepongo. On the other hand, the formation of UROCAL represented the end of a period characterized by peasant organizations that had formed with the sole purpose of acquiring land. Almost all of the land invasions within the zone occurred between 1968 and 1976, and the overwhelming majority took place between the end of 1973 and the end of 1976. In December 1976, when military dictator Rodríguez Lara was removed from power, the military triumvirate that replaced him immediately gutted the political and financial power of IERAC. The Law of Agricultural Development, a reactionary piece of legislation which gave hacendados and military forces capacity to repress land invasions, was soon passed. The principal and most dramatic form of rural popular political activity was thus cut off and popular organizations were forced to reorient themselves (C 103502 1977; C 114002 1979; C 337124 1985; *Diagnostica Zona Baja* n.d.).

In this sense, it is important to remember that UROCAL was formally constituted in 1976 and thus participated in relatively few land invasions. Virtually all of the leaders involved in the formation of UROCAL played a key role in numerous struggles for land. However, although UROCAL was a product of peasant land struggles, the majority of the struggles took place prior to UROCAL's legal constitution. With few exceptions, the base organizations that came to form UROCAL in 1976 were organizations that had already acquired land. Notwithstanding a wide range of differences among organizations and individuals, UROCAL's members had "successfully" struggled to implement agrarian reform and were now landowners. Thus, the formation of UROCAL not only coincided with the end of a period of peasant political activity that was defined first and foremost by land invasions, but also signaled the beginning of a period in which the zone's most established popular political organizations were oriented around the struggle to acquire state resources in order to work newly acquired holdings and build communities. This broad shift, and the contradictions it involved, can be seen in the formation of UROCAL itself.

There was, from the very beginning, a tension between those with and those without land. One group of peasants was trying to cultivate crops and form new communities while the other was still trying to acquire land. Initially, these quite different goals were resolved by the intensity of political activity in the early to mid-1970s. Dozens of peasant groups were passing through similar stages—forming an organization, invading a hacienda, clearing the land, and cultivating crops—at roughly the same time. Isolated groups of smallholders in Shumiral-Mollepongo not only established strong ties with many of their landless counterparts, but also recognized the need for broader sets of alliances and struggles. It was the long history of informal ties between these groups, the intensity and focused nature of political activity between 1973 and 1976, and the participation of regional actors that gave the movement its momentary strength and led to the formation of UROCAL.

Nevertheless, after the military triumvirate of 1976 removed the peasantry's most dramatic form of political activity (invasion) and made it nearly impossible for landless groups to acquire property, it became extremely difficult for UROCAL to maintain ties between the landed and the landless. Within a relatively short period after its formation, UROCAL was consolidated into a regional peasant organization by, and largely for, smallholders involved in the production of cacao. As UROCAL's constituency was forced to abandon one kind of struggle in favor of another, UROCAL itself was transformed from an organization designed to coordinate the struggle for land into one that represented peasants in their struggle to acquire resources from the state.

THE DECLINE OF A REGIONAL MOVEMENT

Despite the effective end of land invasions and the second agrarian reform, there was a remarkable increase in the formation of *peasant* organizations between 1975 and 1985 that corresponded to the growing strength of UROCAL. Yet, as UROCAL grew in importance, both with respect to local organizations and its ability to make demands on the state, the regional movement itself weakened. More peasants were organized than ever before, but cooperatives, communes, and workers' associations weakened as their overall orientation, internal dynamics, and relationships with outside groups were transformed. The focus of these local organizations no longer revolved around the acquisition of land, but centered on the struggle to obtain resources to cultivate crops and build communities (C 103502 1977; C 114002 1979; C 337124 1985; *Diagnostica Zona Baja* n.d.; C 332924 1985; author interviews).

In trying to meet the needs of its base organizations, UROCAL, now led by a younger generation of professional leaders, consciously struggled against a number of problems, including the disintegration of base organizations, their control by the state, the bureaucratization of leaders, and internal stratification. The leaders focused on a concrete set of problems—credit and commercialization—in order to strengthen not only UROCAL and the base organizations/communities which it served, but broader efforts at political transformation. Nevertheless, whereas a local politics of land invasion could easily be tied to a broader politics of liberation, the translation between local needs and large-scale political mobilization became much more difficult as peasants became enmeshed in state development projects and the politics of credit and commercialization. As a new model of state-led development emerged, peasants went from being reluctant rebels struggling for land to state clients petitioning for credit and other resources.

In Search of Capital: From Agrarian Reform to Agricultural Development
In 1978, as part of the World Bank's move toward Integrated Rural Development,[2] the Central Bank of Ecuador, under the direction of the military government, established FODERUMA, the Fund for the Development

of Marginal-Rural Areas. It was an alternative source of credit designed to create ways for peasants to sustain themselves and contribute to the country's economic growth. FODERUMA was a *fund* of money that either financed small projects or was loaned directly to peasants in order to stimulate production and facilitate marketing. Although the major impact of FODERUMA was felt between 1979 and 1984, UROCAL was the principal administrator of the fund in the southern coast between August 1978 and the end of 1987. Flowing through UROCAL, the fund directly benefited over 1000 rural families, allowed peasant organizations to cultivate plots of land collectively ("communal holdings"), and indirectly affected a large portion of rural peoples living in the zone (*Diagnostica Zona Baja* n.d.; C 101602 1979; C 102024 1979; C 220028 n.d.; C 332924 1985).

FODERUMA was also a friendly way of unofficially announcing the death of agrarian reform. It was the first major rural development project that had no pretensions of redistributing land. The initiative was designed to help *organized* groups of *landed* peasants help themselves. It was a "progressive" type of development designed to prevent a sector of the rural poor from losing the few gains they had managed to squeeze out of agrarian reform. Directed at the class of smallholders who had been emerging over the past two decades, FODERUMA filled many of the same roles as UROCAL. It was, however, also designed to control and channel popular organizations and demands, intensifying the uneven process through which peasants became clients of the Ecuadorian state.

The first program that FODERUMA approved for organizations affiliated with UROCAL was designed to facilitate a wide range of development projects, including the commercialization of cacao, the development of cultural centers and child care facilities, as well as creation of health programs and women's organizations. Few of the projects outlived the initial surge of funding. Financial resources allowed communities to start health centers, but rarely provided for the continued maintenance or development of such facilities. Similarly, although short-term loans did allow a small minority to expand individual production, they were not sufficient to allow projects involving collectively owned and operated communal holdings to become self-sustainable.

Despite the limited nature of the projects, the process of development transformed UROCAL. On a basic level, there can be little doubt that the influx of money strengthened the organization. The number of cooperatives, workers' associations, and women's organizations that affiliated with UROCAL quickly doubled (to over thirty) as Padre Hernán became FODERUMA's southern representative and UROCAL became the administrator of state-funded projects. As the administrator and architect of a wide range of development projects, UROCAL controlled considerable resources and represented several thousand rural people. The organization became the major local force behind what constituted marginal development during this period. Not surprisingly, however, UROCAL's transformation and growth involved a number of contradictions.

Most importantly, FODERUMA's project turned UROCAL into an agent of the state. After considerable debate, the peasant leaders and members of UROCAL accepted their new role with great reluctance. They were well aware of the potential dangers of embracing the state's latest initiative, but there was really little choice. UROCAL had no independent source of funding and FODERUMA was a relatively progressive form of state development. In this sense, the intensified relationship between an organized peasantry (in the form of UROCAL) and state-led development (in the form of FODERUMA) was an ambiguous one. On the one hand, through its relationship with FODERUMA, UROCAL became an agent of the state in a very direct and formal sense. It was now administering state-funded and controlled development projects. On the other hand, by accepting this new role, UROCAL hoped that it—and by extension the region's peasantry—would not be incorporated *into* the state, but would gain control and influence *over* the state. By administering credit and development projects on behalf of FODERUMA, UROCAL would control state resources and help determine the nature of state intervention in the southern coast. The program, which addressed an important set of needs for a large portion of the rural population, was going to happen; it was simply a question of how it was to be implemented and who would control it. As a result, UROCAL decided to tentatively embrace the project, defending the initiative's very existence against reactionary groups within the state and demanding its extension to truly marginalized areas.

The difficulty with UROCAL's new role was not so much that it changed the organization's relationship to the state, but that in so doing it transformed the relationship between UROCAL and its peasant constituency. UROCAL's leaders were clearly aware of this possibility. From the beginning of its relationship with FODERUMA, UROCAL recognized that peasant organizations would have to struggle to maintain their autonomy vis-à-vis the state and fight against clientelism, bureaucracy, and paternalism. The problem, however, was that by 1980 over half of the peasant organizations that belonged to UROCAL had joined with the idea of obtaining credit from FODERUMA. When UROCAL became FODERUMA's representative, the number of affiliated organizations more than doubled, but most of these organizations had formed only as a response to the opportunities opened up by the state. When credit ran out, peasants not only severed their relationships with UROCAL, but also terminated their own organizations. One member characterized the relationship between his organization and UROCAL as follows:

> UROCAL gives credit. We wanted to develop a relationship with UROCAL in order to get credit. We asked for credit with the idea that we would grow cacao. The credit was given for an eight year period. UROCAL gave us this loan through the Central Bank of Ecuador. We grew the cacao but with the flood of 1983 we lost everything. We still owe money. We have the intention of paying the loan because if we don't we will never receive another loan from anyone. (M.P. 10/6/95)

As UROCAL became an agent of the state, the group of professionalized leaders who administered state projects and controlled the credit program *became* UROCAL. The base organizations became their clients. The implementation of FODERUMA-sponsored projects, unlike agrarian reform, did not demand that peasants mobilize against the landed oligarchy. It required a new type of organization that depended on the expertise of a small number of professional leaders.

This was one of the key differences that distinguished state agricultural policies in the early 1970s from those in the early 1980s. Agrarian reform institutions and policies occupied a variety of places during the early and mid-1970s, but nowhere were they more visible than in the space between capital and peasant-workers. In contrast, state-sponsored development in the 1980s worked from a quite different location and set of assumptions. As we have seen, agrarian reform encouraged (or forced) large landowners to modernize the most fertile sections of their properties while turning over the more marginal lands to peasant-workers. In so doing, this struggle-filled process helped generate a landowning peasantry *and* a capitalist class of banana producers. Once constituted, each group of landowners confronted a number of problems with respect to production and marketing, but these problems were not seen as a product of conflicting interests between the two groups. By the 1980s, then, the state's development apparatus was (unequally) serving the needs of two seemingly disconnected sectors. Capitalist planters and peasant producers both made quite harsh criticisms of the state's understanding and implementation of development, but they rarely came into contact or conflict with each other. Rather, they competed for the few state resources that were destined for agriculture—a clientelistic competition that was decidedly unequal.

Market Exploitation

If the lack of credit made it impossible for small producers to expand production, middlemen and exploitative market relationships made it difficult for peasants to profit from the products they managed to cultivate (which in turn made it hard to expand production). Consequently, the struggle against exploitative market relations—embodied in the system of middlemen—was seen by UROCAL and others as *the* political issue that would replace "the land" and unify the peasantry on a regional and national level. The problem, however, was that the strategies for organizing around the market were neither clear nor easily implemented (C 103502 1977).

When UROCAL consolidated itself as an organization of smallholders in the mid-1970s, almost all of its members (95 percent) were growing cacao for export. A number of factors made cacao a relatively attractive crop for small producers throughout the Ecuadorian coast in the 1960s and 1970s. Although the industry would remain plagued by a cyclical pattern of high prices followed by overproduction (followed by low prices/underproduction), the 1960s saw a general rise in the price of cacao. Moreover, as peasants were increasingly pushed out of banana production, cacao became the only export crop available. Most combined cacao cultivation with a wide range of food crops (both for consumption and sale in local markets), but cacao remained the crop of choice. It was more profitable and required considerably less work than more labor-intensive crops such as corn and beans. Indeed, it has largely been small and medium-size producers that have made Ecuador one of the top ten cacao-producing countries in the world during the second half of the century.[3]

As cacao producers, UROCAL's constituency has faced serious difficulties in obtaining both credit[4] and a fair price for a product that is eventually sold in the United States and Europe. Although marketing relationships varied, a middleman (of a middleman) would generally come to a given community sometime between January and April before the harvest. It was during these months that families were scrambling to generate an income. Taking advantage of the low cash flow, middlemen would offer to buy the family's cacao before the harvest began. The catch, of course, was that they would buy the ungrown cacao in February at a much lower price than the peasant could sell for in July, when the crop matured.

On a basic level, there was and is an obvious solution. Peasants need to sell directly to exporters or foreign buyers. In practice, however, the situation is quite complicated, involving a considerable amount of coordination and resources. Selling to an exporter requires delivering large quantities of cacao at a designated time. Individual peasants must first dry their cacao and then deliver it to a central holding facility so that enough beans accumulate to warrant the attention of an exporter. If one lacks capital, such an endeavor requires short- and long-term credit. A number of one-time purchases need to be made, including a cacao dryer, trucks, and a warehouse to store the beans. More importantly, UROCAL, as the new middleman, would need to have the money ready at the moment producers delivered the cacao. Few peasants could wait until UROCAL accumulated cacao, sold to an exporter, and then received payment a month later when the product finally arrived in foreign markets.

UROCAL decided to confront the problem from a variety of angles, including an experiment with a cacao dryer. Generated by the peasants themselves, the dryer became a popular example of alternative development, inspiring similar projects throughout the country. It served to increase the number of organizations affiliated with UROCAL while supporting the commercialization and credit programs. The basic idea was that members of base organizations would dry their cacao in the dryer purchased and run by UROCAL. They would be charged a service fee in order to finance the dryer, but would receive higher prices for dry cacao sold in bulk.

Even during its period of initial success, however, the project confronted a number of administrative problems that left little room for error. When the project started (1977–1978) the price for a quintal of cacao was hovering around 4000 sucres (CA 220228 1980). By the end of 1980 the price had fallen to only 1300 sucres. Combined with growing administrative problems, the drop in prices weakened and eventually destroyed the project. By 1985, when the zone was just recovering from a series of devastating floods, the experiment was effectively terminated and producers were confronted with the same sets of problems. More importantly, UROCAL had lost the confidence of a significant number of peasants and the project's failure did little to strengthen the base organizations involved (C 103502 1977; C 113110 n.d.; C 220228 1980; C 466902 1988).

The dramatic drop in cacao prices also led an increasingly large portion of peasants to conclude that small-scale projects were not sufficient. It was at this time that UROCAL became involved in national-level efforts to combat forms of market exploitation.

The Cacao Strike of 1981
Due to a combination of factors, including the return to democracy, the end of the oil boom, neoliberal economic policies, and a general economic crisis, popular political activity re-intensified throughout Ecua-

dor in the late 1970s and early 1980s. The labor movement, temporarily united under a coalition called the Frente Unitario de Trabajadores (FUT), now had strong ties with rural groups and reemerged in the late 1970s as the military government relinquished power and austerity policies were forced on the Ecuadorian nation (Davila Loor 1995; León and Pérez 1986). After a brief honeymoon between the democratically elected government of Roldos/Hurtado and popular groups, FUT returned in the early 1980s and held five national strikes. In alliance with rural groups, these strikes were widely supported by labor, teachers, and popular sectors within the country's major urban centers (León and Pérez 1986).

Although the nationwide growth of popular political activity was motivated by a number of broad factors, its form varied considerably from region to region. In the southern coast, a number of things made the lives of small cacao producers unbearable in the late 1970s and early 1980s. In addition to the general economic crisis and the withdrawal of state resources from rural areas, prices for agricultural products were falling, particularly cacao and other exports. In response, peasants organized for the National Peasant March in October 1980. Despite the long list of peasant demands,[5] it was the extreme drop in cacao prices, combined with state policies favoring "industrial" processors, that motivated the march (C 105324 1980; C 109124 1981).[6]

The march, which successfully mobilized thousands from throughout Ecuador, made it clear that neither the problems nor the peasants were about to disappear. When the government failed to respond, peasant organizations began to plan a national strike of cacao producers. Representing more producers than any other peasant organization in the country, UROCAL was naturally at the center of this movement. The cacao harvest had not yet begun and it was clear that UROCAL's constituency was facing the devastating combination of poor output and exceptionally low prices. The situation was deteriorating on a daily basis and collective solutions such as the cacao dryer were crumbling under the economic pressure. Food prices were rising, gas prices quadrupled, and neoliberal economic policies, government subsidies to cacao processors, as well as the Law of Agricultural Development all made it clear that the government was not going to intervene on behalf of the nation's peasantry. Moreover, repression emanating from the National Security Law insured that anything less than a unified political action would be brutally confronted. A nationwide strike involving producers and exporters of all sizes was the only alternative (C 109124 1981).

As part of the national strike, peasant groups in the southern coast met in Ponce Enríquez, a small town located on the major highway between

Guayaquil and Machala (on the eastern edge of United Fruit's Hacienda Tenguel), early in the morning of July 8, 1981. The men arrived first and began building barricades in order to stop the flow of traffic. The women prepared food for most of the night and then accompanied their husbands, fathers, and brothers at the highway. As one woman participant recalls: "When the women came the men started cheering us. Later the children came. We took them out of school so they could learn" (P.Z. 1/10/96). The blockade stopped everyone from moving along the country's most important economic artery, including military troops, tractor trailers owned by Dole and Chiquita, as well as busloads of commuters. A little after noon about fifty police arrived and without warning began to throw tear gas and fire their guns; an attack from the ground was immediately accompanied by tear gas bombs from circling planes. The peasants were asphyxiated and some began to run. The majority, however, established a front from which they began to defend themselves with rocks, the only weapon they could find. Some women ran to get water to help with the asphyxiation while others supplied the men with rocks. The bombs and bullets continued, but the peasants slowly advanced, pushing the police out of town. At the end, rock-throwing men and women were running full speed behind the fleeing police (CA 219025 1981; author interviews).

After the initial victory the peasants returned to the barricades and prepared for the second attack they knew would come. Within a couple of hours, however, word of the conflict had spread and compañeros not only from UROCAL but from throughout the zone had come to support the cause. The deteriorating situation of small cacao producers had politicized much of the zone's peasantry. UROCAL was the principal organizer, but peasants who knew nothing of UROCAL came to Ponce Enríquez on July 8 in order to support the strike. Three thousand strong and energized by the first confrontation, the peasants were determined to maintain the barricade throughout the night. They did, but were rapidly evicted when military forces came the next day.

The strike produced immediate results and the Congress passed a new law that favored producers-exporters at the expense of industrial processors. The industrialists were beaten but nothing in the law explicitly favored peasants. Power passed from the processors back into the hands of middlemen, large producers, and exporters. The strike, however, gave UROCAL a presence on the national scene, not just as a key participant in national organizations but as an organization that could by itself mobilize enough people to demand the presence of military forces. UROCAL's reputation within the zone was also greatly enhanced. Unorganized peasants had seen what the organization could accomplish and those who had only known UROCAL as a source of credit began to understand the organization's other side.

Women and Organizing: From Compañeras to Wives
Women gave the cacao strike of 1981 its force and were a key factor in the growing strength of UROCAL during this period. It was just before and after the cacao strike that the number of women's organizations affiliated with UROCAL grew dramatically. The widespread struggle for land in the early part of the 1970s had been a turning point in terms of women's political, economic, and familial roles. Women participated in virtually every stage of the land invasions, from confronting police and putting up fences to clearing and cultivating land. As the initial period of invasion gave way to the more mundane tasks of community building, however, women frequently went from being compañeras to wives. With few exceptions, women did not occupy leadership roles in the base organizations that led the invasions and controlled the subsequent development of new communities. UROCAL's record is not much better. With the exception of those leadership positions where one might expect to see their participation (education, health programs, etc.), women have not held key (formal) roles within UROCAL (C 224510 1981; C 331909 n.d.; C 346924 n.d.; C 464424 1987; Systematización Mujer n.d.; author interviews).

Nevertheless, by the end of the 1970s close to one-third of UROCAL's base organizations had been formed by women—that is, organizations by and for women. This transformation did not happen overnight. Women had been struggling to increase their influence since the formation of the zone's earliest peasant organizations. In the early 1960s, for example, women struggled to alter the statutes of the Colonia Agrícola Shumiral in order to allow women to become formal members. Despite these efforts, however, a basic problem persisted both in the Colonia and in peasant organizations in general. Cooperatives, communes, and colonias were organizations of landowners. If one did not own land, as in the case of most women, one could not belong. Moreover, inasmuch as these organizations had been responsible for obtaining the most basic requirement of newly formed peasant communities (the land), they became the central decision-making organizations within communities. In other words, a cooperative's key role in the initial process of land invasion insured that it would be *the* organization that came to represent the entire community (ibid.).

It was this exclusion from key aspects of community life that led to the formation of the earliest women's organizations in the zone. In 1975, close to a year before UROCAL was actually constituted, thirty-five women formed the Comité Feminino Shumiral (CFS). Its explicit goal was to increase women's influence within the community. Not surprisingly, the formation of the CFS occurred during the height of land invasions within the zone. The presence of Padre Hernán and the GP, as well as Shumiral's centrality to organizational efforts in the area, all contributed to the formation of the CFS in Shumiral.[7]

Because of the intensity of conflict during this period, the CFS felt that women and men should unite as peasants in order to combat the zone's dominant classes. It affiliated with UROCAL while maintaining a certain degree of independence as a women's organization. Nevertheless, even as women occupied key roles in land invasions and mass mobilizations, their organizations remained subordinated to UROCAL. The CFS collaborated in *mingas* (collective work), prepared food for UROCAL's meetings, and collected money for organizational efforts and acts of solidarity. They did not, however, participate in formal decision-making processes.[8] As one woman explains:

> We formed [the CFS] during the struggle for land. Women played a key role in these struggles but the men dominated the organizations. So we formed our own organization. We wanted to remain part of the struggle for land but have an independent organization. This gave us [women] some strength. We affiliated with UROCAL just like any other organization [i.e. a cooperative]. But the men remained in control. (C.V. 8/96)

Despite a certain marginalization, women's organizations experienced tremendous growth following the period of land conflicts. This was due mainly to UROCAL's role in administering funds from FODERUMA. Women organized, affiliated with UROCAL, and became a driving force behind the development of FODERUMA-sponsored preschools and health centers. In fact, women were often the key figures behind many of FODERUMA's community-oriented projects, including the acquisition of potable water, electricity, medicine, roads, and schools. Although these activities often reinforced preexisting gender roles, they also succeeded in organizing women.

It was after their participation in the 1981 cacao strike that women began to argue again and more vigorously for a stronger type of participation—one that included more direct access to FODERUMA's resources. They no longer wanted to be wives, but equal members in UROCAL. Their demands met with mixed results. They received credit for small projects, but the loans had to be guaranteed by their husbands. The hypocrisy behind this policy was not lost on women. As one recounts: "This was an insult. We couldn't possibly do worse than the men. Almost no men have paid back all their cacao loans" (R.A. 7/96). Like the men, however, the women quickly learned that FODERUMA-sponsored projects never involved enough money to make the experiments successful. In addition, most of the organizations that formed after 1977, regardless of whether they were run by women or men, affiliated with UROCAL in order to get economic resources from FODERUMA. When credit ended or the state projects ran into trouble, these clients quickly disappeared.

Although UROCAL itself experienced strong growth during the crisis caused by the floods of 1982–1983 (peasants flocked to UROCAL in order to benefit from the surge in funding that accompanied the crisis), the overall number of women's organizations did not grow after 1983. The basic-needs crisis caused by the floods placed even more demands on women who already found it difficult to attend meetings. The subsequent appearance of gold, which was discovered in the foothills as a result of the floods, complicated things even further. Men departed for the mines and women were left with additional agricultural responsibilities. On top of everything, many men continued to restrict women's movement and discourage their organizational efforts. Finally, despite its shortcomings, UROCAL was a key source of support for women's organizations; its decline in the late 1980s, as well as the termination of FODERUMA, did little to help women or their organizations. Women's organizational efforts became plagued with internal problems as development projects failed and base organizations disintegrated. By the late 1980s, none of the women's organizations that had emerged during the 1970s were functioning.

CONCLUSION

UROCAL's emergence as a regional organization in the mid-1970s was rooted in the second agrarian reform and the peasantry's struggle for the land. Shortly after UROCAL's formation, however, the political landscape was transformed by a new military government, the end of agrarian reform, and the emergence of a new agricultural development model. By 1980, UROCAL's ability to mobilize the peasantry derived from the organization's ability to help peasants acquire credit, sell their products, and build communities. With land invasions no longer possible and agrarian reform effectively ended, UROCAL became the principal representative of the zone's landowning peasantry. Dozens of organizations were linked to UROCAL through a variety of projects. As superficial as these relationships sometimes were, they nonetheless put UROCAL in contact with thousands of small producers of cacao. As the cacao strike demonstrated, the organizations existed, they just needed to be infused with political energy.

Nevertheless, although UROCAL's role as an intermediary between the state and local organizations allowed it to funnel resources to peasant groups, it is difficult to conclude that it served to strengthen local and regional attempts at political organizing. UROCAL's relationships with its base organizations became increasingly clientalistic. In times of extreme frustration, UROCAL could call on the zone's peasantry to make vocal demands on the state, but these demands were clientelistic in both form and presentation. As UROCAL became the vehicle through which individual peasants petitioned development offices for credit and other resources, the peasantry's collective capacity for political mobilization was diminished. The base organizations in which peasants were now grouped often existed only on paper and were designed with the sole goal of accessing state largesse. When FODERUMA's funds dried up, most of the base organizations not only severed their relationships with UROCAL but disbanded altogether.

In this sense, not only was the cacao strike not a point of departure for increased political mobilization, but it marked the continuing decline of a regional movement that, in the last analysis, never really coalesced. The strike also represented a turning point in terms of the orientation of peasant-state relations. The land conflicts of the early 1970s were first and foremost against the zone's landlords. The state played a key role in these struggles; the support or hostility of particular state officials and institutions often determined their outcome. But the struggle for land was ultimately between the landless and the landed. It could hardly have been otherwise. After the period of agrarian reform and land invasions, a portion of the landless became owners of small plots. As their status changed, so too did their needs. They struggled to become viable landowners and agricultural producers, a struggle that could be quite politicizing. The conditions, including marginal land, little credit, poor infrastructure, and exploitative market relations, all insured that the beneficiaries of agrarian reform would not become the conservative smallholders envisioned by the state. However, although capitalists, in their control over the region's land and resources, continued to shape the lives of peasants, the orientation of peasant struggle was now directed almost exclusively at the state. The form of political activity varied considerably—from the petitions of clients to the barricades of activists—but the orientation was clear.

Produced by years of political conflict, agrarian reform, and agricultural restructuring, the formation of this class of smallholders, as well as their political orientation, has had a number of advantages for capital. In the struggle to become independent and viable peasants, smallholders have remained every bit as "political" as in earlier periods, but it is a politics that is directed at the clientelist state. Smallholders compete with large capitalists over state resources, but only rarely do they confront capital directly. For the moment, the land question has been resolved and for the most part peasants and capitalists do not produce the same types of crops. Moreover, despite the fact that smallholders earn a significant portion of their income working as wage-laborers on large haciendas, they do not identify themselves as workers or form alliances with the landless. This is due in part to the fact that they engage in wage labor in order *not* to be workers. In their struggle for autonomy—to be free from wage labor and become viable smallholders—most peasant-workers turn to wage labor both for survival and to acquire money in order to reinvest into their own land. This strategy rarely proves successful, but the struggle to become an "independent" peasant is the goal that orients political activity and identity. Thus, in general, large producers and exporters of bananas no longer confront that portion of the agrarian poor who have acquired land through agrarian reform and continue to struggle with the state for the resources to work their small plots. And, as we will see in the following chapter, large capitalists, in conjunction with the state and multinationals, have developed a system of production and marketing that makes it very difficult for the landless to organize on their own (apart from smallholders), or even *be* "workers" in any traditional sense of the word.

10   In Search of Workers: Contract Farming
and Labor Organizing

> The political and ideological requirements of contracting explain why the
> state is imperative in the reproduction of this particular production regime
> — Michael J. Watts, 1994

This chapter explores the legacy of agrarian reform from the perspective of agricultural workers and the contracted banana plantations that
presently surround towns such as Tenguel, Balao, Santa Rosa, and Pasaje
in the heart of the southern coast's fertile agricultural plain. This system of contracting was a long time coming, involving numerous starts
and stops and requiring continuous refinements. Nevertheless, with the
Cavendish variety of banana well established and the period of land conflicts coming to an end, Dole Fruit, followed by Del Monte, Chiquita,
and Bonita Banana, began in 1976 to extend contracts to large landowners, many of whom acquired land through agrarian reform. Once installed, contract farming allowed multinational exporters to reduce their
risk and intensify their control over the industry, while solidifying the
divide between large domestic planters, semi-proletarianized peasants,
and landless plantation workers. It also restructured the zone's physical
landscape; cacao production expanded further into the Andean foothills
as banana production became concentrated in the fertile coastal plain
near towns like Tenguel.

What is the relationship between this system of contracting, associated
forms of state regulation and labor control, and the absence of workers'
organizations within the Ecuadorian banana industry? Why, in a region with such a rich history of labor organizing, are their virtually no
labor unions? Part of the answer, of course, can be found in the history of agrarian reform, popular organization, and state intervention outlined above. Labor unions were dismantled during agrarian reform as
the largest haciendas were broken up and workers joined organizations
designed to acquire land (i.e. cooperatives). Once agrarian reform was
over, plantation workers who had not acquired land found themselves
working on recently formed plantations that had little history and no

labor unions. Nevertheless, neither the end of agrarian reform nor the reshaping of banana plantations fully explains the continued absence of labor unions. The zone remains dominated by plantations that employ thousands of workers who labor under similarly difficult conditions. In this sense, both the region and the industry seem ideally situated for labor unions. To address this question/paradox, we must turn to the current system of production, and the forms of discipline, struggle, identity, and state regulation that surround and shape it.

DISCIPLINE THROUGH DISORGANIZATION

In an effort to establish and maintain a reliable workforce, United Fruit went to considerable trouble to support a stable family and community during the 1940s and 1950s. The irony, of course, was that although the family/community supported the company's enterprise, once that stability was undermined, both the nuclear family and the plantation community became important sources of labor militancy and resistance.

In contrast, contemporary plantation owners work to create a labor force that is *temporary* and *unstable* in several senses. Most simply, plantation workers are not permanent. They receive no benefits, move from one hacienda to the next, and are not organized into unions. A large portion work full time, but they rarely work on the same hacienda for over a year. Workers are also temporary in the sense that they have no future *as* workers. Several factors, including low pay, the intensity of the work, and management policies, cause workers to abandon plantation labor after no more than four or five years; few plantation workers are over the age of thirty. Plantation labor, therefore, underwrites a way of life that cannot possibly reproduce itself over the lifetime of a single individual. Finally, the work is temporary in that both workers and plantation management have devalued it. It has little of the status once associated with plantation labor.

As we have seen, the contemporary system of contract farming emerged through a long, uneven, and conflictive process. By mid-century, and certainly by the 1960s, peasants, workers, agricultural diseases, and Latin American governments had made the traditional system of producing bananas—the foreign-owned enclave—politically and economically untenable from the perspective of multinational corporations. However, if the reproduction of foreign-owned plantations was no longer possible in some places (Ecuador) and increasingly difficult in others (Central America), the unequal power relations on which the industry was based insured that it was primarily multinationals, and not workers, who would determine how production would be organized in the postwar period. Consequently, foreign corporations increasingly turned to a system of contract farming in which they have retained de facto control over the production process while transferring all of the risks associated with direct production to a class of domestic planters who employ a poorly paid and largely nonunionized labor force.

In Ecuador, the tangible rewards of employment under contract farming vary little from one plantation to the next. Owners offer none of the inducements that briefly characterized the large enclaves of the past. Low wages and no benefits are now the rule. Patricio, an agricultural laborer on the 100-hectare Hacienda María Blanca, earns about six dollars a day, has no security, and receives no formal benefits. Ironically, the lands that make up Hacienda María Blanca used to belong to peasants such as Patricio's father, Julio, a former United Fruit employee who participated in the invasion of Hacienda Tenguel and was subsequently incorporated into a state-controlled cooperative. After years of struggling with both debt and local landowners, Julio, along with most of the other cooperative members, sold his land to outsiders like Rafael Sánchez, the current owner of Hacienda María Blanca. Patricio, then, is working on the same land that his father once worked for United Fruit and later owned as a cooperative member. As Patricio astutely noted: "My father worked this land for a company called United Fruit. A foreign company. There was a union, they provided good houses, and the pay was excellent. Today, I work for an Ecuadorian who pays me shit. But he controls nothing. He contracts with Dole. It is also a foreign company" (P.A. 5/19/96).

Like hundreds of other domestic planters, Patricio's boss, Rafael Sánchez, has a contract to produce for Dole Fruit. Sánchez, who is from Machala and has numerous holdings throughout the southern coast, is also a national Congressman. He rarely visits any of his plantations, splitting time between Machala, Guayaquil, and Quito. Hacienda María Blanca is one of the most modern plantations in the zone. Every hectare is filled with banana trees, primary and secondary canals, an underground system of irrigation and drainage, as well as an overhead rail system that moves the bananas from tree to processing facility. Dole, the exporter, provided all of the initial financing, sends a technical expert several times a week, and continues to supply Sánchez with nearly everything from protector bags and insecticides to the familiar cardboard boxes and little Dole stickers that are attached to every cluster of bananas. Dole even holds educational classes for administrators, agronomists, and workers.

Dole does not, of course, do all of this for free. The costs for the protector bags, boxes, chemicals, and advice are all deducted from production every time Hacienda María Blanca places a box of bananas on a

Dole truck. Yet the relationship between Dole and the plantation is so tight that a formal contract is no longer necessary. At least until the next change in the world market, Dole will continue to purchase fruit from María Blanca as long as the hacienda produces a high-quality product—a result that Dole virtually insures. In fact, the relationship between Sánchez and Dole is even more insidious. Sánchez also owns a company that is an intermediary of Dole.[1]

It should be noted that this elaborate system of contracting—the myriad relationships between foreign exporters, domestic landowners, administrators, agronomists, and plantation workers—does little to mask the unequal power relations that sustain the entire industry. As Patricio succinctly explains: "The workers produce the bananas. Rafael Sánchez does nothing. How could he? He is never here. Dole does not produce the bananas. How could they? The Dole technical expert comes twice a week for ten minutes to laugh with the administrator. We produce the bananas, but Dole has control and Sánchez make millions." Although it fools no one, the system of contracting nonetheless provides export companies like Dole, and domestic capitalists like Rafael Sánchez, with a number of political advantages. Dole Fruit, whose signs and advertisements are found in some of the most remote corners of the southern coast, is extremely difficult to *physically* locate. The foreign company, a major player in the global banana industry, maintains a minimal presence in Machala, the banana capital of the world. In rural zones such as Tenguel, the Dole agronomist who travels from hacienda to hacienda *is* Dole Fruit. Dole owns no plantations, directly employs few workers, and has almost no fixed capital in the zone. For his part, Rafael Sánchez, confident that his administrator, in conjunction with the Dole agronomist, will keep the profits flowing, spends little time on Hacienda María Blanca. To workers, he is simply known by his fancy truck: "To tell you the truth," one worker noted, "I don't think I have ever seen him; he is always in his big truck and the windows are darkened." Another worker explained the broader implications of such a system as follows:

> Who would we organize against? I work on a hacienda that pays me little. The owner never comes to the hacienda and makes millions. The exporter is at port, but controls everything. But the exporter is not my employer. It is illegal to organize a big union and if you do you get fired. We make appeals to the state. But the state is controlled by the same people. Sánchez is a Congressman. (A.W. 5/97)

It is difficult to organize against a form of class power that is hard to confront or even locate. Although they frequently hold political office, or are at least well connected to military and political elites, exporters and landowners remain ephemeral figures who spend little time in zones where bananas are actually produced. At the same time, despite the elaborate system of contract farming, bananas must be produced in particular spaces. It is to this labor process, its implications for labor organizing, and the state's roles in its reproduction, that we now turn.

STATE REGULATION: THE MAKING OF A TEMPORARY WORKING CLASS

Banana plantations have two types of work days: normal days and days of *embarque*. On normal days, field workers are paid by task. A worker must complete a certain job, such as spraying chemicals over a particular area. There is little economic incentive to work faster as the task and area are fixed. "Working faster means you can leave early. But if you work too fast they might give you more work." On days of embarque, when the fruit is cut, cleaned, inspected, and boxed, field workers are paid by the number of boxes processed and earn slightly more than on normal days.

Depending on the number of boxes needed by Dole, the field crew, numbering about forty and overwhelmingly male, arrives at the hacienda at around 5:30 A.M. on days of embarque. The crew members are immediately split into groups and sent to different sections of the plantation where they begin removing the banana stems from the trees. The stem is quickly cut and attached to the rail system by male members of the crew; women then prepare the fruit for its short trip to the processing facility at the entrance of the plantation.

By the time the field crew has brought several groups of bananas to the processing facility, the *cuadrilla* has arrived. The cuadrilla, or processing crew, is typically comprised of between ten and fifteen men and women. They come to the hacienda only on days of embarque when the fruit is taken from the trees and boxed. They are responsible for cutting bunches of bananas from the stems, cleaning and inspecting them, and then packaging the fruit in the Dole boxes.

Members of the cuadrilla are paid by the number of boxes processed. Unlike the field crew, however, they are not employees of the hacienda. The administrator of Hacienda María Blanca contracts with the head of the cuadrilla who is responsible for bringing *his* crew to the plantation on days of embarque. He is told how many boxes Dole Fruit wants and is promised a certain amount of money per box. The head of the cuadrilla then pays *his* workers. A typical Dole-contracted hacienda will have two to three embarques every week all year long. However, María Blanca is not Rafael Sánchez's only plantation. The same processing crew is contracted for two slightly smaller haciendas owned by Sánchez. These haciendas border one another and—despite the legal fiction—are effectively run as a single enterprise. Therefore, although they are not technically "employed" by Sánchez, members of the cuadrilla work on one of his three haciendas six days a week. They are full-time workers *on* the hacienda, but are not employees *of* the hacienda.

As a result, although members of the cuadrilla represent about one-quarter of the approximately 100 workers employed on Sánchez's three haciendas, they cannot organize as employees of Sánchez or one of his plantations. According to Ecuadorian law, labor organizations can only be formed on business enterprises with at least twenty *permanent* workers. Members of the cuadrilla, who are not in any legal sense employees of Rafael Sánchez, being neither permanent nor temporary, cannot form organizations on their own or with field workers.

What about field workers such as Patricio who account for three-quarters of the labor force on Sánchez's plantations? Most workers on María Blanca have worked on the hacienda for more than three months and according to law should be classified as *permanent* workers. Some, in fact, have worked on the plantation for years. A number of factors, however, make organizing difficult. To begin, an industry-wide union is simply illegal; labor unions must be attached to specific business enterprises. Workers from Sánchez's plantations cannot form a union with similarly situated workers from plantations throughout Ecuador's coast. Worse yet, although Sánchez has three plantations in the same locale, each is technically owned by a different company. As a result, workers from Sánchez's legally distinct business enterprises cannot even organize together. According to law, it makes little difference that the three plantations have a single administrator, or that the workers are routinely moved from plantation to plantation. Workers from Haciendas María Blanca, Santa Clara, and Florentina, all plantations owned by Rafael Sánchez, may not form a collective labor organization. They work at "distinct" businesses.

The inability to organize *across* plantations serves to isolate organizational efforts on haciendas such as María Blanca. At 100 hectares, Hacienda María Blanca is fairly large by Ecuadorian standards. Once the cuadrilla is excluded, the hacienda employs close to forty workers, about three-quarters of whom should be considered permanent. Thus, even if the legal definition of permanent were enforced, few plantations would have twenty permanent workers, the minimum number required to form a union. However, in the absence of state enforcement, plantation owners and administrators are the ones who decide which workers are considered permanent. In the past, administrators would simply fire and then rehire the same workers every three months. This formality is no longer necessary. As one plantation administrator frankly noted: "I have temporary workers who have worked on the plantation for thirty years. If they try to organize a union we kick them off" (A.P. 8/96). The irony of the situation is not lost on workers. As one pointed out: "To organize a legal union you need *permanent* workers. But we are not considered permanent because the state does not enforce the laws. So to be considered permanent we would first need a union to fight for this right. But we can't form a union if we are not permanent. You can see the problem" (A.W. 8/96).

IN SEARCH OF WORKERS: IDENTITY AND WORK

The current system of contract farming and associated forms of state regulation not only makes labor organizing difficult, it makes it hard to *be* a worker in any subjective sense. In comparison to former workers of United Fruit, most of whom recount with pride the difficulty and intensity of their work, it is remarkable how little contemporary workers have invested in their labor. Most, such as Patricio, insist that they are not even workers.

> No, I am not an agricultural laborer (*trabajabor*). This is just temporary. I am saving money to start a business. Well, yes, I have been working here for almost a year. Before that I worked on another hacienda. We all have to do wage labor sometimes in order to survive. But I am not a wage laborer. It is not my life. (7/96)

Workers invariably explain their presence on plantations as part of a momentary effort to earn cash. Full-time workers, even those who have been working on plantations for over five years, rarely identify themselves as workers. This is in part explained by, and helps explain, the feminized and devalued lens through which the labor itself is now viewed. As an older worker explains:

> The [labor] process is now different. Before things were simpler but much more difficult. It required more strength. There were no boxes. The work today is more delicate because the fruit is more delicate. There are jobs women can do. Cleaning, inspecting the fruit, and putting the stickers [on the bunches] are all things women can do. Many women can do it more quickly. Their hands are better for peeling the stickers. (E.S. 8/96)

A familiar story indeed.

Few male workers have such a detailed and historical explanation for women's presence on banana plantations. Most welcome women, noting that they work hard and are capable of doing virtually all of the work found on plantations. Many also point out that the constant banter between the sexes makes the day go by faster.[2] Moreover, despite the presence of women, banana plantations remain a very masculine domain. Women make up less than 25 percent of the workforce and only one minor task has been thoroughly "feminized." Men are found in every aspect of the production process while women are thoroughly excluded from a number of tasks (such as cutting and carrying the heavy stems). It should also be stressed that women did not cause the devaluation of plantation labor. A temporary, nonunionized, and poorly paid labor force was created by decades of struggle and repression, at which point women were allowed access to plantation labor. In other words, it was because the work had already been devalued that women were allowed on plantations.[3]

That plantation workers, both men and women, do not identify with their work or place much value on plantation labor should not be surprising. On the one hand, workers correctly recognize that they have no real future on the banana plantations where they labor. The production process, combined with state regulation, has created a temporary labor force that receives low wages, no benefits, and faces considerable obstacles with respect to organization. On the other hand, one of the reasons why this oppressive system of production and management has not been more politicizing is that the relationship between plantation labor and daily life has changed dramatically. Banana plantations still surround Tenguel, as well as other towns located in the fertile coastal plain of the southern coast (such as Balao). The town/community of Tenguel does not, however, *belong* to a plantation as it did during the time of United Fruit. In fact, banana plantations, which are generally owned and operated by individuals who live outside of rural towns such as Tenguel, are strangely disconnected from the other sites where people's sense of dignity and self-worth are formed—soccer teams, social clubs, community meetings, food stores, fiestas, etc. Men's economic capacity to join social clubs, play on soccer teams, have families, and otherwise participate in community life depends on their ability to get out of plantation labor and find other sources of income. Men quickly explain their presence on plantations as part of an attempt, almost always failed, to save money and become a "real man" by buying a truck, starting a business, and leaving their parents' house to establish a family. In fact, for the youngest generation of men, masculinity and identity tend to be located off the plantation, particularly in jobs connected to trade and transportation. It is only in these activities where men can become "men" by acquiring a certain freedom from the land, their families, and the economic difficulties associated with plantation labor. Although they uniformly recognize the need for labor unions, male workers—many of whom work full-time on plantations—insist that they themselves have no reason to become involved in organizing. "Why," as one full-time worker and aspiring truck driver noted, "would I involve myself in a union if I am not a worker?" (D.J. 8/96).

Although most men insist that they themselves are not workers, the definition of "worker" remains thoroughly masculinized. Thus, while many men are not workers (by choice, self-definition), women simply cannot *be* workers. They are defined as nonworkers whose "temporary" forays into plantation labor supplement the income of the (often fictitious) male breadwinner. In so doing, women remain wives, mothers, or simply women, but never workers. Femininity and womanhood remain largely in the home, or at least not on the plantation. Their entrance into plantation wage labor, historically the quintessential form of masculine wage labor in the region, has not expanded the range of identities open to women. As one woman, who has worked irregularly on plantations for several years, explains:

> I am not a worker. I am only here because we need money. It's not like in the past. My mom did not have to work, only now and again. But my husband cannot earn enough to support us. He works on another plantation. The woman today has to work just for the family to survive. But we are not workers. Not like the men. (B.G. 8/95)

Implicit in such narratives is a critique of plantation labor and the limited range of economic opportunities in the southern coast. Indeed, it is often women who voice such critiques most loudly. However, work, even economic activity, remain thoroughly masculinized, or at least strongly associated with men. Women's work, in turn, remains invisible. The possibility that they might organize as workers (with or without men) is simply unthinkable.

CONCLUSION

It is tempting to conclude that "Fordist" production, in this case an agricultural model based on the factory-in-the-field, facilitated a strong class consciousness, whereas "post-Fordist" production based on contract farming does not. Although seductive, both the periodization and the terms, as well as underlying assumptions about the relationship between production and the formation of identities, are too simplistic. To maintain, as I have, that workers strongly identified with their work under United Fruit's plantation regime in the 1950s, and to suggest that this led them to take political action once that way of life was threatened, is not to argue that the majority of workers and their families saw themselves as part of a larger working class whose interests were opposed to foreign and domestic capitalists. The ambiguity of the workers' stance toward United Fruit was matched only by the limited nature of their goals; many of those who participated in the invasion actually hoped that the company would return after the Panama Disease was controlled. Similarly, as interviews with contemporary workers suggest, laboring peoples in the southern coast are—perhaps to an even greater extent than in the past—conscious of the class system that impinges on their lives and makes it difficult to organize. They do not need to physically see domestic plantation owners or foreign exporters in order to understand who does and does not control the region's economy. It is patently obvious to just about everyone in Tenguel.

The key difference between the two periods, then, is not whether men did or did not identify as a class, but whether they identified strongly with their work; whether they identified *as* workers whose labor was intimately tied, both materially and subjectively, to the daily life and culture of the entire community; whether this way of life was threatened; and whether the objective conditions were such that they were able to organize. What this suggests is that in order to understand how working-class identities and struggles are formed, it is not enough to locate people within the productive process; the process of production itself must be broadly understood, as part of a way of life. This is precisely why gender and the state are so important.

It was because men (as workers) and women (as housewives) had so much at stake in United Fruit's production regime that they came together as a class and community once that regime, and the way of life it supported, came under attack. In contrast, under the current system of contract farming, plantation labor is not only temporary, unappealing, and devalued, but has, from the point of view of most Tengueleños, been severed from other aspects of daily life. A family's ability to participate in the community—in sporting events, fiestas, and other institutions—depends on the capacity of individual members to disassociate themselves from, and thereby reduce their reliance on, plantation wage labor. As a result, although it is not difficult to imagine Tengueleños organizing as a community in order to confront the state (i.e. for better water, health, infrastructure, etc.), it seems unlikely that their role in banana production will provide the organizational impetus for class action. The temporary nature of work, as well as its partial severing from daily life, is not unique to Tenguel and has profound implications for how, and around what issues, classes will organize. When trying to understand the presence and nature of popular struggles, the question may not revolve around the "consciousness" or "unity" of a particular group, but whether it is possible for that group to claim and organize around certain identities.

Indeed, it is particularly ironic that just as women joined men on banana plantations, thereby sharing a fairly common experience of work, that labor became less meaningful in terms of its connection to daily life, as a source of political conflict, and as a focus of organization. Located on "distinct" business enterprises, wage laborers are not only isolated from one another and the domestic planters and foreign exporters who control the industry, but are alienated from a labor process which seems only tangentially connected to their daily lives. They can no longer identify themselves as workers, economically, emotionally, politically, or subjectively. In contrast, although men and women during the time of United Fruit did not work together in the banana groves, and certainly did not share an identity as workers, they did share a set of collective interests that were directly and transparently connected to the production process. That these interests served to unite the community into a class of land invaders had less to do with the miraculous arrival of class consciousness than it did with the rapid, callous, and devastating way in which those interests were attacked. The workers identified with their work, took action once the way of life it supported was threatened, and were able to justify their actions as part of a nationwide call for agrarian reform. They never saw themselves as part of a national or international proletariat, and did not need to in order to organize as a class.

The transformation of these production regimes, as well as the associated implications for working-class identities and struggles, did not occur by accident. Just as popular struggle played a central role in the withdrawal of multinational corporations from direct production, the state has been implicated in the constitution and transformation of both production and identity. In both periods, the state has been *seemingly* absent on banana plantations. United Fruit was largely on its own when it came to building roads, installing electricity, constructing ports, and controlling workers both on and off the plantation. The company was also on its own when workers began to organize, a process that served to strengthen their identity as workers and ultimately led to the invasion of the hacienda. Today, the situation is very different. On the one hand, the rural interventions of the Ecuadorian state are defined in part by its absent presence; the neoliberal state has basically dismantled "development," particularly programs aimed at poor people living in rural areas. Consequently, as the state's power has become defined in part by what it is *not* doing, rural people have been left even more exposed to various manifestations of capital since the early 1980s. On the other hand, the Ecuadorian state—through legislation, export policies, financial assistance to domestic planters, and the selective implementation of laws regulating labor organizing—actively helps capitalists sustain contract farming through the reproduction of an isolated and unorganized labor force. It supports, in short, a system that makes it impossible to *be* a worker. The difficulty of claiming identity as a worker, of organizing around one's work—the traditional source of working-class politics—is one of the dilemmas that many laboring peoples face as they continue to confront class power in the early twenty-first century.

11 Conclusion

> Capital is a sort of cabalistic word like church or state, or any other of those general terms which are invented by those who fleece the rest of mankind to conceal the hand that shears them. —Thomas Hodgskin, 1825 [1]

During the 1960s and 1970s a powerful current within the interdisciplinary field of agrarian studies worked from the assumption that the economic (i.e. class) location of rural actors determined the forms of political action and consciousness they would adopt. In short, certain groups, whether they be self-sufficient peasants or fully proletarianized workers, were more or less likely to rebel due to the structural position they occupied within agrarian society. Such an economistic approach had, at least, two unfortunate consequences. First, it led to analyses that were *historically* empty. Because scholars often began with hypotheses linking sources of income with political behavior, their case studies served to validate theories that were not particularly useful for understanding the histories of particular rebellions. "Theories" that *assumed* a fairly direct causal relationship between economic position and political behavior could only be "proven" in the absence of historically detailed analyses of particular regions.[2] Second, such assumptions also led to analyses that were *politically* empty. Since the answer to *why* rural peoples rebelled was found in their class position, there was little reason to examine *how* rebellions were actually put together (Roseberry 1993; Smith 1989).

By the early 1980s, this of type of analysis came under attack from anthropologists, historians, and others for being too economistic or structural.[3] In an admirable desire to expand the definition of peasant politics, scholars began to examine a wider range of political practices, including, for example, forms of protest, resistance, and ideology that were not immediately related to large scale revolutions (Scott 1985). Similarly, an increased concern with gender and ethnicity has not only served to broaden the field of agrarian studies, but has forced scholars to rethink and expand their understandings of politics, culture, and ideology. As a result, even older, more traditional, areas of inquiry such as the state (Nugent 1994; Walton 1992), the development of capitalism (Jacobsen 1993; Larson 1988; Mallon 1983; Roseberry 1983; Tomich 1990; Troulliot 1988; Walton 1992; Wolf 1982), and agrarian protest (Feierman 1990; Beinhart and Bundy 1987; Gould 1990; Luong 1992; Nugent 1993; Pearce 1986; Rodney 1981; G. Smith 1989; Stern 1987) have received renewed interest from more nuanced perspectives.

As necessary as the recent critique and partial correction of economistic approaches has been, there have been some unfortunate consequences. Most importantly, although most scholars now *situate* the political activities of popular groups in relation to "larger structures," those activities themselves are rarely seen as central forces that drive the uneven histories of capitalist development. Part of this tendency, particularly during the 1980s, derived from a populist/postmodern desire to celebrate the agency of subaltern groups while simultaneously rejecting "metanarratives" (particularly those associated with Marxism). Yet the tendency also emerged because of the genuine and admirable discomfort that many scholars felt toward the way in which older paradigms conceptualized the relationships between popular political activity and "larger structures." With increasing frequency, scholars discarded many of the oppositions that had characterized and plagued an earlier generation of scholarship:

structure	vs.	agency
economy	vs.	politics
capitalism/state	vs.	ethnography/local/subaltern

The difficulty, however, is that although these oppositions must be rejected, they nonetheless point to crucial questions regarding the nature of capitalism and social change that need to be addressed, not avoided.

In this sense, the problem with much of agrarian studies during the 1960s and 1970s was not that scholarship was too economic or too structural, but that economic and structural processes were understood in a rigid, static, and largely apolitical manner that necessarily excluded a range of important actors and stories (Roseberry 1993). Florencia Mallon was, I think, suggesting something quite similar when she recently wrote:

> The task at hand, it seems to me, is not the building of new, hard-and-fast, "correct" paradigms—understood as attempts to dismiss troublesome anomalies and questions as unimportant externalities —but rather the redefinition of paradigms as open-ended yet committed attempts to find principles of unity, patterns of meaning, among the fragments. . . . It . . . means a recommitment, on redefined

terms, to the importance of understanding broader narratives, structures, and power relations. If our previous versions of these narratives and structures were too rigid, recent treatments of discourse and culture have sometimes treated power and narrative line as if they were endlessly variable and diffuse. (Mallon 1993: 372)

"Many of us" she continues, "feel uneasy about how best to reconnect apparently economic concepts—the labor process, capital accumulation, absolute versus relative surplus value—to our increasingly complex and multilayered understandings of politics" (ibid.: 378). The challenge, according to Mallon, "is to rebuild a sense of explanation and causation without silencing important stories" (ibid.: 395). It is to the importance of such a project that this present study speaks.

The main reason I have spent so much time talking about the "state" and "capital" is in order to better understand capitalism and the role that subaltern groups play in its transformation. Once the political struggles of differently situated actors are placed at the center of our understandings of capitalism, it becomes very difficult to sustain a number of rather simplistic oppositions that have, explicitly or implicitly, characterized many studies. The challenge, however, is not so much to "reconnect apparently economic concepts . . . to our increasingly complex and multilayered understandings of politics" (ibid.: 378) as it is to place politically engaged people at the center of those seemingly economic concepts and processes. The preceding historical narrative tried to dissolve such dichotomies, placing "agency" at the center of "structure" and structure at the center of agency; economy at the center of politics and politics at the center of economy. I have attempted to understand capitalism through the ethnographic study of a particular locale while at the same time making capitalism, that is, broader forces, central to my understanding of that locale.

Part of the way in which I have done this is by not reducing agency to something that only subaltern groups possess. Quite often it seems as though peasants and workers "possess" varying degrees of agency that come into conflict with rather static and all-powerful forces such as state and capital. The constraints that peasants and workers confront are not structures, in the sense of a faceless and omnipotent state or capital, but are real agents that occupy particular places within specific governments, institutions, and corporations (all of which have their own histories and levels of resources).

In the case at hand, even when reduced to an exceptionally powerful company operating in a particular place and time, "capital" did not represent anything resembling a *structure,* if by structure we mean something static, unmovable, and all-powerful. To remove the mask of such "structures" is not, for even a moment, to suggest that there were not quite serious *structural* contradictions between United Fruit's Hacienda Tenguel and the zone's peasant-workers. Nor does it imply that, as a group, capitalists do not wield considerable power. Even on its own, United Fruit was considerably more powerful than many of the nation-states in which it operated, let alone the workers it employed. Foreign companies such as Dole and Chiquita do not have to act in concert in order to structure the investment opportunities of domestic capitalists, the actions of state officials, or the lives of workers and peasants.

What our historical examination does suggest, however, is that at the core of what we call capital, or other structural determinants of social relations such as the state, are human *agents*. I have recognized the agency that capital and state, or more accurately, certain capitalists, companies, ministries, agencies, and officials, have exercised in order to demonstrate this precise fact—to demystify the abstraction or structure that we frequently refer to as "capital" or "the state."

At the same time, I have suggested that the emergence and actions of capital and state—including Charles Sinners's initial search for property in 1924; the attempt by United Fruit's manager to evict the Mollepongo squatters; the Teniente's recognition of the Mollepongo Commune; the Intendente's refusal to evict the squatters; the "impartial" study conducted by the inspector of Labor; United Fruit's decision to withdrawal from direct production; the military's invasion of Hacienda Tenguel; IERAC's decision to give 400 hectares of Cooperative San Rafael to a group of capitalists—cannot be separated from the struggles that capitalists and state actors had with each other and a wide range of other groups. The fragmented and complex nature of capital and state is directly related to the struggle-filled process through which they are formed. If we do not place human actors at the center of abstract categories such as capital, the state, the church, or "the popular," then we not only miss the complex nature of such actors, but fail to understand how the struggles through which they are formed propel processes of capitalist transformation—how, in this particular case, a form of accumulation characterized by enclave production was slowly transformed into one based on contract farming. In other words, we are left with a historically and politically empty understanding of capitalism.

This deconstruction of state and capital has two important implications for how we understand capitalism and the role that various actors play in its emergence, expansion, retraction, and transformation. First, once we have a better understanding of what actually constitutes state and capital, it becomes impossible to see the actions of subaltern groups as a response, or even an initiative, to something we might call capitalism (or structure). This is due in part to the fact that the driving force behind capitalist expansion can no longer be attributed solely to the actions of "larger forces" such as state and capital. The attempts on the part of the Mollepongo peasants to clear and cultivate forest, acquire political allies, confront hacienda police, contact government ministries, and sign contracts to produce bananas for United Fruit were not so much responses or initiatives to capitalist expansion as they were its very core. In other words, it is impossible to separate what we traditionally think of as capitalism—including the dismantling of enclaves, capital's reentrance and expansion into the southern coast, and the rise of contract farming—from the political alliances and confrontations that the Mollepongo peasants had with each other, representatives of United Fruit, state officials, and labor organizers. The very way in which capital and state were formed, accumulated, reconfigured, and fragmented was shaped by the actions of peasant-workers. Political practices and motivations should not simply be "situated" in relation to larger forces, but should be historically and theoretically examined as integral parts of capitalist transformation.

In the case at hand, such an understanding allows us to recognize and decipher the role played by popular struggle in shaping both the activities of United Fruit and the broader transition to contract farming. Put another way, the actions of peasant-workers in Ecuador's southern coast influenced the movement of what has arguably been the quintessential form of "capital" in Latin America during the twentieth century—the United Fruit Company. In so doing, peasant-workers also helped generate a form of capitalism—contract farming—that has not only transformed the global banana industry but has been considered a defining feature of late capitalism. To be sure, such struggles have been laced with irony, rarely producing the outcomes desired by their rural protagonists. Peasant-workers, with considerable help from agricultural diseases, labor organizations, and even Latin American governments, may have been able to push foreign multinationals out of direct production, but they could not determine the broad contours of the subsequent system of production. The point here is not that peasant-workers defeated United Fruit, or that they were able to replace one method of growing bananas with a less repressive system of production based on contract farming. To the contrary, United Fruit was not defeated, and contract farming has not been kind to smallholders, plantation workers, or their organizations. Nevertheless, although Ecuadorian peasant-workers have not *determined* the exact path of the banana industry, they (along with their comrades in other banana-producing regions of Latin America) have played a decisive role in undermining the foreign-owned enclave—a system that was not only once the paragon of U.S. imperialism and hegemony in Latin America, but which from the vantage point of the first half of the twentieth century appeared as invincible as contract farming seems today. It is worth remembering that the foreign-owned enclave emerged and was eventually dismantled through a series of struggles that were located somewhere between the extremes of full-scale revolution and everyday resistance; and that contract farming was a product of these struggles and the emergence of contradictory state forms that could (at times) be simultaneously reactionary and empowering (i.e. agrarian reform). This is not to argue that contracting, whether in agriculture or industry, has emerged and been reproduced in the same way in all times and places. Rather, it is to insist that contracting, as well as other forms of capitalist production and accumulation, must be seen in its political form, where working-class people are not merely responding to structural processes, but are in fact central to the (at times highly unequal) struggles that drive those processes.

It is particularly important that political practices and motivations be placed at the heart of socioeconomic transformations during a historical moment when scholars, politicians, and the media seem intent on emptying capitalism of its social and political content. Even for the left, and particularly its more pessimistic manifestations, it seems as though the only groups involved in the making of history are large corporations and a handful of states. In such scenarios, struggle becomes not only futile, but foolish, as something carried out only by groups who have not wised up and recognized their inevitable fate at the hands of globalization or flexible accumulation (Wood 1995).

Second, although our scripts must incorporate a broader range of "important characters," including peasants, workers, ethnic groups, women, and other subalterns, that have frequently been excluded from "conventional stories of how a world system was made" (Mallon 1993: 395), it is important that such narratives also include a critical reexamination of other important actors, including capitalists, the state, the church, nongovernmental organizations, and international organizations such as the World Bank. In so doing, we will not only have a more complete and complex analysis of capitalism, but will have a better understanding of the role that subaltern groups play in processes of capitalist transformation, without either removing their political activities from the wider relationships in which they are enmeshed, or concluding that their actions are controlled by structures they play no role in shaping.

This type of understanding is particularly important in situations where forms of popular political activity do not approach the intensity or scope of a "revolution," or even serve as the precursor on which a subsequent revolution occurs; that is, in cases where the actions of subaltern groups do not alter, in an immediately visible manner, the foundations of state power and capital accumulation. The rare occasions when peasants and workers overthrow governments are not the only times when they shape history. Nor is their political and economic influence limited to what have been called "everyday forms of resistance" (Scott 1985). The central protagonists of this particular history were not revolutionaries struggling for a socialist future or victims that passively watched as capitalism ran them over. Most were in search of economic autonomy, a quest that could, depending on political and economic conditions, lead them down a variety of revolutionary and nonrevolutionary paths. That these paths did not lead to some sort of promised land does not mean that the political actions of peasant-workers were historically unimportant. Their "failed" actions not only shaped processes of state formation and capital accumulation, including the long transition to contract farming, but provided the foundation on which subsequent struggles will emerge, challenge, and transform existing forms of exploitation and domination.

Notes

1 CAPITALIST TRANSFORMATIONS

1 This fragile consistency is destroyed periodically by massive flooding associated with El Niño.

2 Like people in Ecuador's southern coast, I generally use the terms *hacienda* and *plantation* interchangeably. However, at times I use the term hacienda to refer to an exceptionally large property that contains several plantations. It should be noted that (as I use it) the term hacienda does not necessarily carry any particular connotation with respect to its efficiency or productivity, though it is never applied to a property of less than twenty-five hectares.

3 For an important exception with respect to contract farming and popular struggle in banana-producing regions, see Soluri (1998).

4 See Maiguashca (1994) and Clark (1998) for a discussion of history and region in Ecuador. Redclift (1978) also has a nice discussion of the relationships between agricultural development and Ecuador's "regions."

5 "Marginal land" refers to land that is located in the foothills of the Andes and is both hilly and somewhat rocky. By highland standards, this is very fertile land and is generally occupied by smallholders who produce cacao as well as food crops. It was not, however, suitable for large-scale banana production after the introduction of disease-resistant strains in the 1960s (see introduction to part two).

6 The boundaries of Hacienda Tenguel varied over time and depend on the particular source cited. In general, however, the hacienda began at the ocean in the west and went well into the mountains to the east. The northern boundary almost reached the town of Balao, while the southern border crossed well over into the province of El Oro (see Map 2).

7 The archives of CECCA, a Catholic organization run by Padre Hernán Rodas, are incredibly well organized and provide excellent information on peasant organizations and political activity in the southern coast during the 1960s and 1970s.

INTRODUCTION TO PART ONE

1 For the cacao period see Chiriboga (1980), Crawford de Roberts (1980), and Guerrero (1980).

2 In addition to Cueva (1982, 1988), see de la Torre (1993), Miño Grijalva (1988), Robalino Dávila (1973), Pareja Andrade (1991), and Maiguashca and North (1991) for a discussion of the July Revolution, Velasco, and the crisis of the 1920s and 1930s.

3 The owners of Hacienda Tenguel were not the only ones to turn to foreign capital. Periods of financial crisis sometimes forced the richest families to form corporations, sell shares, and modernize their holdings. The Seminarios, for instance, formed the Compañia Agricola Colon in Hamburg in 1912 in order to improve the hacienda and resolve a temporary financial crisis. The infusion of foreign capital allowed the family to regain complete control over the property. The Duran-Ballén family also incorporated their largest holding in the 1890s. Here, the infusion of capital led to foreign control and a German group held the hacienda until World War II (Crawford de Roberts 1980; Chiriboga 1980).

4 Quotes from interviews done by the author are referenced by the initials of the interviewee and the date of the interview. All interviews were conducted in Ecuador.

5 The *Remate* was essentially an auction list that included everything of economic value contained on the property.

2 THE BANANA BOYS COME TO ECUADOR

1 The process has been much more uneven than this brief outline suggests. Contracting has existed from the earliest days of the banana industry (Bourgois 1989; LaBarge 1959; Chomsky 1996). However, the current system is significantly different from earlier forms in that it dominates the industry and involves exceptionally tight relationships between large domestic capitalists and multinational agro-exporters.

2 As Miño Grijalva notes (1988), this period has received little historical attention. The lack of detailed studies of the state or particular governments during this period is undoubtedly due to the fact that between 1925 and 1948 the central government changed hands over twenty times (i.e. every year). For a decent review of the various governments see Cueva (1988). For a general treatment of the 1920s, see Carlos Marchán Romero (1987).

3 Kepner's main studies (Kepner and Soothill 1935; Kepner 1936) were published at almost the exact moment when United Fruit came to Ecuador. They remain two of the key studies on the banana industry and multinational involvement. The activities of United Fruit and other banana companies have, however, received considerable scholarly interest (Adams 1914; Davies 1990; Ellis 1983; LaBarge 1959; May and Plaza 1958; McCann 1976; Watt 1964; Wilson 1948). For recent and more historically/ethnographically detailed studies see Bourgois (1989), Chomsky (1996), LeGrand (1984), Grossman (1998), Moberg (1997), Putnam (2000), and Soluri (1998).

4 Between 1913 and 1933, United Fruit's cultivations in Costa Rica dropped from a peak of close to 50,000 acres to less than 5000 (Kepner 1936: 51). In Panama, the company would lose a remarkable 50,000 acres of bananas during the first three decades of the century (LaBarge 1959: 39–40; Kepner 1936: 49–50). To compensate, United Fruit expanded production in Guatemala as well as Honduras, Colombia, and Mexico. For a broader, and more sophisticated treatment of the Panama Disease and the biological nature of banana production, see Soluri (2000).

5 For example, in 1926, after combating the Panama Disease for close to two decades on its Costa Rican plantations, United Fruit acquired almost three-quarters of its exports from local planters. In Honduras, where the company had arrived later and diseases were much less developed, the exact opposite situation developed during the same period; United Fruit's own plantations supplied 85 percent of the company's Honduran exports (Labarge 1959).

6 Mexico implemented progressive labor codes after its revolution, Colombia was not far behind, and by July 1934 all of the Central American countries had drafts of national labor codes pending before their respective congresses (Kepner 1936: 108–112). Other sources also point to the myriad problems that United Fruit was having with both labor and states during this period (Chomsky 1996; Moberg 1997; Bourgois 1989; Acuña 1984; Valadès 1975; Gaspar 1979; Dosal 1993; Flores 1987).

7 This section is based on documents from the United States National Archives in College Park, Maryland. "NA" refers to National Archives which is then followed by the number of the record group (RG), the folder, and the date.

8 It is worth noting that the situation was probably much more complicated that the sources suggest. There were undoubtedly a whole range of domestic and foreign actors who were exploring banana production in Ecuador during this period that have simply not entered into the historical record.

9 In the case of Tenguel, for example, opponents argued that United Fruit's purchase was in violation of a law that made it illegal for foreigners to own land within fifty kilometers of the Ecuadorian coastline. Yet, as was often the case, legal battles revolved around social questions. Opponents called for the immediate expropriation of the property not because of any deep commitment to the law, but because it was at Tenguel where United Fruit's productive operations were most rapidly expanding. If United Fruit produced its own bananas at Tenguel, it would not—so the argument went—buy from Ecuadorian capitalists (some of whom were members of Congress). Indeed, when United Fruit finally admitted that it owned the property, company representatives did little to challenge the law. Instead, they noted that in 1935 Ecuadorians had produced over 90 percent of the company's exports and that this figure would remain stable (NA RG59 822.6156/27, 12/3/35). In other words, the company essentially ignored the

legal question and assured domestic capitalists that there was plenty of banana pie to go around. United Fruit's battles with different sectors of the Ecuadorian state over laws regulating export taxes and the foreign ownership of land can also be seen in this light.

3 THE BIRTH OF AN ENCLAVE: LABOR CONTROL AND WORKER RESISTANCE

1 This figure was repeated by numerous ex-workers and probably represents exports during peak periods. It is important to note that the hacienda produced more than just bananas. Hundreds of acres were devoted to cacao and pasture, and the hacienda produced a significant share of its own food needs. All production within the core of the hacienda was carried out by wage labor.

2 The case of Abdón Calderón is a perfect example of the impact of the hacienda's growth on the local and regional economy. Arriving in Tenguel as an engineer's assistant, Calderón developed friendly contacts with a number of United Fruit's top administrators. Quickly realizing that there was more to be made in the local market than as an engineer's assistant, he left the company after working for only two years. He maintained his contacts, however, and was able to obtain a special permit to market a wide variety of goods to the growing population in Tenguel. The contacts and permit were crucial to his success as the company strictly controlled entrance to the zone and access to the market. Calderón would expand his business over the years and eventually take advantage of the company's departure, becoming one of the zone's major landowners. The immediate point, however, is that the arrival of United Fruit and the development of an "enclave" generated a wide range of marketing opportunities for local and regional entrepreneurs such as Calderón (A.C. 9/12/95). On a somewhat smaller scale, his story was repeated numerous times during the 1940s and 1950s.

3 Workers also recall United Fruit's preference for married men. The belief that married men were more stable/docile was not limited to United Fruit but can be found in many company towns (see Klubock 1998; Shifflett 1991). See Moberg (1997: 118–26) for an interesting comparison.

4 Klubock (1998) outlines a similar pattern at a foreign-owned copper mine in Chile.

5 Workers frequently remarked on the company's obsession with cleanliness. This included street cleaning, constantly spraying for mosquitoes, and a series of other practices designed to keep public areas clean. The company also offered women classes on hygiene and housekeeping.

6 On the gendered nature of banana production also see Putnam (2000).

7 By any standards, United Fruit has not treated workers at any of its divisions particularly well. However, as LaBarge points out (1959), there was considerable variation from division to division—variations that de-

pended on the administrators involved, the respective governments, the relative development of labor unions, as well as the nature of the hacienda. Moreover, by the 1940s and 1950s, governments and workers had forced United Fruit to become more sophisticated in its labor relations. Thus, to the extent that the company was using the carrot as opposed to the stick with increasing frequency after World War II its paternalistically decent treatment of workers at Tenguel may not have been that unusual. See Carr (1998) for a somewhat similar case.

8 This is not to suggest that the company did not make money off the sale of various goods to its employees. However, it did sell meat, milk, and other products at less than the market price.

9 Barry Carr (1998) also points to United Fruit's willingness to buy off workers in exchange for political stability and labor control.

10 In a context that shares the unequal power relations of plantations, Sider (1986) explores the "logic of paternalism" in ways that speak to the case at hand (also see Moberg 1997).

11 These events were by no means new, even if company sponsorship and organization was. Although hacienda-sponsored social clubs were brought by United Fruit, the sponsorship of fiestas by hacendados has a long history in Ecuador and Latin America, particularly in the highlands where most of the workers came from.

12 Although agricultural laborers came to the zone from virtually every province, they were all Ecuadorian and almost exclusively mestizo. Very few Indians or blacks migrated to the hacienda. With the exception of the highest levels of hacienda management, occupational hierarchies were not based on intercultural divisions and the company could not manipulate ethnic divisions as it did on Central American plantations (Bourgois 1989).

13 After considerable struggle, the Código de Trabajo (Labor Code) was passed in 1938. Then, during much of the 1940s, popular groups struggled for its defense and serious enforcement (Ycaza 1991).

14 Also see Cueva (1982). For the development of the labor movement during this period see Paez Cordero (1988) and Ycaza (1984).

15 See Almeida Vinueza (1988) and Ibarra (1984) for general treatments of peasant movements during this period.

16 The most immediate response—before agrarian reform began in earnest in 1964—came from the government of Camilo Ponce which enacted an Emergency Law in July 1959; the law placed the National Institute of Colonization in charge of dividing up *state* haciendas and distributing them to landless peasants. This limited process of land redistribution was funded by the U.S. government and explicitly aimed at calming an increasingly active peasantry. A multitude of state and quasi-state committees and commissions formed during this period with the express purpose of exploring the possibilities of reform and/or developing a plan. See Barsky (1984),

Saad (1976), and Santos Ditto (1986) for general treatments of agrarian reform. See Uggen (1993) and Redclift (1978) for the reform process in the coast.

17   Velasco implemented a highly visible, personalistic, and quite limited type of reform in which he positioned himself as the grand mediator between the isolated (evil) landlord and the helpless peasants. This, of course, was part of his style. Landlords as a class were never seriously confronted, but Velasco nonetheless appeared as the savior of the poor and the enemy of privilege (de la Torre 1993).

4   ON THE MARGINS OF AN ENCLAVE: THE FORMATION OF STATE, CAPITAL, AND COMMUNITY

1   For a variety of reasons, including the fact that the central government changed hands almost once a year during the 1930s and 1940s, there has been little detailed research on the state or state-community relations during this period. Although clearly biased, the sources used here—the internal correspondence between United Fruit officials—help to partially fill this gap and provide a unique view into the relationships between peasants, state, and capital. The correspondence took place between the general manager of United Fruit's operations in Ecuador (Carlos Estrada) and the company's Quito-based lawyer (Adriano Cobo). It was most frequently written in English. Reference is made simply by "UFC" and the exact date or month. I would like to give special thanks to Manuel Chiriboga for generously sharing these documents.

2   UFC 3/40–7/45.

3   On the regional nature of the Ecuadorian nation, see Maiguashca (1994).

4   It was leaders from the CTE/FPTG who helped the peasants form a commune and then pushed their case through a number of different bureaucracies. It is important to note that all of these organizations—the CTE, the FPTG, as well as the Mollepongo Commune—formed during the organizing surge surrounding the May Revolution of 1944 and Velasco's return to power. It was no coincidence that the key moments of the Mollepongo conflict coincided with Velasco's second administration (1945–1947).

5   The peasants, however, were involved in their own maneuvers. Less then a week later, Cobo reported that Eloy Barros (president of the commune), despite being denied authorization to organize the commune, was continuing to "cause trouble" at the ministry by insisting that Mollepongo's boundaries extended much further than the company admitted (UFC 9/19, 9/21/45).

6   Company officials appealed once again to President Velasco, complaining that local authorities refused to act on behalf of the multinational. While United Fruit was awaiting the president's response, the situation became even more complicated when Oramas, the legal representative of the com-

mune and secretary general of the FPTG, arrived at the offices of United Fruit in Guayaquil. He informed Estrada that the Ministry of Defense was going to investigate the matter of the boundaries between Mollepongo and Tenguel. Not satisfied with subverting unfavorable reports from the responsible ministries, the peasants had gone in search of a ministry that — a month before the military would overthrow Velasco — might conduct a more sympathetic study. The Ministry of Defense was not only increasingly autonomous from the Velasco government during this period, but was generally nationalistic and had a long-standing dispute with the company. Nothing came of the study due to the fact that the ministry had no jurisdiction, but the peasants' appeal revealed their quite sophisticated understanding of the Ecuadorian state and the evolution of a particularly effective strategy: petition enough state offices, agencies, and authorities and someone will eventually listen.

7 Not surprisingly, United Fruit officials had close contacts in the U.S. embassy. However, embassy officials managed to stay out of the conflict by using the convenient excuse that United Fruit was running its Ecuadorian operations through a *Canadian* subsidiary. To my knowledge, United Fruit did not enlist the aid of the Canadian embassy (UFC).

8 A tentative agreement was reached, the peasants remained on the disputed territory, and the commune was finally legalized in 1955. It is important to note that although the Mollepongo peasants, as well as those in Shumiral (chapter 5), won significant quantities of land, they were never able to acquire the resources to bring it all into production. As a result, they sold much of their land to landless peasant-workers in the region.

9 United Fruit turned to the state in the first place because company officials felt that an eviction by state authorities would be much cleaner and avoid a public relations disaster.

5 IMAGINING NEW WORLDS

1 This section on the formation of Shumiral was put together almost exclusively through interviews with ten or so of the town's founders.

2 On the expansion of peasant protest throughout Ecuador in the 1960s, see Barsky (1984), Bustamante and Prieto (1986), and Ycaza (1992). With respect to the coast, see Uggen (1993), Redclift (1978), and Rivera et al. (1986).

3 Designed to facilitate the colonization of state-owned land, the National Institute of Colonization was the precursor to IERAC, the first real agrarian reform agency created by the state in 1964.

4 A colonia, in contrast to a commune, was a form of organization designed to colonize state land.

5 Although provincial boundaries were poorly defined, Shumiral is now part of the province of Azuay. The reason why this tactic was so effective was

that police in Tenguel-Balao were more beholden to company demands than authorities in the province of Azuay.

6 I would like to thank Rafael León for sharing these documents.

6 THE END OF AN ENCLAVE

1 The case of Shumiral, for example, differed in two quite important ways from that of Tenguel. First, the Colonia Agricola Shumiral had taken over lands that had never been cultivated. There was no infrastructure in the area and the lands were marginal. Second, and to a certain extent as a result of the marginal nature of the lands, the colonia was able to purchase the lands in question. The situation in Tenguel, by contrast, was infinitely more complicated. To begin, there were 20,000 hectares as opposed to 2500. In addition, Tenguel was complete with a massive infrastructure—towns, light, rail systems, a port, an airport, etc.—and possessed some of the highest-quality agricultural lands in Ecuador.

2 See Barsky (1984), Santos (1986), and Saad (1976) on agrarian reform and peasant protest. For more treatments of peasant political activity during this period see Bustamante and Prieto (1986) and Ycaza (1992). With respect to the coast, see Uggen (1993), Redclift (1978), and Rivera et al. (1986).

3 I relied largely on *El Universo,* the coast's most important daily, for this section, though other newspapers gave similar reports. It should pointed out that although some of these reports were simply inaccurate, or colored by the political milieu in which they were written, others were entirely fabricated. For example, a number of photos showing blown-up buildings and mass destruction were simply false.

4 There was definitely an upside to being pioneers. Cooperative Juan Quirumbay was organized and run by the workers. In contrast, cooperatives formed after 1972 were often organized and run by the state.

5 Although members of Juan Quirumbay had a different interpretation of the events, there was enough truth in the reports to cause problems. Juan Quirumbay felt that the state's promised takeover of the hacienda had made all previous rental contracts between United Fruit and private individuals null and void. As such, the cooperative, which was made up of ex-workers to whom the hacienda had been promised, began to take back land, cattle, and other property that had once been part of United Fruit's Hacienda Tenguel. Unfortunately, some of the sectors in question had been dismembered and *sold* to the above-cited capitalists about a year prior to the invasion. Similarly, Juan Quirumbay's threat to invade Gala's 3000 hectares—land that the state was going to appropriate anyway—was also taken as a sign of the communist menace and an attack on private property.

6 For excellent, and extremely detailed, treatments of this moment in Ecuadorian history, see Pyne (1975) and Needler (1964). Both give a good sense

of how ideologically polarized the early 1960s were in Ecuador, particularly with respect to the fear of communism. Also see Cueva (1982) and Ayala Mora (1983: vol. 11). On Velasco's populism, see Cueva (1982), de la Torre (1993), and Maiguashca and North (1991).

7 Although there have been some general studies of this period, I know of none that have explored the impact of the military government on the constitution of particular ministries. However, labor activists from this period, many of whom had found employment in state bureaucracies during the 1940s and 1950s, recall being fired en masse when the junta came to power. The Ministry of Social Welfare received much of this attention.

INTRODUCTION TO PART TWO

1 In 1964, United Fruit and Standard Fruit handled only 30 percent of the country's total banana exports and were producing virtually no fruit. The Panamanian-based Fruit Trading Corporation, which cultivated close to 7000 hectares of bananas and was a major exporter in the early 1950s, virtually disintegrated in the early 1960s. The Chilean Compañia Frutera, owner of Balao Chico, an immense property located just to the north of Tenguel, was exporting more than 5 percent of the country's fruit before collapsing in the 1960s. Workers carried out a major strike against the Swedish-owned ASTRAL banana plantations in the northern coast in 1955, eventually forcing the foreign company out of Ecuador. Four years later, in 1959, there was a violent eight-month strike on U.S.-owned plantations in the Quevedo region. Even a conglomeration of German companies could not avoid the forces that were converging on foreign-owned plantations in the late 1950s and early 1960s (Larrea 1987c: 51, 1987d: 70–75; Sylva 1987: 116; Handleman 1980: 4).

2 Prior to 1964, the United States absorbed about 60 percent of Ecuador's exports. Between 1964 and 1973, Ecuador's exports to this key market were cut almost in half. In contrast, exports to the United States from the four principal Central American producers almost tripled during the same period; most of this production came from multinational-owned plantations (Larrea 1987c, 1992).

3 This change was a significant blow to United Fruit whose domination of the industry partially rested on its control over immense tracts of land. However, although the new variety served to restructure power relations among the major agro-exporters, weakening United Fruit while strengthening Standard Fruit, Del Monte, and Noboa, it did not reduce the control that a handful of foreign companies had over the industry as a whole. During the 1950s, two multinationals, United Fruit and Standard Fruit, had about 80 percent of the U.S. market. In 1964, the same two companies controlled about 65 percent of world banana trade, with six other companies accounting for an additional 30 percent (Larrea 1992: 169–

71). Since the early 1970s, the world banana trade has been controlled by three multinationals, Chiquita Brands (United Brands/Fruit), Castle and Cooke (Standard Fruit/Dole), and Del Monte, with Ecuadorian-based Noboa (Bonita Bananas) and Colombian-based Uniban occupying important places (Larrea 1987b: 22; Porras 1988: 27). In the case of Ecuador, fewer companies are presently involved in the exportation of bananas than in the past. Standard Fruit, Noboa, and, to a lesser extent, Del Monte have controlled most of the country's exports since the late 1970s. In 1984, for example, the three multinationals exported about 85 percent of the country's fruit. Along with Chiquita Brands, these three companies control most of the world's banana trade (Larrea 1987).

4　Because the Cavendish was so much more productive, the number of hectares devoted to banana cultivation was quickly reduced by more than half and became concentrated in Ecuador's southern coast (Larrea 1987; Sylva 1987). The region possesses high-quality land and is located close to Machala and Guayaquil, Ecuador's principal ports. It was and is ideal for a fragile fruit that must be produced under the right conditions and cannot sustain long trips over poorly maintained roads.

5　For a broader, comparative understanding of the spread and impact contract farming in other banana producing regions see: Larrea 1987; Roberto Lopez 1986; FLACSO 1988; Bourgois 1989; Martínez Cuenca 1991; Vallejo Mejía 1982; Slutsky and Alonso 1980; Nurse and Sandiford 1995; Grossman 1998; Marie 1979; Carías Velasquez 1991; Welch 1996; Fonsah and Chidebelu 1995.

6　The literature on agrarian reform in Ecuador is quite extensive. Barsky (1984) provides a broad overview as does Cosse (1984). On the coast, both Redclift (1978) and Uggen (1975, 1993) contributed excellent case studies on the relationship between political mobilization and agrarian reform. Also see Zuvekas (1976) and Handelman (1980).

7　The CFP was a populist party founded and rooted in Guayaquil. In part a vehicle for Bucaram's political ambitions, the CFP mobilized largely urban, working-class voters around attacks on the oligarchy and clientelist networks. See Conaghan (1988).

8　The differences between "labor" and "peasant" organizations were often hard to decipher in the sense that labor organizations such as the CTE and CEDOC had been helping agricultural workers and peasants organize since the 1930s. Moreover, even after strong peasant organizations such as FENOC emerged, they often worked closely with so-called labor organizations.

9　From the perspective of peasant-workers, workers' associations, cooperatives, communes, and colonias were all forms of organization created by the state that, under the right circumstances, allowed popular groups to acquire land. Cooperatives and workers' associations were the main forms of organization adopted by peasant-workers during the agrarian reform period. As in the case of Hacienda Tenguel, cooperatives were often formed within the context of a formal agrarian reform project, involved a high level of state intervention, and legally required that members work at least a portion of the land collectively. In contrast, workers' associations allowed a group of peasant-workers to acquire the land collectively, divide it, and then work their plots on an individual basis. In the southern coast, this was the favored form of organization by the early 1970s.

7   FROM WORKERS TO PEASANTS AND BACK AGAIN: AGRARIAN REFORM AT THE CORE OF AN ENCLAVE

1   This chapter is based on interviews, government archives, and court proceedings. The people interviewed, including large landowners, agrarian reform officials, and cooperative leaders, members, and their families all have their own perspectives. Similarly, the archival materials, gathered and organized by the Ministry of Agriculture, IERAC, and a military court, were authored by a wide range of differentiated actors, including peasants and capitalists involved in conflicts, as well as state officials with varying capacities, statuses, interests, and motives. I have tried to use the range of sources to interrogate each other.

2   IERAC, 1964. At nearly 150 pages, this plan provides a wealth of information about both the project at Tenguel and the condition of the hacienda in the mid-1960s. It is complemented by an even longer report that evaluated the agrarian reform project in Tenguel in May 1968 (OAS 1968). Conducted in the later part of 1967, this independent report was conducted by the Centro de Investigaciones y Ensenanza en Reforma Agraria of the Instituto Interamericano de Ciencias Agricolas de la O.E.A. Both sources are exceptionally rich and are complemented by interviews with peasants and agrarian reform officials who participated in the project.

3   In this respect, the cooperatives in Tenguel were significantly different from the vast majority of cooperatives formed in Ecuador during the 1960s and 1970s. Most cooperatives were not created, supported, or directly administered by the state, but—as we will see in chapters eight and nine— were created by peasants as a means to acquire land. Few cooperatives were monitored as closely as those in Tenguel, let alone placed under the rubric of a specific agrarian reform project.

4   One thousand hectares remained in forest projects and another 2000 were considered "reserve." Both the savannah (6395 hectares) and the mangroves (3103 hectares) were being studied to determine their economic potential. IERAC appropriated the property in the sense that United Fruit was forced to sell to the agency; but the multinational did receive money for Hacienda Tenguel and cooperative members would eventually have to pay IERAC for the property.

5   Exactly what the "collective work method of the company" was remains

something of a mystery. Only a very peculiar understanding of "collective" would allow the label to be applied to United Fruit's hierarchical productive system.

6 Over half of the workers had more than fifteen years of experience in agriculture. Yet Cooperative Israel, which was comprised of ex-members of the military, was made up almost entirely of twenty-year-old men who had just been released from their year of obligatory service. They, along with Cooperatives Balarezo (field bosses) and Ferroviarios (train workers), had relatively high levels of education but little experience in agriculture. Similarly, although the great majority had been agricultural laborers ("peons") in the time of the company, there were also rail workers, field bosses, and tractor operators (OAS 1968; author interviews).

7 It should be noted that the lack of resources was more debilitating than the evaluation concluded. As of late 1967, not a single cooperative member had received any credit and at least one-third of the members were working full-time on neighboring haciendas. This, along with the general lack of resources, helps explain why such a low percentage of the lands were cultivated. Members were not unwilling to innovate. The overwhelming majority wanted access to fertilizers, pesticides, and modern machinery, but IERAC did not provide them and the cooperatives could not afford them.

8 In addition to interviews with former cooperative members, this section on the Empresa Repobladora is based on several sources: (1) the joint proposal put forth by the Repobladora and the cooperatives (IERAC 1967); (2) the contract between IERAC, the Repobladora, and the cooperatives (Contrato 1966); (3) the minutes from the Comité de Vigilancia, an oversight committee that watched the Repobladora project during its short life; and (4) the legal findings of the military tribunal that investigated the failed project (Tribunales Especiales n.d.; Contraloría General 1973). I would like to thank Alberto Baquero for access to these documents and his insightful perspective on this period.

9 Although it was not clear at the time, the project's problems began in August 1968 when Juan Moreno left the zone. The Oversight Committee began to meet with less regularity and subsequent IERAC representatives spent more time in Quito and less in Tenguel. The membership of the committee lost its continuity and the inspections were increasingly carried out by third parties who then submitted reports to the committee.

10 There was at least a degree of truth in Cornejo's account. A number of payments had been delayed and there was speculation that this was due to IERAC's obligations in other areas. The money was, however, guaranteed and the delay does not excuse the missing funds. As far as the peasants' "invasion" of the hacienda, it did not stop the Repobladora from working. To the contrary, the peasants invaded *because* the Repobladora had ceased working and began looting the hacienda, removing machinery and other

equipment necessary for the maintenance of the plantations. It also seems worth pointing out that the cooperative members "invaded" lands that they owned and had been working as employees of a company who paid them with a loan guaranteed by themselves.

11   This section on the conflict between Cooperative San Rafael and Oro Cavendish is based both on interviews with former members of Cooperative San Rafael and documents from IERAC (since renamed INDA). These documents, coming in a variety of shapes and sizes, all pertain to this conflict and are in IERAC's archives. Using IERAC's own, rather inconcistent system of organization, these documents are simply referred to as IERAC 2.117.

12   Fauller's manager was expelled for selling twenty-seven hectares of pasture that did not belong to him. Similar sorts of violations plagued all of the cooperatives by the early 1970s. Although seemingly minor, they generated considerable internal dissension and corruption, often consuming general assemblies and inhibiting more productive discussion.

13   See Uggen (1975, 1993) and Redclift (1978) for the complex relationship between rice production, agrarian reform in the coast, and popular political activity.

14   In addition to interviews with former members, this section on Cooperative Fauller is based on documents from the Ministry of Agriculture. The ministry has numerous folders on each of the cooperatives in Tenguel. Theoretically, these folders contain all of the correspondence between the cooperative and the state. I referred to these documents as MAG-Fauller.

15   In fact, in the case of Cooperative Fauller, the same story was repeated with different landlords. With a growing debt, internal problems, and no possibility of cultivating its communal lands, the cooperative sold off well over half of its communal section during the late 1970s. In 1976 and 1977, for example, there were a series of meetings between the executive director of IERAC, the cooperative's leaders, and Francisco Murillo, one of the zone's emerging hacendados. The reason for this particular sale was explained as follows: "The cooperative received a loan from Hannover Trust Bank which it was unable to pay . . . but had led to the cultivation of approximately 50 hectares of [Cavendish]. In order to pay this debt, the cooperative will sell this land to . . . Murillo." Once again, IERAC's rationale for the sale leaves much unsaid. The loan from Hannover Trust was not, as the correspondence suggests, obtained independently by the cooperative. It was secured by IERAC as part of the project with the Empresa Repobladora. IERAC's own role in the cooperative's inability to pay is conveniently ignored (MAG-Fauller).

16   In addition to lands sold to the Maldonados and Murillo, Cooperative Fauller sold 140 hectares of savanna to Walter Semiglia and an additional 80 hectares to Juan Baidal. Baidal, using the same tactics he had perfected with Cooperative San Francisco, had invaded the property and con-

structed various works. Unable to reimburse Baidal for his trouble, Cooperative Fauller was forced to sell.

17 There were, as is always the case, a number of exceptional success stories which everyone can point to. An extremely small minority left the agrarian reform period with more than their original ten hectares. They either purchased communal holdings from the cooperative or acquired individual lands from less fortunate members. Some even obtained land by reducing the cooperative's membership and then dividing the remaining communal holdings among themselves. Yet these individual cases, and the circumstances that made them possible, only serve to prove the rule. All but a handful came out of agrarian reform with little land and few resources.

18 In 1986, when Cooperative San Rafael formally disbanded, IERAC conducted a survey in order to determine who owned what (and thus distribute land titles to individual members). This statistical view of Cooperative San Rafael is based on this survey.

19 Thirty percent had no land, and of those who still owned property, 70 percent had less than ten hectares; 95 percent owned less than fifteen. Six members had managed to accumulate more than fifteen hectares and only one had more than twenty-five (thirty-nine hectares). In short, no one from San Rafael had acquired a particularly large amount of the cooperative's lands.

20 Although the fragmentation of holdings has made it more difficult for local capitalists to purchase additional land within the cooperatives' boundaries, this rather complicated landholding pattern was not the result of any individual or collective strategy on the part of members. A large single holding is always preferred to numerous small plots. The coast is not the Andean highlands where peasants often acquire multiple plots in different climatic zones in order to ensure survival. The quality of land within the boundaries of San Rafael does vary, but within a fairly narrow range that simply effects the relative productivity of a small number of crops.

21 It is important to stress that Cooperative San Rafael was among the more successful cooperatives. In the less successful cooperatives, under one-quarter of the former members have any land, collectively owning less than 10 percent of the cooperatives' lands.

8 FROM STRUGGLES TO MOVEMENT: THE EXPANSION OF PROTEST AND COMMUNITY FORMATION

1 Although few peasants benefited from the first agrarian reform, it succeeded in raising expectations among the nation's peasantry and put a number of key issues on the table. In addition, the production of food products destined for the domestic market was declining and it was widely believed that archaic tenancy arrangements were responsible. The fact

that Ecuador was now importing rice was the most glaring example; see Uggen (1975, 1993) and Redclift (1978). Tenants' demands for reform in the rice-growing region of the Guayas basin were now being echoed by popular organizations, sectors within the state, and even groups of modernizing capitalist farmers. Moreover, the rhetoric that surrounded Velasco's candidacy raised expectations and stimulated popular organizing. To no one's surprise, a central issue of the 1968 campaign was a second agrarian reform.

2   This section on La Florida is based on interviews with inhabitants of the zone who, at one time or another, worked as administrators/workers on haciendas, owned small plots of land, formed cooperatives and other peasant organizations, and invaded uncultivated land.

3   The Chiribogas, owners of Haciendas Mirador and Santa Rosa, signed contracts with the company as quickly as Moncada. Don Julio Gutièrrez, as well as Roberto Froman and Carolina Morla of Hacienda Guatemala, also entered into similar arrangements.

4   Haciendas Santa Rosa and Mirador were claimed by several groups, none of which had real ties to the land. Adelina's ownership was complicated by the feud between Aragundi and Moncada, and a foreigner owned Hacienda Guatemala.

5   The southern coast was just one site where popular political activity around agrarian reform increased during this period. See Barsky (1984), Saad (1976), Murmis (1986), and Quintero and Silva (1991) for more general treatments. For other areas in the coast, see Uggen (1975, 1993), Redclift (1978), and Santos (1986, 1991).

6   Like the section on La Florida, this section on Luz y Guia is based largely on interviews.

7   Cooperative Eloy Alfaro was located on what was formerly Hacienda Plantaciones Ecuatorianas, a property that United Fruit had rented. When things fell apart in Tenguel, the company abruptly pulled out of Plantaciones Ecuatorianas, leaving over 1000 workers without salaries or food. The workers, who refused to leave the property, seemed to be in a relatively ideal situation for agrarian reform. However, Plantaciones Ecuatorianas received almost none of the public attention bestowed on Tenguel. The workers had not invaded the hacienda; they had been left with it. Because United Fruit had abandoned the hacienda prior to agrarian reform, the property simply reverted back to its Ecuadorian owner and was eventually parceled off to local capitalists and peasant organizations, including Cooperative Eloy Alfaro, which bought part of what used to be Plantaciones Ecuatorianas.

8   The exact nature of this decree, which was aimed largely at the rice-producing region of the Guayas Basin, is not as important as the fact that it further stimulated popular political organizing around agrarian reform. See Santos (1986, 1991), Uggen (1975, 1993), and Redclift (1978) for a more

detailed discussion of this particular agrarian reform law and its impact in other regions.

9 A pre-cooperative is a cooperative going through the procedures of becoming a fully legalized cooperative. Prior to finishing this process, the members of Santa Martha decided to form a workers' association because it was easier to form and did not require land to be worked collectively.

10 Along with the CTE, CEDOC has (since its inception in the late 1930s) been one of the major labor organizations in the country (see Ycaza 1991). FENOC, which was essentially consolidated during the second agrarian reform period and has (at times) worked closely with CEDOC, has been the major national peasant organization in the southern coast. Although UROCAL has been closely affiliated with FENOC (and later FENOC-I), the national peasant organization does not have the resources to maintain a sustained presence in the region.

9 THE RECONSTITUTION OF STATE, CAPITAL, AND POPULAR STRUGGLE

1 This section on Padre Hernán Rodas, the Grupo Pucara, UROCAL, and their involvement in the zone is based on interviews with numerous people, including Padre Hernán, local activists, and peasant-workers, as well as an incredibly well-organized archive developed by Padre Hernán and a Catholic Organization (CECCA) he helps run. References to this archive correspond to its own system of organization (C followed by a number). Where such numbers did not exist I simply give the title of the document and (when possible) its date. These documents are varied, ranging from local and/or popular histories and reports to political pamphlets and minutes from meetings.

2 Integrated Rural Development (IRD) works from the distinction between "agricultural" and "rural" development with the latter being a broader-based type of development that seeks not only to increase agricultural output but to improve the lives of the poor. IRD assumes that various aspects of rural poverty need to be addressed simultaneously, including agricultural production, social services, and infrastructure (Lacroix 1985).

3 Although a significant producer, Ecuador is virtually always behind a number of West African countries, as well Nigeria and Brazil, in terms of total production. Eighty-five percent of producers have less than 100 hectares, and over half own fewer than 50 (Chiriboga and Piccino 1982).

4 Because cacao trees take years to mature, peasants find it difficult to start production without credit. Although they were sometimes able to obtain reasonable credit from the state in the 1970s, this source has been all but cut off to small producers since the mid-1980s. As a result, they have struggled, with minimal success, to obtain credit from international sources.

5 The demands of the march were varied, but reflected the legacy of agrarian

reform and the twin problems of credit and commercialization. The peasants' central demands included: (1) guaranteed cacao prices; (2) the repeal of recent laws affecting the price and sale of cacao; (3) a genuine attempt on the part of the government to form alliances with other cacao producing countries; (4) the availability of long-term loans at low interest and without red tape; (5) the completion of the legalization process for peasants who had been left hanging after the end of agrarian reform; (6) and the repeal of the Law of Agricultural Development and the National Security Law, which were seen as favoring the landed oligarchy while repressing the peasantry.

6   In order to stimulate industry, the national government subsidized the purchase price of cacao for those who were involved in its processing. Processors, numbering fewer than twenty, also benefited from favorable tax policies. As a result, the export of semi-processed cacao expanded dramatically in the mid- to late 1970s (see Chiriboga and Piccino 1982; Conaghan 1988). In contrast, the government made it more and more difficult to export cacao in its natural form, forcing producers to sell to processors at artificially low prices.

7   Virtually all women's organizations in the zone have been somehow related to UROCAL.

8   Such exclusion was even more complete in local community organizations (i.e., cooperatives, workers' associations). At the very least, UROCAL supported and created a space for women's organizations. Most local organizations did not even make this gesture.

10   IN SEARCH OF WORKERS: CONTRACT FARMING AND LABOR ORGANIZING

1   Dole fills its export needs in one of two ways. First, it contracts directly with haciendas such as Maria Blanca. Second, it purchases fruit from relatively large companies which act as middlemen. These companies, such as the one owned by Sánchez, are responsible for establishing relationships, both formal and informal, with other haciendas.

2   Although I suspect flirting and banter were intensified for my benefit, they are an integral part of the work process. As one woman explained: "Most women work in shrimp plants. But it's all women. Here [on the plantation] there are men [chicos] and women [chicas]. It's more fun" (B.A. 5/95). We could view this as something resembling everyday forms of resistance, in which workers turn the disciplinary space of the hacienda into a location of friendship and camaraderie. However, to the extent that friendly relations are necessary to the production process they also support the overall enterprise. Moreover, although camaraderie may be the seed from which future political actions emerge, such relations have yet to take on a more (organized) political form (see Farnsworth-Alvear 1997).

3   The feminized, devalued, and temporary natures of plantation labor are

intertwined. Even the most masculine of tasks has been denigrated. As one woman explains: "We [the women] cannot carry the stem from the tree to the rail. It can weigh close to one hundred pounds. Even most men cannot do the job. It is for the brutish. It is fine to do for a day. But only an animal could do it every day" (C.S. 3/96).

11 CONCLUSION

1 Hodgskin's quote comes from his *Labour Defended against the Claims of Capital* and then was quoted by Marx in *Capital* vol. 1. I found the quote in Corrigan (1980).

2 Paige's *Agrarian Revolution* (1975) is the classic example of this tendency, though there are many more (Beckford 1972). Even Wolf's (1969) and Scott's early (1976) works exhibit certain aspects of this trend.

3 There were, of course, quite nuanced studies dealing with peasant politics before the 1980s (see Wolf 1969; Womack 1968). Unfortunately, they did not explicitly engage in a dialogue with the more economistic approaches that dominated agrarian studies during the 1960s and 1970s.

Bibliography

ARCHIVES

NA United States National Archives, College Park, Maryland
C CECCA Archives (Catholic Organization based in Cuenca)
MAG Ministry of Agriculture, Ecuador
IERAC National Agrarian Reform Institute, Ecuador

PERIODICALS AND UNPUBLISHED REPORTS

El Pueblo, Guayaquil
El Nacional
El Universo, Guayaquil
TURIPAC, Cuenca

BOOKS AND ARTICLES

Abrams, Philip. [1977] 1980. "Notes on the Difficulty of Studying the State." *Journal of Historical Sociology* 1 (1): 58–89.

Acuña Ortega, Víctor H. 1984. *La Huelga Bananera de 1934.* Costa Rica: CENAP.

Adams, Frederick Upham. 1914. *Conquest of the Tropics: The Story of the Creative Enterprises Conducted by the United Fruit Company.* Garden City, N.J.: Doubleday, Page and Company.

Almeida Vinueza, Josè. 1988. "Luchas campesinas del siglo XX (primera parte)." In *Nueva Historia del Ecuador Vol. 10,* ed. Enrique Ayala Mora. Quito: Corporación Editora Nacional.

Ayala Mora, Enrique, ed. 1983. *Nueva Historia del Ecuador. Vol. 11.* Quito: Corporación Editora Nacional.

Barsky, Osvaldo. 1984. *La Reforma Agraria Ecuatoriano.* Quito: CEN FLACSO.

Beckford, George. 1972. *Persistent Poverty: Underdevelopment in Plantation Economies of the Third World.* Oxford: Oxford University Press.

Beinhart, W. and Colin Bundy. 1987. *Hidden Struggles: Rural Politics and Popular Consciousness in South Africa.* London: University of California.

Bernstein, Henry, et al., eds. 1990. *The Food Question: Profits Versus People.* New York: Monthly Review Press.

Bonanno, A., et al., eds. 1994. *From Columbus to ConAgra: The Globalization of Agriculture and Food.* Lawrence: University of Kansas Press.

Botero Herrera, Fernando and Diego Sierra Botero. 1981. *El Mercado de Fuerza de Trabajo en la Zona Bananera de Urabá.* Colombia: Editorial Lealon.

Bourgois, Philippe. 1989. *Ethnicity at Work. Divided Labor on a Central American Banana Plantation.* Baltimore: Johns Hopkins University Press.

Brenner, Robert and Mark Glick. 1991. "The Regulation Approach: Theory and History." *New Left Review* 188: 45–119.

Bucheli, Marcelo. 1997. "United Fruit Company in Colombia: Impact of Labor Relations and Governmental Regulations on its Operations, 1948–1968." *Essays in Economic and Business History* 17: 65–84.

———. 1998. "United Fruit Company in Latin America: Institutional Uncertainties and Changes in Operations, 1900–1970." Paper presented at the Annual Meeting of the American Anthropological Association, December, Philadelphia, PA.

Bustamante, Teodoro and Mercedes Prieto. 1986. "Formas de organización y de acción campesina e indígena: experiencias en tres zonas del Ecuador." In *Clase y Región en el Agro Ecuatoriano,* ed. Miguel Murmis. Quito: Corporación Editora Nacional/CERLAC/FLACSO.

Carías Velásquez, Marco Virgilio. 1990. *La Guerra del Banano.* Honduras: Ediciones Paysa.

Carney, Judith. 1988. "Struggles over Crop Rights and Labour within Contract Farming Households in a Gambian Irrigated Rice Project." *Journal of Peasant Studies* 15(3): 334–49.

———. 1994. "Contracting a Food Staple in The Gambia." In *Living under Contract: Contract Farming an Agrarian Transformation in Sub-Saharan Africa,* ed. Peter D. Little and Michael J. Watts. Madison: University of Wisconsin Press.

Carney, Judith and Michael Watts. 1990. "Manufacturing Dissent: Work, Gender and the Politics of Meaning in a Peasant Society." *Africa* 60(2): 207–41.

Carr, Barry. 1998. "Omnipotent and Omnipresent? Labor Shortages, Worker Mobility, and Employer Control in the Cuban Sugar Industry, 1910–1934." In *Identity and Struggle at the Margins of the Nation-State: Laboring Peoples of Central America and Hispanic Caribbean,* ed. Aviva Chomsky and Aldo Lauria-Santiago. Durham, N.C.: Duke University Press.

Chiriboga, Manuel. 1980. *Jornaleros y gran propietarios en 135 años de exportación cacaotera (1790–1925).* Quito: Consejo Provincial Pichincha.

Chiriboga, Manuel and Renato Piccino. 1982. *La Producción Campesina and Cacaotera: Problemas and Perspectivas.* Quito: CAAP/CECCA.

Chomsky, Aviva. 1996. *West Indian Workers and the United Fruit Company in Costa Rica, 1870–1940.* Baton Rouge: Louisiana State University Press.

Clapp, Roger A. J. 1988. "Representing Reciprocity, Reproducing Domination: Ideology and the Labor Process in Latin American Contract Farming." *Journal of Peasant Studies* 16(1): 5–39.

Clark, A. Kim. 1998. *The Redemptive Work. Railway and Nation in Ecuador, 1895–1930.* Wilmington, Del.: SR Books.

Collins, Jane L. 1993. "Gender, Contracts, and Wage Work: Agricultural Restructuring in Brazil's Sao Francisco Valley." *Development and Change* 24: 53–82.

Conaghan, Catherine M. 1988. *Restructuring Domination: Industrialists and the State in Ecuador.* Pittsburgh: University of Pittsburgh Press.

Cooper, Frederick, et al. 1993. *Confronting Historical Paradigms: Peasants, Labor, and the Capitalist World System in Africa and Latin America.* Madison: University of Wisconsin Press.

Corrigan, Philip, ed. 1980. *Capitalism, State Formation and Marxist Theory. Historical Investigations.* London: Quartet Books.

Corrigan, Philip, and Derek Sayer. 1985. *The Great Arch: English State Formation as Cultural Revolution.* Oxford: Basil Blackwell.

Corrigan, Philip, Harvie Ramsay, and Derek Sayer. 1980. "The State as a Relation of Production." In *Capitalism, State Formation and Marxist Theory: Historical Investigations,* ed. Philip Corrigan. London: Quartet Books.

Cosse, Gustavo. 1984. *Estado y Agro en el Ecuador.* Quito: FLACSO-Corporación Editora Nacional.

Cox, Robert W. 1981. "Social Forces, States and World Orders: Beyond International Relations Theory." *Millennium* 10: 126–55.

Crawford de Roberts, Lois. 1980. *El Ecuador en La Epoca Cacaotera.* Quito: Editorial Univerisitaria.

Cueva, Agustín. 1982. *The Process of Political Domination in Ecuador.* New York: Transaction Books.

———. 1988. "El Ecuador de 1925 a 1960." In *Nueva Historia del Ecuador Vol. 10,* ed. Enrique Ayala Mora. Quito: Corporación Editora Nacional.

Davies, Peter. 1990. *Fyffes and the Banana Musa sapientum: A Centenary History, 1888–1988.* London: Althone.

Dávila Loor, Jorge. 1995. *El FUT: trayectoria y perspectivas.* Quito: Corporación Editora Nacional.

de la Torre, Carlos. 1993. *La Seducción Velasquista.* Quito: Ediciones Libri Mundi.

Dosal, Paul J. 1993. *Doing Business with the Dictators: A Political History of United Fruit in Guatemala 1899–1944.* New York: SR Books.

Edelman, Marc. 1996. "Reconceptualizing and Reconstituting Peasant Struggles: A New Social Movement in Central America." *Radical History Review* 65: 26–47.

Ellis, Frank. 1983. *Las Transnacionales del banano en Centroamèrica.* San José, Costa Rica: Editorial Universitaria Centroamericana.

Evans, Peter. 1985. "Transnational Linkages and the Economic Role of the State: An Analysis of Developing and Industrialized Nations in the Post-World War II Period." In *Bringing the State Back In,* ed. Peter Evans, Dietrich Rueschemeyer, and Theda Skocpol. New York: Cambridge University Press.

Farnsworth-Alvear, Ann. 1997. "Talking, Fighting, Flirting: Workers' Sociability in Medellin Textile Mills, 1935–1950." In *The Gendered Worlds of Latin American Women Workers: From Household and Factory to the Union Hall and Ballot Box,* ed. John D. French and Daniel James. Durham, N.C.: Duke University Press.

Feierman, Steven. 1990. *Peasant Intellectuals*. Madison: University of Wisconsin Press.

FLACSO. 1987. *Cambio y Continuidad en la Economía Bananera*. San José, Costa Rica: FLACSO/CEDAL/FES.

Flores Valeriano, Enrique. 1987. *La Explotación Bananera en Honduras*. Honduras: Editorial Universitaria.

Fonsah, Esenduge Gregory and Angus S. N. D. Chidebelu. 1995. *Economics of Banana Production and Marketing in the Tropics (A Case Study of Cameroon)*. London: Minerva Press.

Gaspar, Jeffrey Casey. 1979. *Limón, 1880-1940*. Costa Rica: Editorial Costa Rica.

Glover, David and Ken Kusterer. 1990. *Small Farmers, Big Business: Contract Farming and Rural Development*. New York: St. Martin's Press.

Gómez, Nelson E. 1990. *Atlas del Ecuador: Geografía y Economía*. Quito: Ediguias C. Ltda.

Goodman, David and Michael Watts. 1994. "Reconfiguring the Rural or Fording the Divide? Capitalist Restructuring and the Global Agro-Food System." *Journal of Peasant Studies* 22(1): 1-49.

Gordon, David C. 1988. "The Global Economy: New Edifice or Crumbling Foundations?" *New Left Review* 168: 24-66.

Gould, Jeffry. 1990. *To Lead as Equals: Rural Protest and Political Consciousness in Chinandega, Nicaragua, 1912-1979*. Chapel Hill: University of North Carolina Press.

Grossman, Lawrence. 1998. *The Political Ecology of Bananas. Contract Farming, Peasants, and Agrarian Change in the Eastern Caribbean*. Chapel Hill: University of North Carolina Press.

Guerrero, Andrés. 1980. *Los Oligarcas del cacao*. Quito: Editorial el Conejo.

Handelman, Howard. 1980. "Ecuadorian Agrarian Reform: The Politics of Limited Change." Hanover: American Universities Field Staff Reports, No. 49.

Herrera Soto, Roberto and Rafael Romero Castañeda. 1979. *La zona bananera del Magdalena*. Colombia: Imprenta Patriótica del Instituto Caro y Cuervo.

Hirst, Paul and Jonathan Zeitlin. 1991. "Flexible Specialization versus Post-Fordism: Theory, Evidence and Policy Implications." *Economy and Society* 20 (1): 1-56.

Horsman, Mathew and Andrew Marshall. 1994. *After the Nation State: Citizen, Tribalism, and the New World Disorder*. London: HarperCollins.

Ibarra, Hernán. 1984. *La Formación del Movimiento Popular: 1925-1936*. Quito: CEDIS.

Jackson, Jeremy C. and Angela P. Cheater. 1994. "Contract Farming in Zimbabwe: Case Studies of Sugar, Tea, and Cotton." In *Living under Contract: Contract Farming and Agrarian Transformation in Sub-Saharan Africa*, ed. Peter D. Little and Michael J. Watts. Madison: University of Wisconsin Press.

Jacobsen, Nils. 1993. *Mirages of Transition: The Peruvian Altiplano, 1780-1930*. Berkeley: University of California Press.

Joseph, Gilbert and Daniel Nugent. 1994. *Everyday Forms of State Formatiom. Revolution and Rule in Modern Mexico*. Durham, N.C.: Duke University Press.

Kepner, Charles. 1936. *Social Aspects of the Banana Industry.* New York: Columbia University Press.

Kepner, Charles and Jay Soothill. 1935. *The Banana Empire: A Case Study of Economic Imperialism.* New York: Vanguard Press.

Kim, Chul-Kyoo and James Curry. 1993. "Fordism, Flexible Specialization, and Agri-Industrial Restructuring." *Sociologia Ruralis* 33: 61–80.

Korovkin, Tanya. 1992. "Peasants, Grapes, and Corporations: The Growth of Contact Farming in a Chilean Community." *Journal of Peasant Studies* 19(2): 228–254.

Klubock, Thomas Miller. 1998. *Contested Communities: Class, Gender, and Politics in Chile's El Teniente Copper Mine, 1904–1951.* Durham, N.C.: Duke University Press.

LaBarge, Richard Allen. 1959. "A Study of United Fruit Company Operations in Isthmian America, 1946–1956." Ph.D. dissertation, Duke University, Department of Economics.

Lacroix, Richard L. J. 1985. "Integrated Rural Development in Latin America." World Bank Staff Working Papers, Number 716. Washington, D.C.: World Bank.

Larrea, M. Carlos. 1985. "El Agroexportador y su articulación con la economía Ecuatoriana durante La Etapa Bananera (1948–1972)." In *Economía Política del Ecuador: Campo, Region, Nación,* ed. Louis Lefeber. Quito: Corporacion Editora Nacional/FLACSO.

———. 1987a. "Introducción." In *El Banano en el Ecuador: Transnacionales, Modernización y Subdesarrollo,* ed. Carlos Larrea. Quito: FLACSO.

———. 1987b. "Marco Conceptual y tesis centrales del estudio." In *El Banano en el Ecuador: Transnacionales, Modernización y Subdesarrollo,* ed. Carlos Larrea. Quito: FLACSO.

———. 1987c. "Auge y Crisis de la producción bananera (1948–1976)." In *El Banano en el Ecuador: Transnacionales, Modernización y Subdesarrollo,* ed. Carlos Larrea. Quito: FLACSO.

———. 1987d. "Empresas Exportadoras y Concentración Económica." In *El Banano en el Ecuador: Transnacionales, Modernización y Subdesarrollo,* ed. Carlos Larrea. Quito: FLACSO.

———. 1992. "Empresas Transnacionales y Cambios en la Exportación Bananera Ecuatoriana: Una Reinterpretación." In *El Ecuador de la Postguerra Vol. I,* ed. Banco Central. Quito: Banco Central del Ecuador.

Larrea, M. Carlos, ed. 1987. *El Banano en el Ecuador: Transnacionales, Modernización y Subdesarrollo.* Quito: FLACSO.

Larson, Brooke. 1988. *Colonialism and agrarian transformation in Bolivia: Cochabamba, 1550–1900.* Princeton, N.J.: Princeton University Press.

Lefeber, Louis. 1985. *Economía Política del Ecuador: Campo, Región, Nación.* Quito: FLACSO/CERLAC.

LeGrand, Catherine. 1984. "Colombian Transformations: Peasants and Wage Laborers in the Santa Marta Banana Zone." *Journal of Peasant Studies* 11(2): 178–200.

León, J. and J. P. Pérez. 1986. "Crisis y movimiento sindical en Ecuador: Las huelgas nacionales del FUT (1981–1983)." In *Movimientos Sociales en el Ecuador,* ed. Manuel Chiriboga et al. Quito: CLACSO.

Little, Peter D. and Michael J. Watts, eds. 1994. *Living Under Contract: Contract Farming an Agrarian Transformation in Sub-Saharan Africa.* Madison: University of Wisconsin Press.

Lopez, Josè Roberto. 1984. *La Economía del Banano en Centroamèrica.* Costa Rica: Editorial DEI.

Luong, Hy V. 1992. *Revolution in the Village.* Honolulu: University of Hawaii Press.

Maiguashca, Juan. 1994. *Historia y Region en el Ecuador.* Quito: FLACSO.

Maiguashca, Juan and Liisa North. 1991. "Orígenes y significado del velasquismo: Lucha de clases y participación política en el Ecuador, 1920–1972," In *La cuestión regional y el poder,* ed. Rafael Quintero. Quito: Corporación Editora Nacional.

Mallon, Florencia. 1983. *The Defense of Community in Peru's Central Highlands: Peasant Struggle and Capitalist Transition, 1860–1940.* Princeton, N.J.: Princeton University Press.

———. 1993. "Dialogues Among the Fragments: Retrospect and Prospect." In *Confronting Historical Paradigms: Peasants, Labor, and the Capitalist World System in Africa and Latin America,* ed. Cooper et al. Madison: University of Wisconsin Press.

Marchán Romero, Carlos. 1987. *Crisis y Cumbios de la Economía Ecuatoriana en los Años Viente.* Quito: Banco Central del Ecuador.

Marie, J. M. 1979. *Agricultural Diversification in a Small Economy—The Case for Dominica.* Cave Hill, West Indies: Institute of Social and Economic Research, University of the West Indies.

Martínez Cuenca, Alvaro. 1991. *Banana Libre.* Managua: Editorial Nueva Nicaragua.

Martz, John D. 1972. *Ecuador: Conflicting Political Culture and the Quest for Progress.* Boston: Allyn and Bacon.

Martz, Mary. 1968. "Ecuador and the Eleventh Inter-American Conference." *Journal of Inter-American Studies* 10(2): 306–27.

Massey, Doreen. 1984. *Spatial Divisions of Labour.* London: Macmillan.

May, Stacy and Galo Plaza. 1958. *The United Fruit Company in Latin America.* Washington, D.C.: National Planning Association.

McCann, Thomas, P. 1976. *An American Company: The Tragedy of the United Fruit Company.* New York: Crown.

McMichael, Philip. 1991. "Food, the State, and the World Economy." *International Journal of Sociology of Agriculture and Food* 1: 71–85.

McMichael, Philip, ed. 1994. *The Global Restructuring of Agro-Food Systems.* Ithaca, N.Y.: Cornell University Press.

McMichael, Philip and David Myhre. 1991. "Global Regulation vs. the Nation-State: Agro-Food Systems and the New Politics of Capital." *Capital and Class* 43: 83–105.

Miño Grijalva, Wilson. 1988. "La economía ecuatoriana de la gran recesión a la crisis bananera." In *Nueva Historia del Ecuador Vol. 10,* ed. Enrique Ayala Mora. Quito: Corporación Editora Nacional.

Mitchell, Timothy. 1991. "The Limits of the State: Beyond Statist Approaches and Their Critics." *American Political Science Review* 85(1): 77–96.

Moberg, Mark. 1997. *Myths of Ethnicity and Nation. Immigration, Work, and Identity in the Belize Banana Industry.* Knoxville: University of Tennessee Press.

Murmis, Miguel, ed. 1986. *Clase y Región en el Agro Ecuatoriano.* Quito: CEN/CERLAC/FLACSO.

Murray, Robin. 1971. "The Internationalisation of Capital and the Nation State." *New Left Review* 67: 84–110.

Needler, Martin C. 1964. "Anatomy of a Coup d'Etat: Ecuador 1963." Washington, D.C.: ICOPS, Special Article Series No. 1.

Nugent, Daniel. 1993. *Spent Cartridges of Revolution: An Anthropological History of Namiquipa, Chihuahua.* Chicago: University of Chicago Press.

Nurse, Keith and Wayne Sandiford. 1995. *Windward Islands Bananas: Challenges and Options under the Single European Market.* Kingston, Jamaica: Friedrich Ebert Shiftung.

Ohmae, K. 1990. *The Borderless World.* New York: Harper Business.

Páez Cordero, Alexei. 1988. "El movimiento obrero ecuatoriano en el periodo (1925–1960)." In *Nueva Historia del Ecuador Vol. 9,* ed. Enrique Ayala Mora. Quito: Corporación Editora Nacional.

Paige, Jeffery. 1975. *Agrarian Revolution.* New York: Free Press.

Pareja Andrade, Armando. 1991. "La Revolución Liberal del 9 de Julio de 1925." In *El Liberalismo en el Ecuador,* ed. Blasco Penaherrera Padilla. Quito: Colección Temas.

Pearce, Jenny. 1986. *Promised Land: Peasant Rebellion in Chalatenango El Salvador.* Latin American Bureau.

Picciotto, Sol. 1991. "The Internationalisation of the State." *Capital and Class* 43: 43–63.

Pineo, Ronn F. 1996. *Social and Economic Reform in Ecuador: Life and Work in Guayaquil.* Gainesville: University Press of Florida.

Pooley, Sam. 1991. "The State Rules, OK? The Continuing Political Economy of Nation-States." *Capital and Class* 43: 65–82.

Porras, Celso. 1988. *Cambio y Continuidad en la Economía Bananera.* FLACSO.

Putnam, Lara. 2000. "Public Women and One-Pant Men: Production and Politics on Costa Rica's Caribbean Coast, 1870 to 1960." Ph.D. dissertation, University of Michigan.

Pyne, Peter. 1975. "The Politics of Instability in Ecuador: The Overthrow of the President, 1961." *Journal of Latin American Studies* 7(1): 109–33.

Quintero, Rafael L. and Erika Silva C. 1991. *Ecuador: Una Nación en Ciernes* (Vol. I–III). Quito: ABYA-YALA.

Redclift, M. R. 1978. *Agrarian Reform and Peasant Organization on the Ecuadorian Coast.* London: University of London.

Rivera V., Fredy, J. C. Ribadeniera, and Jorge Mora A. Altafuya. 1986. *Campesinado y Organización en Esmeraldas.* Quito: CAAP.

Robalino Dávila, Luis. 1973. *El 9 de Julio de 1925.* Quito: Editorial "La Union."

Roberto Lopez, José. 1986. *La Economía del Banano en Centroamèrica.* San José, Costa Rica: Editorial Departamento Ecumenico de Investigaciones.

Rodney, Walter. 1981. *A History of the Guyanese Working People.* Baltimore, Md.: Johns Hopkins University Press.

Roseberry, William. 1983. *Coffee and Capitalism in the Venezuelan Andes.* Austin: University of Texas Press.

————. 1993. "Beyond the Agrarian Question in Latin America." In *Confronting Historical Paradigms: Peasants, Labor, and the Capitalist World System in Africa and Latin America,* ed. Cooper et. al. Madison: University of Wisconsin Press.

————. 1994. "Hegemony and the Language of Contention." In *Everyday Forms of State Formation: Revolution and the Negotiation of Rule in Modern Mexico,* ed. Gilbert Joseph and Daniel Nugent. Durham, N.C.: Duke University Press.

————. 1995. "Understanding Capitalism—Historically, Structurally, Spatially." Paper prepared for the session, "Papers on the influence of Joan Vincent: locating capitalism in time and space, I: empire, state, region, frontier," at the 1995 Annual Meeting of the American Anthropological Association, Washington, D.C.

————. 1996. "The Rise of Yuppie Coffees and the Reimagination of Class in the United States." *American Anthropologist* 98(4): 762–775.

Saad, Pedro. 1987. *La Reforma Agraria Democratica.* Guayaquil: Departmento de Publicaciones de la Facultad de Ciencias Economicas de la Universidad de Guayaquil.

Santos Ditto, José. 1986. *Leyes y Sangre en El Agro.* Guayaquil: Universidad de Guayaquil.

————. 1991. *La lucha de los campesinos por la Reforma Agraria.* Quito: Manana Editores.

Sayer, Derek. 1994. "Everyday Forms of State Formation: Some Dissident Remarks on 'Hegemony.'" In *Everyday Forms of State Formation: Revolution and the Negotiation of Rule in Modern Mexico,* ed. Gilbert Joseph and Daniel Nugent. Durham, N.C.: Duke University Press.

Scott, James. 1976. *The Moral Economy of the Peasant.* New Haven, Conn.: Yale University Press.

————. 1985. *Weapons of the Weak.* New Haven, Conn.: Yale University Press.

Shifflett, Crandall A. 1991. *Coal Towns: Life, Work, and Culture in Company Towns of Southern Appalachia, 1880–1960.* Knoxville: University of Tennessee Press.

Sider, Gerald. 1986. *Culture and Class in Anthropology and History: A Newfoundland Illustration.* Cambridge: Cambridge University Press.

Slutsky, Daniel and Esther Alonso. 1980. *Empresas Transnacionales y Agricultura: El Caso del Enclave Bananero en Honduras.* Tegucigalpa, Honduras: Editorial Universitaria.

Smith, Gavin. 1989. *Livelihood and Resistance: Peasants and the Politics of Land in Peru.* Berkeley: University of California Press.

———. 1991. "Writing for Real. Capitalist Constructions and Constructions of Capitalism." *Critique of Anthropology* 11(3): 213–32.

Soluri, John. 1998. "Landscape and Livelihood: An Agroecological History of Export Banana Growing in Honduras, 1870–1975." Ph.D. dissertation, University of Michigan.

———. 2000. "People, Plants, and Pathogens: The Eco-Social Dynamics of Export Banana Production in Honduras." *Hispanic American Historical Review* 80(3): 463–501.

Stern, Steve. 1987. *Resistance, Rebellion, and Consciousness in the Andean Peasant World.* Madison: University of Wisconsin Press.

Stoler, Ann. 1985. *Capitalism and Confrontation in Sumatra's Plantation Belt, 1870–1979.* New Haven, Conn.: Yale University Press.

Striffler, Steve. 1998. "In the Shadows of State and Capital: The United Fruit Company and the Politics of Agricultural Restructuring in Ecuador, 1900–1995." Ph.D. dissertation, New School for Social Research.

———. 1999. "Wedded to Work: Class Struggles and Gendered Identities in the Restructuring of the Ecuadorian Banana Industry." *Identities: Global Studies in Culture and Power* 6(1): 91–120.

Sylva Charvet, Paola. 1987. "Los Productores de Banano." In *El Banano en el Ecuador: Transnacionales, Modernización y Subdesarrollo,* ed. Carlos Larrea. Quito: FLACSO.

Tomich, Dale. 1990. *Slavery in the Circuit of Sugar: Martinique and the World Economy, 1830–1848.* Baltimore, Md.: Johns Hopkins University Press.

Trouillot, Michel-Rolph. 1988. *Peasants and Capital.* Baltimore, Md.: Johns Hopkins University Press.

Uggen, John, F. 1975. "Peasant Mobilization in Ecuador: A Case Study of Guayas Province." Ph.D. dissertation, University of Miami.

———. 1993. *Tenencia de la tierra y movilizaciones campesinas: zona de Milagro.* Quito: ACLAS.

Valadès, Edmundo. 1975. *Los contratos del diablo.* Mexico: Editores Asociados.

Vallejo Mejía, Hernán. 1982. *Productos Básicos Dependencia y Subdesarrollo. El problema bananero.* Bogotá, Colombia: Ediciones Tercer Mundo.

Walton, John. 1992. *Western Times and Water Wars: State, Culture, and Rebellion in California.* Berkeley: University of California Press.

Watt, Stewart. 1964. *Keith and Costa Rica. A Biographical Study of Minor Cooper Keith.* Albuquerque: University of New Mexico Press.

Watts, Michael J. 1992. "Living under Contract: Work, Production Politics, and the Manufacture of Discontent in a Peasant Society." In *Reworking Modernity: Capitalisms and Symbolic Discontent,* ed. Allan Pred and Michael John Watts. New Brunswick, N.J.: Rutgers University Press.

———. 1994a. "Epilogue: Contracting, Social Labor, and Agrarian Transitions." In *Living under Contract: Contract Farming an Agrarian Transformation in Sub-*

Saharan Africa, ed. Peter D. Little and Michael J. Watts. Madison: University of Wisconsin Press.

————. 1994b. "Life under Contract: Contract Farming, Agrarian Restructuring, and Flexible Accumulation." In *Living under Contract: Contract Farming an Agrarian Transformation in Sub-Saharan Africa,* ed. Peter D. Little and Michael J. Watts. Madison: University of Wisconsin Press.

Weiss, Linda. 1997. "Globalization and the Myth of the Powerless State." *New Left Review* 225.

Welch, Barbara M. 1996. *Survival by Association: Supply Management Landscapes of the Eastern Caribbean.* London: McGill-Queen's University Press.

Wickizer. Vernon Dale. 1951. *Coffee, Tea, and Cocoa: An Economic and Political Analysis.* Stanford, Calif.: Stanford University Press.

Wilson, Charles. 1947. *Empire in Green and Gold: The Story of the American Banana Trade.* New York: Henry Holt and Co.

Wolf, E.R. 1969. *Peasant Wars of the Twentieth Century.* New York: Harper and Row.

Womack, John. 1968. *Zapata and the Mexican Revolution.* New York: Vintage Books.

Wood, Ellen Meiksins. 1995. *Democracy against Capitalism: Renewing Historical Materialism.* New York: Cambridge University Press.

Ycaza, Patricio. 1984. *Historia del movimiento obrero ecuatoriano.* Quito: CEDIME.

————. 1991. *Historia del movimiento obrero ecuatoriano II.* Quito: CEDIME.

————. 1992. "Lucha Sindical y popular en un periodo de transición." In *El Ecuador de la Postguerra,* ed. Banco Central del Ecuador. Quito: Banco Central del Ecuador.

Zuvekas, Clarence, Jr. 1976. "Agrarian Reform in Ecuador's Guayas River Basin." *Land Economics* 52(3): 314–329.

Index

Agrarian reform: debates about, 56–57, 95–96, 106, 119–121; and Ecuador, 4, 16, 55, 94, 104, 119–127, 130, 193, 210; and La Florida, 151–158; and legislation, 57, 96, 120; and Luz y Guia, 158–163; and Rio Gala, 168–171; and Santa Martha, 164–168; and Tenguel, 129–150
Agrarian restructuring, 5–9, 115. *See also* Contract farming
Agrarian studies, 5, 205
Agricultural Workers' Association, 99, 125, 126, 164
Arosemena Monroy, Carlos Julio, 56–57, 101, 105, 107

Bananas: and Ecuador, 34–37, 40–42, 115–119, 160, 193; as global industry, 31–33, 194–195; and Tenguel, 1–3, 42, 136–138

Cacao, 2, 10, 11, 12, 13, 21–28, 65, 71, 140, 147, 175, 180–190
Castro Jijón, Ramón, 107, 119, 129, 151. *See also* Military
Cavendish, 117–119, 136, 157, 193
CEDOC, 52, 124, 167, 168
CFP, 123
Chiquita Brands, 1, 2, 4, 118, 208. *See also* United Fruit Company
Clientelism, 74, 80–82, 124–127, 149–150, 182–185, 190–192
Commune, 66–67, 125–126. *See also* Mollepongo
Communism: and agrarian reform,

95, 104, 129; and organizations, 52, 162; paranoia of, 52–53, 56–57, 78, 94–97, 100, 101–111, 124, 166. *See also* CTE
Contract farming, 1, 4, 5, 6–9, 13, 15, 16, 29, 32, 83, 90–91, 98, 110, 116, 118–119, 126–127, 152–156, 175, 193–204, 209–210
Cooperatives, 99, 132–150
CTE, 52, 56, 68, 94, 99, 108, 124, 125, 160, 168. *See also* FPTG

Del Monte, 4, 193
Dole Fruit, 1, 4, 116, 118, 175, 193, 195–198, 208

Enclave, 4, 13, 15, 16, 29, 43, 61, 115, 194, 208

FENOC, 124, 168
FODERUMA, 180–185, 189, 190
Fordism, 5, 6, 48, 201
FPTG, 52, 68, 73, 74, 94, 99, 125, 160, 168. *See also* CTE

Gender, 45–46, 49–50, 58–60, 99 100, 172–173, 188–190, 199–204
Guayaquil, 10, 11, 22, 25, 26, 34, 36, 40, 41, 42, 44, 52, 66, 70, 71, 72, 118, 132, 152, 153, 156, 160, 161, 162, 168, 171, 195

Hacienda Balao Chico, 13, 14, 159–163

STEVE STRIFFLER is Assistant Professor of Anthropology
and Latin American Studies at the University of Arkansas.

Library of Congress Cataloging-in-Publication Data
Striffler, Steve.
In the shadows of state and capital : the United Fruit Company,
popular struggle, and agrarian restructuring in Ecuador,
1900–1995 / Steve Striffler.
p. cm. — (American encounters/global interactions)
Includes bibliographical references and index.
ISBN 0-8223-2836-4 (cloth : alk. paper)
ISBN 0-8223-2863-1 (pbk. : alk. paper)
1. Banana trade—Employees—Ecuador—Pacific Coast—
Political activity—History—20th century.   2. United Fruit
Company—History.   3. Peasantry—Ecuador—Political activity
—History—20th century.   4. Land reform—Ecuador—History
—20th century.   5. Ecuador—Politics and government—20th
century.   6. Capitalism—Ecuador—History—20th century.
I. Title.
HD8039.B232 E27   2002
338.7′634772′09866—dc21   2001046027